PHILOSOPHY
of
ARTHUR SCHOPENHAUER

Translated by
BELFORT BAX and
BAILEY SAUNDERS

———

With a Special Introduction by
JAMES GIBSON HUME, M.A., Ph.D.
Professor of Philosophy, University of Toronto

TUDOR PUBLISHING CO.
NEW YORK

PRINTED IN THE UNITED STATES OF AMERICA
1946

SPECIAL INTRODUCTION

THE Essays of Schopenhauer comprised in this volume are well designated by the title which specially pertains to the first Essay. It will be noticed that the earlier essays are predominantly theoretical or metaphysical, the later practical or ethical. Hence we have in these Essays Schopenhauer's views upon a number of important problems in Metaphysics and Ethics, valuable, as an introduction to his more abstract expositions, to the specialist in philosophy, and yet presented in such a manner as to appeal to the general reader and student of literature.

Among philosophical writers Schopenhauer enjoys the advantage of standing alone. He cannot be classified. He thus escapes being lost in the crowd. It is indeed true that a great deal of what he writes is taken from his predecessors. It is, however, borrowed, not stolen. It is in each case acknowledged and accredited to the original authors, and while it is adopted by Schopenhauer it is so assimilated and transmuted as to become his own, bearing his image and superscription.

He also possesses the advantage of a distinctive and polished literary style. He has a highly developed artistic sense and in accordance with this selects and arranges his material in a form of expression pleasing to his readers. Although a recluse and given to the habit of talking to himself, when he writes he talks to his reader frankly and entertainingly. While he does not even pretend to practice what he preaches in regard to ethical matters, it will be found that his views on the writing of literature are practiced by himself. For instance, note the advice to writers upon the choice of a title. How well has he succeeded in this. Each of his writings has a title appropriate, striking, suggestive, illuminating.

Another advantage that Schopenhauer has, is, that while posing as a critic, he is also the advocate of a positive belief. His criticism is not merely fault-finding without any substitute proposed. His confidence in his own theory, whether justifiable or not, makes him earnest at all times, and this makes even his petty moods and savage attacks attain a certain dignity that covers a multitude of sins.

An additional advantage that Schopenhauer has is in possessing a unique and striking personality. This always attracts notice and interest even if it does not evoke admiration or elicit approval. On the whole there is more of what we can in a sense admire than there is of what we can commend in Schopenhauer's personality. Nevertheless one is fascinated with the peculiarities of this eccentric individual. He is a problem as complex as his philosophy. Indeed they are the same problem, for, as much as any writer not excepting Fichte, and much more than most other writers, Schopenhauer's philosophy is an expression of himself. His own peculiar character is the "will" of which his philosophy is the "presentation," to use his own phraseology. From this one would naturally be led to expect a consistent and harmonious system, but this presupposes a unitary character. Such, however, is just the reverse of the facts in this case. Schopenhauer's character is a walking contradiction. No delineation of a Dr. Jekyll and Mr. Hyde can approach to the weird and uncanny way in which the two natures are bound together, forever fiercely fighting, not alternating, in Schopenhauer. He himself is well aware of this, and in his own way tries to account for it first by heredity and secondly by a philosophy of the Universe. His philosophy of the Universe is just himself "writ large," just as his remarks on women are just a detailed account of his mother, as he views her.

Arthur Schopenhauer was born in 1788, died in 1860.* His

---

*For Schopenhauer's "Life and Writings," see Article "Arthur Schopenhauer" in Encyclopædia Britannica, Vol. XXI., pp. 448–458; also "Life of Arthur Schopenhauer," by William Wallace, with Bibliography, by J. P. Anderson, up to 1890; published by Walter Scott, London.

For a criticism of Schopenhauer's system see article by R. Adamson in "Mind," Vol. I., 1876, pp. 491–509.

father, Heinrich Schopenhauer, was a wealthy merchant of Dantzic, of strong political opinions, cosmopolitan interests, and independence of thought. His mother was Johanna Schopenhauer, a graceful and refined lady of literary instincts and ambitions, who, after her husband's death, attained to some degree of success as an authoress. From the standpoint of heredity Schopenhauer was unfortunate on the father's side, as there were in the father strong tendencies to mental alienation that appeared in the son in the form of eccentricities, groundless fears, and suspiciousness. On his mother's side he also suffered in environment, for according to Schopenhauer's testimony, her method of dealing with him was unsympathetic. It must be granted that he was not an easy individual to deal with. His mother's butterfly vanity and her selfishness, her method of snubbing, mortifying, and disparaging her son were unfortunate and injurious in their influence. She did not seem to have the true mother instinct of love which Schopenhauer sadly needed. While Kant could recall the tender solicitude and pious influence of a godly and deeply affectionate mother molding his whole life, Schopenhauer could accuse his mother of frivolity and heartlessness. Not that she was positively cruel, but simply lacking in regard for her son.

With natural tendencies that dragged him to the earth, there was conjoined a genius that turned his gaze upward persistently. This was his love for the beautiful and his interest in reflective contemplation. From the poet-philosopher Plato he appropriated a vision of the ideal world in contrast with the fleeting shadows that mock us. Plato's story of the Cave is Schopenhauer's philosophy in its main features. He turns with eager interest to the neo-Platonic adaptations of the original Plato. From this he is led back to Oriental speculation with its Buddhistic self-obliteration, its annihilation of the Will-to-live, its Nirvana. He studied Kant assiduously and made himself familiar with the leading features of this great modern thinker. When he began to write his own views he claimed to be the true disciple of Kant, but in reality he translates, selects, rejects, adapts, and modifies Kant to

suit his own predilections. He was the first to call attention to the differences in the two editions of Kant's
« Critique of the Pure Reason,» and fiercely attacks Kant
for modifications introduced into the second edition.
Among English readers both Kant and Hegel have suffered to some extent from the fact that in many cases
they have been first looked at through the spectacles of
Schopenhauer's presentation, which is often a misrepresentation. The fault is partly with Kant and Hegel. What
Schopenhauer says about the style or rather lack of style
in much that they wrote is — unfortunately too true. It
is not surprising that the majority of those to whom
German is a foreign language should begin their acquaintance with German philosophy through the reading of
Schopenhauer, because of the elegance, simplicity, and
charm of his exposition. But Schopenhauer is not a trustworthy expositor or critic of others. He can speak for
himself and he warns his readers against accepting any
exposition of an author, earnestly advises them to go to
the originals and not take their impressions from the
« cast of a cast,» blurred and indistinct like old type. A
knowledge of Kant will help much in the comprehension
and correction of Schopenhauer. A knowledge of Hegel
is almost as essential to the philosophical student as an
antidote against Schopenhauer's onesidedness.*

It would be the easiest thing in the world to trace
contradictions in Schopenhauer. According to his theory
the whole Universe is a mighty contradiction where the
false appearances continually strive to usurp the place
that rightfully belongs to the deeper, more abiding Will.
What Schopenhauer means by "Will" is a puzzle not
easily solved. The reader should be warned against
lightly identifying the term with his own previous conceptions. In connection with this chief term we may
find opposite poles of meaning from the crudest materialistic to the most refined idealistic. It would be tedious
to enumerate the ambiguities whereby he alternately pleases
and displeases all sorts and conditions of theorizers and

---

*The following writers in English have been in various degrees
influenced by Hegel: Morris, Wallace, Green, John and Edward
Caird, Watson, Royce, Ritchie, Dewey, Harris.

anti-theorizers. He declares that a man's creed should be
" I must have a metaphysic," and then elaborately argues
that all metaphysic is foolishness. He asserts that speculation is for action, wisdom for life, and then sophistically
argues that we should not expect a metaphysician to be
a saint, and as usual proves (?) it by a misleading analogy
from the sculptor who does not need to be himself beautiful to make a beautiful statue. He does not claim consistency between his theory and his practice. Although
he discovers the root of all morality and religion in a basal
sympathy due to the fact that in the last resort all beings are but passing phases of the one identical striving;
the chief characteristic in Schopenhauer is his misan-
thropic lack of sympathy. Although he outruns the mystics, the pietists and the pantheists in his demand not
only for the renunciation of the joys of life but also of the
love of life, he cleverly refutes the foolishness of suicide.

In spite of contradictions sometimes amusing, often
tragic, due to the conflict of his own character, we may
gather much of what is true and excellent from Schopenhauer. His claim that a man should have a theory of
life that is really his own and not one blindly adopted
on authority is a truth that needs to be reasserted in
every age. Without this insight, no progress. Schopenhauer has been accused of repudiating history altogether.
What he despises and condemns is the mere enumeration
of incidents without discerning their deeper meaning.
It may be granted that he does more to state the problem of life than he does toward solving it. He refers to
" Will " as his ultimate metaphysical reality, and to
" Sympathy " as his ultimate ethical principle. The problem he leaves to his successors is to discover in what
sense " Will " and " Sympathy " must be understood, if
they are to result in self-conservation and not in self-
destruction as in Schopenhauer. Even Schopenhauer's
pessimistic conclusion has a philosophical value. Unlike
such writers as John Locke and John Stuart Mill, who
start with a narrow theory and end with many excellent
truths that are brought in not because of their theory,
but in spite of it, whereby the original jackdaw gets
decked in borrowed plumage, Schopenhauer with all his

waywardness is at least in his final conclusion consistent with his fundamental philosophy. To those who reject his "materialistic pantheism," the gloomy pessimism in which it is seen to issue will be regarded as a truer insight than the somewhat shallow optimism that characterizes other recent theosophical pantheistic systems. The pessimistic conclusion is more likely to lead to a reconsideration of the original presuppositions.

Schopenhauer explicitly announces that he is in open revolt against every so-called orthodox position. His work is throughout a protest. He naturally attracts to him every one who is dissatisfied, and where can we find anyone who thinks seriously who does not find something needing emendation? It will not be surprising if the majority of those who would in varying degrees accept Schopenhauer's denunciations of established opinions should also see equal force in the objections that could be urged against his own position. The result might be that instead of saying that nothing was left over worthy of being retained, the point of view gained by the discovery of inadequacy in each one-sided position might lead to the stereoscopic combination whereby a new result would be gained far in advance of either Schopenhauer or his opponents, for which we should give both of them humble and hearty thanks.

Schopenhauer, in spite of all his faults, is a mine of suggestion both to the literary and to the philosophical student. If we understand the secret of his waywardness and extend our sympathy, we shall reap much benefit and not waste our efforts in too harsh criticism.

James Gibson Hume.

CONTENTS

THE WISDOM OF LIFE

ESSAYS

(xi)

INTRODUCTION.

In these pages I shall speak of "The Wisdom of Life" in the common meaning of the term, as the art, namely, of ordering our lives so as to obtain the greatest possible amount of pleasure and success; an art the theory of which may be called Eudæmonology, for it teaches us how to lead a happy existence. Such an existence might perhaps be defined as one which, looked at from a purely objective point of view, or rather, after cool and mature reflection — for the question necessarily involves subjective considerations,— would be decidedly preferable to non-existence; implying that we should cling to it for its own sake, and not merely from the fear of death; and further, that we should never like it to come to an end.

Now whether human life corresponds, or could possibly correspond, to this conception of existence, is a question to which, as is well known, my philosophical system returns a negative answer. On the eudæmonistic hypothesis, however, the question must be answered in the affirmative; and I have shown, in the second volume of my chief work (ch. 49), that this hypothesis is based upon a fundamental mistake. Accordingly, in elaborating the scheme of a happy existence, I have had to make a complete surrender of the higher metaphysical and ethical standpoint to which my own theories lead; and everything I shall say here will to some extent rest upon a compromise; in so far, that is, as I take the common standpoint of every day, and embrace the error which is at the bottom of it. My remarks, therefore, will possess only a qualified value, for the very word eudæmonology is a euphemism. Further, I make no claims to completeness; partly because the subject is inexhaustible, and partly because I should otherwise have to say over again what has been already said by others.

I

The only book composed, as far as I remember, with a like purpose to that which animates this collection of aphorisms, is Cardan's *De utilitate ex adversis capienda*, which is well worth reading, and may be used to supplement the present work. Aristotle, it is true, has a few words on eudæmonology in the fifth chapter of the first book of his "Rhetoric;" but what he says does not come to very much. As compilation is not my business, I have made no use of these predecessors; more especially because in the process of compiling individuality of view is lost, and individuality of view is the kernel of works of this kind. In general, indeed, the wise in all ages have always said the same thing, and the fools, who at all times form the immense majority, have in their way, too, acted alike, and done just the opposite; and so it will continue. For, as Voltaire says, WE SHALL LEAVE THIS WORLD AS FOOLISH AND AS WICKED AS WE FOUND IT ON OUR ARRIVAL.

THE WISDOM OF LIFE.

CHAPTER I.

DIVISION OF THE SUBJECT.

ARISTOTLE divides the blessings of life into three classes — those which come to us from without, those of the soul, and those of the body. Keeping nothing of this division but the number, I observe that the fundamental differences in human lot may be reduced to three distinct classes :

(1) What a man is : that is to say, personality, in the widest sense of the word; under which are included health, strength, beauty, temperament, moral character, intelligence and education.

(2) What a man has : that is, property and possessions of every kind.

(3) How a man stands in the estimation of others : by which is to be understood, as everybody knows, what a man is in the eyes of his fellow-men, or, more strictly, the light in which they regard him. This is shown by their opinion of him; and their opinion is in its turn manifested by the honor in which he is held, and by his rank and reputation.

The differences which come under the first head are those which Nature herself has set between man and man; and from this fact alone we may at once infer that they influence the happiness or unhappiness of mankind in a much more vital and radical way than those contained under the two following heads, which are merely the effect of human arrangements. Compared with GENUINE PERSONAL ADVANTAGES, such as a great mind or a great heart, all the privileges of rank or birth, even of royal birth, are but as kings on the stage to kings in real life. The same thing was said long ago by Metrodorus, the earliest disciple of Epicurus, who wrote as the title of one of his chapters, THE HAPPINESS WE RECEIVE FROM OURSELVES IS GREATER THAN THAT WHICH WE OBTAIN FROM OUR SURROUNDINGS. And it is an obvious fact, which cannot be called in question, that the principal element in a man's well-being,— indeed, in the whole tenor of his existence,— is what he is made of, his inner constitution. For this is the immediate source of that inward satisfaction or dissatisfaction resulting from the sum total of his sensations, desires and thoughts; while his surroundings on the other hand, exert only a mediate or indirect influence upon him. This is why the same external events or circumstances affect no two people alike; even with perfectly similar surroundings every one lives in a world of his own. For a man has immediate apprehension only of his own ideas, feelings and volitions; the outer world can influence him only in so far as it brings these to life. The world in which a man lives shapes itself chiefly by the way in which he looks at it, and so it proves different to different men; to one it is barren, dull, and superficial; to another rich, interesting, and full of meaning. On hearing of the interesting events which have happened in the course of a man's experience, many people will wish that similar things had happened in their lives too, completely forgetting that they should be envious rather of the mental aptitude which lent those events the significance they possess when he describes them. To a man of genius they were interesting adventures; but to the dull perceptions of an ordinary individual they would have been stale, everyday occurrences. This is in the highest degree the case with many of Goethe's and Byron's poems, which are obviously founded upon actual facts; where it is open to a foolish reader to envy the poet because so many delightful things happened to him, instead of envying that mighty power of phantasy which was capable of turning a fairly common experience into something so great and beautiful.

In the same way, a person of melancholy temperament will make a scene in a tragedy out of what appears to the sanguine man only in the light of an interesting conflict, and to a phlegmatic soul as something without any meaning. This all rests upon the fact that every event, in order to be realized and appreciated, requires the co-operation of two factors, namely, a subject and an object; although these are as closely and necessarily connected as oxygen and hydrogen in water. When therefore the objective or external factor in an experience is actually the same, but the subjective or personal appreciation of it varies, the event is just as much a different one in the eyes of different persons as if the objective factors had not been alike; for to a blunt intelligence the fairest and best object in the world presents only a poor reality and is therefore only poorly appreciated,—like a fine landscape in dull weather, or in the reflection of a bad *camera obscura*. In plain language, every man is pent up within the limits of his own consciousness, and cannot directly get beyond those limits any more than he can get beyond his own skin; so external aid is not of much use to him. On the stage, one man is a prince, another a minister, a third a servant or a soldier or a general, and so on, mere external differences; the inner reality, the kernel of all these appearances is the same — a poor player, with all the anxieties of his lot. In life it is just the same. Differences of rank and wealth give every man his part to play, but this by no means implies a difference of inward happiness and pleasure; here, too, there is the same being in all — a poor mortal, with his hardships and troubles. Though these may, indeed, in every case proceed from dissimilar causes, they are in their essential nature much the same in all their forms, with degrees of intensity which vary, no doubt, but in nowise correspond to the part a man has to play, or the presence or absence of position and wealth. Since everything which exists or happens for a man exists only in his consciousness and happens for it alone, the most essential thing for a man is the constitution of this consciousness, which is in most cases far more important than the circumstances which go to form its contents. All the pride and pleasure of the world, mirrored in the dull consciousness of a fool, is poor indeed compared with the imagination of Cervantes writing his "Don Quixote" in a miserable prison. The objective half of life and reality is in the hand of fate, and accordingly takes various forms in different cases: the subjective half is ourself, and in essentials it always remains the same.

Hence the life of every man is stamped with the same character throughout, however much his external circumstances may alter; it is like a series of variations on a single theme. No one can get beyond his own individuality. An animal, under whatever circumstances it is placed, remains within the narrow limits to which nature has irrevocably consigned it; so that our endeavors to make a pet happy must always keep within the compass of its nature, and be restricted to what it can feel. So it is with man; the measure of the happiness he can attain is determined beforehand by his individuality. More especially is this the case with the mental powers, which fix once for all his capacity for the higher kinds of pleasure. If these powers are small, no efforts from without, nothing that his fellow-men or that fortune can do for him, will suffice to raise him above the ordinary degree of human happiness and pleasure, half animal though it be. His only resources are his sensual appetite, a cosy and cheerful family life at the most, low company and vulgar pastime; even education, on the whole, can avail little, if anything, for the enlargement of his horizon. For the highest, most varied and lasting pleasures are those of the mind, however much our youth may deceive us on this point; and the pleasures of the mind turn chiefly on the powers of the mind. It is clear, then, that our happiness depends in a great degree upon what we ARE, upon our individuality, while lot or destiny is generally taken to mean only what we HAVE, or our REPUTATION. Our lot, in this sense, may improve; but we do not ask much of it if we are inwardly rich: on the other hand, a fool remains a fool, a dull blockhead, to his last hour, even though he were surrounded by houris in paradise. This is why Goethe, in the "West-östlicher Divan," says that every man, whether he occupy a low position in life, or emerges as its victor, testifies to personality as the greatest factor in happiness: —

> Volk und Knecht und Ueberwinder
> Sie gestehen, zu jeder Zeit,
> Höchstes Glück der Erdenkinder
> Sei nur die Persönlichkeit.

Common experience shows that the subjective element in life is incomparably more important for our happiness and pleasure than the objective, from such sayings as HUNGER IS THE BEST SAUCE, and YOUTH AND AGE CANNOT LIVE TOGETHER, up to the life of the Genius and the Saint. Health outweighs all other blessings so much that one may really say that a healthy beggar is happier than an ailing king. A quiet and cheerful temperament, happy in the enjoyment of a perfectly sound physique, an intellect clear, lively, penetrating and seeing things as they are, a moderate and gentle will, and therefore a good conscience — these are privileges which no rank or wealth can make up for or replace. For what a man is in himself, what accompanies him when he is alone, what no one can give or take away, is obviously more essential to him than everything he has in the way of possessions, or even what he may be in the eyes of the world. An intellectual man in complete solitude has excellent entertainment in his own thoughts and fancies, while no amount or diversity of social pleasure, theatres, excursions and amusements, can ward off boredom from a dullard. A good, temperate, gentle character can be happy in needy circumstances, while a covetous, envious and malicious man, even if he be the richest in the world, goes miserable. Nay more; to one who has the constant delight of a special individuality, with a high degree of intellect, most of the pleasures which are run after by mankind are perfectly superfluous; they are even a trouble and a burden. And so Horace says of himself, that, however many are deprived of the fancy-goods of life, there is one at least who can live without them : —

> Gemmas, marmor, ebur, Tyrrhena sigilla, tabellas,
> Argentum, vestes Gætulo murice tinctas
> Sunt qui non habeant, est qui non curat habere;

and when Socrates saw various articles of luxury spread out for sale, he exclaimed : How MUCH THERE IS IN THE WORLD THAT I DO NOT WANT.

So the first and most essential element in our life's happiness is what we are, our personality, if for no other reason than that it is a constant factor coming into play under all circumstances. Besides, unlike the blessings which are described under the other two heads, it is not the sport of destiny and cannot be wrested from us; and, so far, it is endowed with an absolute value in contrast to the merely relative worth of the other two. The consequence of this is that it is much more difficult than people commonly suppose to get a hold on a man from without. But here the all-powerful agent, Time, comes in and claims its rights, and before its influence physical and mental advantages gradually waste away. Moral character alone remains inaccessible to it. In view of the destructive effect of time, it seems, indeed, as if the blessings named under the other two heads, of which time cannot directly rob us, were superior to those of the first. Another advantage might be claimed for them, namely, that being in their very nature objective and external, they are attainable, and every one is presented with the possibility, at least, of coming into possession of them; while what is subjective is not open to us to acquire, but making its entry by a kind of DIVINE RIGHT, it remains for life, immutable, inalienable, an inexorable doom. Let me quote those lines in which Goethe describes how an unalterable destiny is assigned to every man at the hour of his birth, so that he can develop only in the lines laid down for him, as it were, by the conjunctions of the stars; and how the Sibyl and the prophets declare that HIMSELF a man can never escape, nor any power of time avail to change the path on which his life is cast:—

> Wie an dem Tag, der dich der Welt verliehen,
> Die Sonne stand zum Grusse der Planeten,
> Bist alsobald und fort und fort gediehen,
> Nach dem Gesetz, wonach du angetreten.
> So musst du sein, dir kannst du nicht entfliehen,
> So sagten schon Sibyllen und Propheten;
> Und keine Zeit und keine Macht zerstückelt
> Geprägte Form, die lebend sich entwickelt.

The only thing that stands in our power to achieve, is to make the most advantageous use possible of the personal qualities we possess, and accordingly to follow such pursuits only as will call them into play, to strive after the kind of perfection of which they admit and to avoid every other; consequently, to choose the position, occupation and manner of life which are most suitable for their development.

Imagine a man endowed with herculean strength who is compelled by circumstances to follow a sedentary occupation, some minute exquisite work of the hands, for example, or to engage in study and mental labor demanding quite other powers, and just those which he has not got, compelled, that is, to leave unused the powers in which he is pre-eminently strong; a man placed like this will never feel happy all his life through. Even more miserable will be the lot of the man with intellectual powers of a very high order, who has to leave them undeveloped and unemployed, in the pursuit of a calling which does not require them, some bodily labor, perhaps, for which his strength is insufficient. Still, in a case of this kind, it should be our care, especially in youth, to avoid the precipice of presumption, and not ascribe to ourselves a superfluity of power which is not there.

Since the blessings described under the first head decidedly outweigh those contained under the other two, it is manifestly a wiser course to aim at the maintenance of our health and the cultivation of our faculties, than at the amassing of wealth; but this must not be mistaken as meaning that we should neglect to acquire an adequate supply of the necessaries of life. Wealth, in the strict sense of the word, that is, great superfluity, can do little for our happiness; and many rich people feel unhappy just because they are without any true mental culture or knowledge, and consequently have no objective interests which would qualify them for intellectual occupations. For beyond the satisfaction of some real and natural necessities, all that the possession of wealth can achieve has a very small influence upon our happiness, in the proper sense of the word; indeed, wealth rather disturbs it, because the preservation of property entails a great many unavoidable anxieties. And still men are a thousand times more intent on becoming rich than on acquiring culture, though it is quite certain that what a man is contributes much more to his happiness than what he HAS. So you may see many a man, as industrious as an ant, ceaselessly occupied from morning to night in the endeavor to increase his heap of gold. Beyond the narrow horizon of means to this end, he knows nothing; his mind is a blank, and consequently unsusceptible to any other influence. The highest pleasures, those of the intellect, are to him inaccessible, and he tries in vain to replace them by the fleeting pleasures of sense in which he indulges, lasting but a brief hour and at tremendous cost. And if he is lucky, his struggles result in his having a really great pile of gold, which he leaves to his heir, either to make it still larger or to squander it in extravagance. A life like this, though pursued with a sense of earnestness and an air of importance, is just as silly as many another which has a fool's cap for its symbol.

WHAT A MAN HAS IN HIMSELF is, then, the chief element in his happiness. Because this is, as a rule, so very little, most of those who are placed beyond the struggle with penury, feel at bottom quite as unhappy as those who are still engaged in it. Their minds are vacant, their imagination dull, their spirits poor, and so they are driven to the company of those like them — for *similis simili gaudet* — where they make common pursuit of pastime and entertainment, consisting for the most part in sensual pleasure, amusement of every kind, and finally, in excess and libertinism. A young man of rich family enters upon life with a large patrimony, and often runs through it in an incredibly short space of time, in vicious extravagance; and why? Simply because, here too, the mind is empty and void, and so the man is bored with existence. He was sent forth into the world outwardly rich but inwardly poor, and his vain endeavor was to make his external wealth compensate for his inner poverty, by trying to obtain everything FROM WITHOUT, like an old man who seeks to strengthen himself as King David or Maréchal de Retz tried to do. And so in the end one who is inwardly poor comes to be also poor outwardly.

I need not insist upon the importance of the other two kinds of blessings which make up the happiness of human life; nowadays the value of possessing them is too well known to require advertisement. The third class, it is

true, may seem, compared with the second, of a very
ethereal character, as it consists only of other people's
opinions. Still everyone has to strive for reputation, that
is to say, a good name. Rank, on the other hand, should
be aspired to only by those who serve the State, and fame
by very few indeed. In any case, reputation is looked
upon as a priceless treasure, and fame as the most precious of all the blessings a man can attain, the Golden
Fleece, as it were, of the elect: while only fools will prefer rank to property. The second and third classes, moreover, are reciprocally cause and effect; so far that is, as
Petronius' maxim, *habes habeberis*, is true; and conversely,
the favor of others, in all its forms, often puts us in the
way of getting what we want.

CHAPTER II.

PERSONALITY, OR WHAT A MAN IS.

WE HAVE already seen, in general, that what a man IS contributes much more to his happiness than what he HAS, or how he is regarded by others. What a man is, and so what he has in his own person, is always the chief thing to consider; for his individuality accompanies him always and everywhere, and gives its color to all his experiences. In every kind of enjoyment, for instance, the pleasure depends principally upon the man himself. Every one admits this in regard to physical, and how much truer it is of intellectual, pleasure. When we use that English expression, "to enjoy oneself," we are employing a very striking and appropriate phrase; for observe — one says not "he enjoys Paris," but "he enjoys himself in Paris." To a man possessed of an ill-conditioned individuality, all pleasure is like delicate wine in a mouth made bitter with gall. Therefore, in the blessings as well as in the ills of life, less depends upon what befalls us than upon the way in which it is met, that is, upon the kind and degree of our general susceptibility. What a man is and has in himself, — in a word, personality, with all it entails, is the only immediate and direct factor in his happiness and welfare. All else is mediate and indirect, and its influence can be neutralized and frustrated; but the influence of personality never. This is why the envy which personal qualities excite is the most implacable of all, — as it is also the most carefully dissembled.

Further, the constitution of our consciousness is the ever present and lasting element in all we do or suffer; our individuality is persistently at work, more or less, at every moment of our life; all other influences are temporal, incidental, fleeting, and subject to every kind of chance and change. This is why Aristotle says: IT IS NOT WEALTH BUT CHARACTER THAT LASTS. And just for the same reason we can more easily bear a misfortune which comes to us entirely from without, than one which we have drawn upon ourselves; for fortune may always change, but not character. Therefore, subjective blessings,—a noble nature, a capable head, a joyful temperament, bright spirits, a well-constituted, perfectly sound physique, in a word, *mens sana in corpore sano*, are the first and most important elements in happiness; so that we should be more intent on promoting and preserving such qualities than on the possession of external wealth and external honor.

And of all these, the one which makes us the most directly happy is a genial flow of good spirits; for this excellent quality is its own immediate reward. The man who is cheerful and merry has always a good reason for being so, the fact, namely, that he is so. There is nothing which, like this quality, can so completely replace the loss of every other blessing. If you know anyone who is young, handsome, rich and esteemed, and you want to know, further, if he is happy, ask, is he cheerful and genial? and if he is, what does it matter whether he is young or old, straight or humpbacked, poor or rich? he is happy. In my early days I once opened an old book and found these words: IF YOU LAUGH A GREAT DEAL, YOU ARE HAPPY; IF YOU CRY A GREAT DEAL, YOU ARE UNHAPPY; a very simple remark, no doubt; but just because it is so simple I have never been able to forget it, even though it is in the last degree a truism. So if cheerfulness knocks at our door, we should throw it wide open, for it never comes inopportunely. Instead of that, we often make scruples about letting it in. We want to be quite sure that we have every reason to be contented; then we are afraid that cheerfulness of spirits may interfere with serious reflections or weighty cares. Cheerfulness is a direct and immediate gain, the very coin, as it were, of happiness, and not, like all else, merely a cheque upon the bank; for it alone makes us immediately happy in the present moment, and that is the highest blessing for beings like us, whose existence is but an infinitesimal moment between two eternities. To secure and promote this feeling of cheerfulness should be the supreme aim of all our endeavors after happiness.

Now it is certain that nothing contributes so little to cheerfulness as riches, or so much, as health. Is it not in the lower classes, the so-called working classes, more especially those of them who live in the country, that we see cheerful and contented faces? and is it not among the rich, the upper classes, that we find faces full of ill-humor and vexation? Consequently we should try as much as possible to maintain a high degree of health; for cheerfulness is the very flower of it. I need hardly say what one must do to be healthy — avoid every kind of excess, all violent and unpleasant emotion, all mental overstrain, take daily exercise in the open air, cold baths and such like hygienic measures. For without a proper amount of daily exercise no one can remain healthy; all the processes of life demand exercise for the due performance of their functions, exercise not only of the parts more immediately concerned, but also of the whole body. For, as Aristotle rightly says, LIFE IS MOVEMENT; it is its very essence. Ceaseless and rapid motion goes on in every part of the organism. The heart, with its complicated double systole and diastole, beats strongly and untiringly; with twenty-eight beats it has to drive the whole of the blood through arteries, veins and capillaries; the lungs pump like a steam-engine, without intermission; the intestines are always in peristaltic action; the glands are all constantly absorbing and secreting; even the brain has a double motion of its own, with every beat of the pulse and every breath we draw. When people can get no exercise at all, as is the case with the countless numbers who are condemned to a sedentary life, there is a glaring and fatal disproportion between outward inactivity and inner tumult. For this ceaseless internal motion requires some external counterpart, and the want of it produces effects like those of emotion which we are obliged to suppress. Even trees must be shaken by the wind, if they are to thrive. The rule which finds its application here may be most briefly expressed in Latin: *omnis motus, quo celerior, eo magis motus.*

How much our happiness depends upon our spirits, and these again upon our state of health, may be seen by comparing the influence which the same external circumstances or events have upon us when we are well and strong with the effect which they have when we are depressed and troubled with ill-health. It is not what things are objectively and in themselves, but what they are for us, in our way of looking at them, that makes us happy or the reverse. As Epictetus says, MEN ARE NOT INFLUENCED BY THINGS BUT BY THEIR THOUGHTS ABOUT THINGS. And, in general, nine-tenths of our happiness depends upon health alone. With health, everything is a source of pleasure: without it, nothing else, whatever it may be, is enjoyable; even the other personal blessings,— a great mind, a happy temperament — are degraded and dwarfed for want of it. So it is really with good reason that, when two people meet, the first thing they do is to inquire after each other's health, and to express the hope that it is good; for good health is by far the most important element in human happiness. It follows from all this that the greatest of follies is to sacrifice health for any other kind of happiness, whatever it may be, for gain, advancement, learning or fame, let alone, then, for fleeting sensual pleasures. Everything else should rather be postponed to it.

But however much health may contribute to that flow of good spirits which is so essential to our happiness, good spirits do not entirely depend upon health; for a man may be perfectly sound in his physique and still possess a melancholy temperament and be generally given up to sad thoughts. The ultimate cause of this is undoubtedly to be found in innate, and therefore unalterable physical constitution, especially in the more or less normal relation of a man's sensitiveness to his muscular and vital energy. Abnormal sensitiveness produces inequality of spirits, a predominating melancholy, with periodical fits of unrestrained liveliness. A genius is one whose nervous power or sensitiveness is largely in excess; as Aristotle has very correctly observed, MEN DISTINGUISHED IN PHILOSOPHY, POLITICS, POETRY OR ART, APPEAR TO BE ALL OF A MELANCHOLY TEMPERAMENT. This is doubtless the passage which Cicero has in his mind when he says, as he often does, *Aristoteles ait omnes ingeniosos melancholicos esse.* Shakespeare has very neatly expressed this radical and innate diversity of temperament in those lines in "The Merchant of Venice":

> Nature has framed strange fellows in her time;
> Some that will evermore peep through their eyes,
> And laugh, like parrots at a bag-piper;
> And others of such vinegar aspect,
> That they'll not show their teeth in way of smile,
> Though Nestor swear the jest be laughable.

This is the difference which Plato draws between εὔκολος and δύσκολος — the man of EASY, and the man of DIFFICULT disposition — in proof of which he refers to the varying degrees of susceptibility which different people show to pleasurable and painful impressions; so that one man will laugh at what makes another despair. As a rule, the stronger the susceptibility to unpleasant impressions, the weaker is the susceptibility to pleasant ones, and *vice versa*. If it is equally possible for an event to turn out well or ill, the δύσκολοι will be annoyed or grieved if the issue is unfavorable, and will not rejoice, should it be happy. On the other hand, the εὔκολος will neither worry nor fret over an unfavorable issue, but rejoice if it turns out well. If the one is successful in nine out of ten undertakings, he will not be pleased, but rather annoyed that one has miscarried; while the other, if only a single one succeeds, will manage to find consolation in the fact and remain cheerful. But here is another instance of the truth, that hardly any evil is entirely without its compensation; for the misfortunes and sufferings which the δύσκολοι, that is, people of gloomy and anxious character, have to overcome, are, on the whole, more imaginary and therefore less real than those which befall the gay and careless; for a man who paints everything black, who constantly fears the worst and takes measures accordingly, will not be disappointed so often in this world, as one who always looks upon the bright side of things. And when a morbid affection of the nerves, or a derangement of the digestive organs, plays into the hand of an innate tendency to gloom, this tendency may reach such a height that permanent discomfort produces a weariness of life. So arises an inclination to suicide, which even the most trivial unpleasantness may actually bring about; nay, when the tendency attains its worst form, it may be occasioned by nothing in particular, but a man may resolve to put an end to his existence, simply because he is permanently unhappy, and then coolly and firmly carry out his determination; as may be seen by the way in which the sufferer, when placed under supervision, as he usually is, eagerly waits to seize the first unguarded moment, when, without a shudder, without a struggle or recoil, he may use the now natural and welcome means of effecting his release. Even the healthiest, perhaps even the most cheerful man, may resolve upon death under certain circumstances; when, for instance, his sufferings, or his fears of some inevitable misfortune, reach such a pitch as to outweigh the terrors of death. The only difference lies in the degree of suffering necessary to bring about the fatal act, a degree which will be high in the case of a cheerful, and low in that of a gloomy man. The greater the melancholy, the lower need the degree be; in the end, it may even sink to zero. But if a man is cheerful, and his spirits are supported by good health, it requires a high degree of suffering to make him lay hands upon himself. There are countless steps in the scale between the two extremes of suicide, the suicide which springs merely from a morbid intensification of innate gloom, and the suicide of the healthy and cheerful man, who has entirely objective grounds for putting an end to his existence.

Beauty is partly an affair of health. It may be reckoned as a personal advantage; though it does not, properly speaking, contribute directly to our happiness. It does so indirectly, by impressing other people; and it is no unimportant advantage, even in man. Beauty is an open letter of recommendation, predisposing the heart to favor the person who presents it. As is well said in those lines of Homer, the gift of beauty is not lightly to be thrown away, that glorious gift which none can bestow save the gods alone —

οὔτοι ἀπόβλητ᾽ ἐστὶ θεῶν ἐρικυδέα δῶρα,
ὅσσα κεν αὐτοὶ δῶσιν, ἑκὼν δ᾽οὐκ ἄν τις ἕλοιτο.

2

The most general survey shows us that the two foes of human happiness are pain and boredom. We may go further, and say that in the degree in which we are fortunate enough to get away from the one, we approach the other. Life presents, in fact, a more or less violent oscillation between the two. The reason of this is that each of these two poles stands in a double antagonism to the other, external or objective, and inner or subjective. Needy surroundings and poverty produce pain; while, if a man is more than well off, he is bored. Accordingly, while the lower classes are engaged in a ceaseless struggle with need, in other words with pain, the upper carry on a constant and often desperate battle with boredom.* The inner or subjective antagonism arises from the fact that, in the individual, susceptibility to pain varies inversely with susceptibility to boredom, because susceptibility is directly proportionate to mental power. Let me explain. A dull mind is, as a rule associated with dull sensibilities, nerves which no stimulus can affect, a temperament, in short, which does not feel pain or anxiety very much, however great or terrible it may be. Now, intellectual dullness is at the bottom of that VACUITY OF SOUL which is stamped on so many faces, a state of mind which betrays itself by a constant and lively attention to all the trivial circumstances in the external world. This is the true source of boredom — a continual panting after excitement, in order to have a pretext for giving the mind and spirits something to occupy them. The kind of things people choose for this purpose shows that they are not very particular, as witness the miserable pastimes they have recourse to, and their ideas of social pleasure and conversation; or again, the number of people who gossip on the doorstep or gape out of the window. It is mainly because of this inner vacuity of soul that people go in quest of society, diversion, amusement, luxury of every sort, which lead many to extravagance and misery. Nothing is so good a protection against such misery as inward

---

*And the extremes meet; for the lowest state of civilization, a nomad or wandering life, finds its counterpart in the highest, where everyone is at times a tourist. The earlier stage was a case of necessity; the latter is a remedy for boredom.

wealth, the wealth of the mind, because the greater it
grows, the less room it leaves for boredom.   The inexhaustible activity of thought! finding ever new material
to work upon in the multifarious phenomena of self and
nature, and able and ready to form new combinations of
them, there you have something that invigorates the
mind, and apart from the moments of relaxation, sets it
far above the reach of boredom.

But, on the other hand, this high degree of intelligence
is rooted in a high degree of susceptibility, greater strength
of will, greater passionateness; and from the union of these
qualities comes an increased capacity for emotion, an en-
hanced sensibility to all mental and even bodily pain,
greater impatience of obstacles, greater resentment of interruption; all of which tendencies are augmented by the
power of the imagination, the vivid character of the whole
range of thought, including what is disagreeable.   This
applies, in varying degrees, to every step in the long scale
of mental power, from the veriest dunce to the greatest
genius that ever lived.   Therefore the nearer anyone is,
either from a subjective or from an objective point of view,
to one of these sources of suffering in human life, the
farther he is from the other.   And so a man's natural
bent will lead him to make his objective world conform
to his subjective as much as possible; that is to say, he
will take the greatest measures against that form of suffering to which he is most liable.   The wise man will,
above all, strive after freedom from pain and annoyance,
quiet and leisure, consequently a tranquil, modest life,
with as few encounters as may be; and so, after a little
experience of his so-called fellow-men, he will elect to live
in retirement, or even, if he is a man of great intellect,
in solitude.   For the more a man has in himself, the less
he will want from other people, the less, indeed, other people can be to him.   This is why a high degree of intellect
tends to make a man unsocial.   True, if QUALITY of intellect could be made up for by QUANTITY, it might be worth
while to live even in the great world; but, unfortunately,
a hundred fools together will not make one wise man.

But the individual who stands at the other end of the
scale is no sooner free from the pangs of need than he

endeavors to get pastime and society at any cost, taking up with the first person he meets, and avoiding nothing so much as himself. For in solitude, where every one is thrown upon his own resources, what a man has in himself comes to light: the fool in fine raiment groans under the burden of his miserable personality, a burden which he can never throw off, while the man of talent peoples the waste places with his animating thoughts. Seneca declares that folly is its own burden, *omnis stultitia laborat fastidio sui*, a very true saying, with which may be compared the words of Jesus, the son of Sirach, THE LIFE OF A FOOL IS WORSE THAN DEATH. And, as a rule, it will be found that a man is sociable just in the degree in which he is intellectually poor and generally vulgar. For one's choice in this world does not go much beyond solitude on one side and vulgarity on the other. It is said that the most sociable of all people are the negroes, and they are at the bottom of the scale in intellect. I remember reading once in a French paper that the blacks in North America, whether free or enslaved, are fond of shutting themselves up in large numbers in the smallest space, because they cannot have too much of one another's snub-nosed company.

The brain may be regarded as a kind of parasite of the organism, a pensioner, as it were, who dwells with the body; and leisure, that is, the time one has for the free enjoyment of one's consciousness or individuality, is the fruit or produce of the rest of existence, which is in general only labor and effort. But what does most people's leisure yield? boredom and dullness; except, of course, when it is occupied with sensual pleasure or folly. How little such leisure is worth may be seen in the way in which it is spent; and, as Ariosto observes, how miserable are the idle hours of ignorant men!—*ozio lungo d'uomini ignoranti*. Ordinary people think merely how they shall SPEND their time; a man of any talent tries to USE it. The reason why people of limited intellect are apt to be bored is that their intellect is absolutely nothing more than the means by which the motive power of the will is put into force; and whenever there is nothing particular to set the will in motion, it rests, and their intellect takes

a holiday, because, equally with the will, it requires something external to bring it into play. The result is an
awful stagnation of whatever power a man has — in a
word, boredom. To counteract this miserable feeling, men
run to trivialities which please for the moment they are
taken up, hoping thus to engage the will in order to rouse
it to action, and so set the intellect in motion; for it is
the latter which has to give effect to these motives of the
will. Compared with real and natural motives, these are
but as paper money to coin; for their value is only arbitrary — card games and the like, which have been invented
for this very purpose. And if there is nothing else to be
done, a man will twirl his thumbs or beat the devil's tat-
too; or a cigar may be a welcome substitute for exercis-
ing his brains. Hence, in all countries the chief occupation
of society is card-playing and it is the gauge of its value,
and an outward sign that it is bankrupt in thought. Because people have no thoughts to deal in, they deal cards,
and try and win one another's money. Idiots! But I do
not wish to be unjust; so let me remark that it may
certainly be said in defense of card-playing that it is a
preparation for the world and for business life, because
one learns thereby how to make a clever use of fortuitous
but unalterable circumstances (cards, in this case), and to
get as much out of them as one can; and to do this a
man must learn a little dissimulation, and how to put a
good face upon a bad business. But, on the other hand,
it is exactly for this reason that card-playing is so demor-
alizing, since the whole object of it is to employ every
kind of trick and machination in order to win what belongs
to another. And a habit of this sort, learned at the card-
table, strikes root and pushes its way into practical life;
and in the affairs of every day a man gradually comes to
regard *meum* and *tuum* in much the same light as cards,
and to consider that he may use to the utmost whatever
advantages he possesses, so long as he does not come within
the arm of the law. Examples of what I mean are of
daily occurrence in mercantile life. Since, then, leisure is
the flower, or rather the fruit, of existence, as it puts a
man into possession of himself, those are happy indeed
who possess something real in themselves. But what do

you get from most people's leisure? only a good-for-nothing fellow, who is terribly bored and a burden to himself. Let us, therefore, rejoice, dear brethren, for WE ARE NOT CHILDREN OF THE BONDWOMAN, BUT OF THE FREE.

Further, as no land is so well off as that which requires few imports, or none at all, so the happiest man is one who has enough in his own inner wealth, and asks little or nothing from outside for his maintenance. For imports are expensive things, reveal dependence, entail danger, occasion trouble, and, when all is said and done, are a poor substitute for home produce. No man ought to expect much from others, or, in general, from the external world. What one human being can be to another is not a very great deal; in the end every one stands alone, and the important thing is WHO it is that stands alone. Here, then, is another application of the general truth which Goethe recognizes in "Dichtung und Wahrheit" (Bk. III.), that in everything a man has ultimately to appeal to himself; or, as Goldsmith puts it in "The Traveller":

> Still to ourselves in every place consign'd
> Our own felicity we make or find.

Himself is the source of the best and most a man can be or achieve. The more this is so — the more a man finds his sources of pleasure in himself — the happier he will be. Therefore, it is with great truth that Aristotle says, TO BE HAPPY MEANS TO BE SELF-SUFFICIENT. For all other sources of happiness are in their nature most uncertain, precarious, fleeting, the sport of chance; and so even under the most favorable circumstances they can easily be exhausted; nay, this is unavoidable, because they are not always within reach. And in old age these sources of happiness most necessarily dry up: love leaves us then, and wit, desire to travel, delight in horses, aptitude for social intercourse; friends and relations, too, are taken from us by death. Then more than ever, it depends upon what a man has in himself; for this will stick to him longest; and at any period of life it is the only genuine and lasting source of happiness. There is not much to be got anywhere in the world. It is filled with misery and pain; and if a man escapes these, boredom

lies in wait for him at every corner. Nay more; it is
evil which generally has the upper hand, and folly makes
the most noise. Fate is cruel, and mankind pitiable. In
such a world as this, a man who is rich in himself is like
a bright, warm, happy room at Christmastide, while without are the frost and snow of a December night. Therefore, without doubt, the happiest destiny on earth is to
have the rare gift of a rich individuality, and, more especially, to be possessed of a good endowment of intellect;
this is the happiest destiny, though it may not be, after
all, a very brilliant one. There was great wisdom in that
remark which Queen Christina of Sweden made, in her
nineteenth year, about Descartes, who had then lived for
twenty years in the deepest solitude in Holland, and,
apart from report, was known to her only by a single
essay: M. DESCARTES, she said, IS THE HAPPIEST OF MEN,
AND HIS CONDITION SEEMS TO ME MUCH TO BE ENVIED. Of
course, as was the case with Descartes, external circumstances must be favorable enough to allow a man to
be master of his life and happiness; or, as we read in
"Ecclesiastes," WISDOM IS GOOD, TOGETHER WITH AN INHER-
ITANCE, AND PROFITABLE UNTO THEM THAT SEE THE SUN.
The man to whom nature and fate have granted the blessing of wisdom, will be most anxious and careful to keep
open the fountains of happiness which he has in himself;
and for this, independence and leisure are necessary. To
obtain them, he will be willing to moderate his desires
and harbor his resources; all the more because he is not,
like others, restricted to the external world for his pleasures. So he will not be misled by expectations of office,
or money, or the favor and applause of his fellow-men,
into surrendering himself in order to conform to low desires and vulgar tastes; nay, in such a case he will follow
the advice that Horace gives in his epistle to Mæcenas.
It is a great piece of folly to sacrifice the inner for the
outer man, to give the whole or the greater part of one's
quiet leisure and independence for splendor, rank, pomp,
titles and honor. This is what Goethe did. My good
luck drew me quite in the other direction.

The truth which I am insisting upon here, the truth,
namely, that the chief source of human happiness is

internal, is confirmed by that most accurate observation
of Aristotle in the "Nichomachean Ethics," that every
pleasure presupposes some sort of activity, the application
of some sort of power, without which it cannot exist.
The doctrine of Aristotle's, that a man's happiness consists in the free exercise of his highest faculties, is also
enunciated by Stobæus in his exposition of the Peripa-
tetic philosophy: HAPPINESS, he says, MEANS VIGOROUS AND
SUCCESSFUL ACTIVITY IN ALL YOUR UNDERTAKINGS; and he
explains that by VIGOR (ἀρέτη) he means MASTERY in anything, whatever it be. Now, the original purpose of those
forces with which nature has endowed man is to enable
him to struggle against the difficulties which beset him
on all sides. But if this struggle comes to an end, his
unemployed forces become a burden to him; and he has
to set to work and play with them, use them, I mean,
for no purpose at all, beyond avoiding the other source
of human suffering, boredom, to which he is at once
exposed. It is the upper classes, people of wealth, who
are the greatest victims of boredom. Lucretius long ago
described their miserable state, and the truth of his
description may be still recognized to-day in the life of
every great capital — where the rich man is seldom in his
own halls, because it bores him to be there, and still he
returns thither, because he is no better off outside; or
else he is away in posthaste to his house in the country,
as if it were on fire; and he is no sooner arrived there,
than he is bored again, and seeks to forget everything
in sleep, or else hurries back to town once more.

> *Exit saepe foras magnis ex ædibus ille,*
> *Esse domi quem pertaesum est, subitoque reventat;*
> *Quippe foris nihilo melius qui sentiat esse.*
> *Currit, agens mannos, ad villam precipitanter,*
> *Auxilium tectis quasi ferre ardentibus instans:*
> *Oscitat extemplo, tetigit quum limina villae;*
> *Aut abit in somnum gravis, atque oblivia quaerit;*
> *Aut etiam properans urbem petit atque revisit.*

In their youth, such people must have had a superfluity
of muscular and vital energy, powers which, unlike those
of the mind, cannot maintain their full degree of vigor
very long; and in later years they either have no mental

powers at all, or cannot develop any for want of employment which would bring them into play; so that they are
in a wretched plight. WILL, however, they still possess,
for this is the only power that is inexhaustible; and they
try to stimulate their will by passionate excitement, such
as games of chance for high stakes — undoubtedly a most
degrading form of vice. And one may say generally that
if a man finds himself with nothing to do, he is sure to
choose some amusement suited to the kind of power in
which he excels, bowls, it may be, or chess; hunting or
painting; horse-racing or music; cards, or poetry, heraldry,
philosophy, or some other dilettante interest. We might
classify these interests methodically, by reducing them to
expressions of the three fundamental powers, the factors,
that is to say, which go to make up the physiological
constitution of man; and further, by considering these
powers by themselves, and apart from any of the definite
aims which they may subserve, and simply as affording
three sources of possible pleasure, out of which every
man will choose what suits him, according as he excels
in one direction or another.

First of all come the pleasures of VITAL ENERGY, of food,
drink, digestion, rest and sleep; and there are parts of the
world where it can be said that these are characteristic
and national pleasures. Secondly, there are the pleasures
of MUSCULAR ENERGY, such as walking, running, wrestling,
dancing, fencing, riding and similar athletic pursuits, which
sometimes take the form of sport, and sometimes of a
military life and real warfare. Thirdly, there are the
pleasures of SENSIBILITY, such as observation, thought, feeling, or a taste for poetry or culture, music, learning, reading, meditation, invention, philosophy and the like. As
regards the value, relative worth and duration of each of
these kinds of pleasure, a great deal might be said, which,
however, I leave the reader to supply. But every one will
see that the nobler the power which is brought into play,
the greater will be the pleasure which it gives; for pleasure always involves the use of one's own powers, and happiness consists in a frequent repetition of pleasure. No
one will deny that in this respect the pleasures of sensibility occupy a higher place than either of the other two

fundamental kinds; which exist in an equal, nay, in a greater degree in brutes; it is his preponderating amount of sensibility which distinguishes man from other animals. Now, our mental powers are forms of sensibility, and therefore a preponderating amount of it makes us capable of that kind of pleasure which has to do with mind, so-called intellectual pleasure; and the more sensibility predominates, the greater the pleasure will be.*

The normal, ordinary man takes a vivid interest in anything only in so far as it excites his will, that is to say, is a matter of personal interest to him. But constant excitement of the will is never an unmixed good, to say the least; in other words, it involves pain. Card-playing,

---

* Nature exhibits a continual progress, starting from the mechanical and chemical activity of the inorganic world, proceeding to the vegetable, with its dull enjoyment of self, from that to the animal world, where intelligence and consciousness begin, at first very weak, and only after many intermediate stages attaining its last great development in man, whose intellect is Nature's crowning point, the goal of all her efforts, the most perfect and difficult of all her works. And even within the range of the human intellect, there are a great many observable differences of degree, and it is very seldom that intellect reaches its highest point, intelligence properly so-called, which in this narrow and strict sense of the word, is Nature's most consummate product, and so the rarest and most precious thing of which the world can boast. The highest product of Nature is the clearest degree of consciousness in which the world mirrors itself more plainly and completely than anywhere else. A man endowed with this form of intelligence is in possession of what is noblest and best on earth; and accordingly, he has a source of pleasure in comparison with which all others are small. From his surroundings he asks nothing but leisure for the free enjoyment of what he has got, time, as it were, to polish his diamond. All other pleasures that are not of the intellect are of a lower kind; for they are, one and all, movements of will — desires, hopes, fears and ambitions, no matter to what directed: they are always satisfied at the cost of pain, and in the case of ambition, generally with more or less of illusion. With intellectual pleasure, on the other hand, truth becomes clearer and clearer. In the realm of intelligence pain has no power. Knowledge is all in all. Further, intellectual pleasures are accessible entirely and only through the medium of the intelligence, and are limited by its capacity. For all THE WIT THERE IS IN THE WORLD IS USELESS TO HIM WHO HAS NONE. Still this advantage is accompanied by a substantial disadvantage; for the whole of Nature shows that with the growth of intelligence comes increased capacity for pain, and it is only with the highest degree of intelligence that suffering reaches its supreme point.

that universal occupation of "good society" everywhere
is a device for providing this kind of excitement, and
that, too, by means of interests so small as to produce
slight and momentary, instead of real and permanent,
pain. Card-playing is, in fact, a mere tickling of the
will.*

On the other hand, a man of powerful intellect is
capable of taking a vivid interest in things in the way of
mere KNOWLEDGE, with no admixture of WILL; nay, such
an interest is a necessity to him. It places him in a
sphere where pain is an alien, a diviner air where the
gods live serene :

θεοὶ ῥ῀εια ζώοντες.

Look on these two pictures — the life of the masses,
one long, dull record of struggle and effort entirely devoted to the petty interests of personal welfare, to misery
in all its forms, a life beset by intolerable boredom as
soon as ever those aims are satisfied and the man is
thrown back upon himself, whence he can be roused
again to some sort of movement only by the wild fire of
passion. On the other side you have a man endowed
with a high degree of mental power, leading an existence
rich in thought and full of life and meaning, occupied by

---

* VULGARITY is, at bottom, the kind of consciousness in which the
will completely predominates over the intellect, where the latter does
nothing more than perform the service of its master, the will. Therefore, when the will makes no demands, supplies no motives, strong or
weak, the intellect entirely loses its power, and the result is complete
vacancy of mind. Now WILL WITHOUT INTELLECT is the most vulgar and
common thing in the world, possessed by every blockhead, who, in the
gratification of his passions, shows the stuff of which he is made. This
is the condition of mind called VULGARITY, in which the only active
elements are the organs of sense, and that small amount of intellect
which is necessary for apprehending the data of sense. Accordingly,
the vulgar man is constantly open to all sorts of impressions, and
immediately perceives all the little trifling things that go on in his
environment: the lightest whisper, the most trivial circumstance, is sufficient to rouse his attention; he is just like an animal. Such a man's
mental condition reveals itself in his face, in his whole exterior; and
hence that vulgar, repulsive appearance, which is all the more offensive,
if, as is usually the case, his will — the only factor in his consciousness
— is a base, selfish and altogether bad one.

worthy and interesting objects as soon as ever he is free
to give himself to them, bearing in himself a source of
the noblest pleasure. What external promptings he wants
come from the works of nature, and from the contemplation of human affairs and the achievements of the great
of all ages and countries, which are thoroughly appreciated
by a man of this type alone, as being the only one who
can quite understand and feel with them. And so it is
for him alone that those great ones have really lived; it
is to him that they make their appeal; the rest are but
casual hearers who only half understand either them or
their followers. Of course, this characteristic of the intellectual man implies that he has one more need than the
others, the need of reading, observing, studying, meditat-
ing, practicing, the need, in short, of undisturbed leisure.
For, as Voltaire has very rightly said, THERE ARE NO REAL
PLEASURES WITHOUT REAL NEEDS; and the need of them is
why to such a man pleasures are accessible which are
denied to others, the varied beauties of nature and art
and literature. To heap these round people who do not
want them and cannot appreciate them, is like expecting
gray hairs to fall in love. A man who is privileged in
this respect leads two lives, a personal and an intellectual,
life; and the latter gradually comes to be looked upon as
the true one, and the former as merely a means to it.
Other people make this shallow, empty and troubled existence an end in itself. To the life of the intellect such a
man will give the preference over all his other occupations: by the constant growth of insight and knowledge,
this intellectual life, like a slowly-forming work of art,
will acquire a consistency, a permanent intensity, a unity
which becomes ever more and more complete; compared
with which, a life devoted to the attainment of personal
comfort, a life that may broaden indeed, but can never
be deepened, makes but a poor show: and yet, as I have
said, people make this baser sort of existence an end in
itself.

The ordinary life of every day, so far as it is not
moved by passion, is tedious and insipid; and if it is so
moved, it soon becomes painful. Those alone are happy
whom nature has favored with some superfluity of intel-

lect, something beyond what is just necessary to carry out the behests of their will; for it enables them to lead an intellectual life as well, a life unattended by pain and full of vivid interests. Mere leisure, that is to say, intellect unoccupied in the service of the will, is not of itself sufficient: there must be a real superfluity of power, set free from the service of the will and devoted to that of the intellect; for, as Seneca says, *otium sine litteris mors est et vivi hominis sepultura*—illiterate leisure is a form of death, a living tomb. Varying with the amount of the superfluity, there will be countless developments in this second life, the life of the mind; it may be the mere collection and labelling of insects, birds, minerals, coins, or the highest achievements of poetry and philosophy. The life of the mind is not only a protection against boredom, it also wards off the pernicious effects of boredom; it keeps us from bad company, from the many dangers, misfortunes, losses and extravagances which the man who places his happiness entirely in the objective world is sure to encounter. My philosophy, for instance, has never brought me in a sixpence; but it has spared me many an expense.

The ordinary man places his life's happiness in things external to him, in property, rank, wife and children, friends, society, and the like, so that when he loses them or finds them disappointing, the foundation of his happiness is destroyed. In other words, the centre of gravity is not in himself; it is constantly changing its place, with every wish and whim. If he is a man of means, one day it will be his house in the country, another buying horses, or entertaining friends, or traveling, a life, in short, of general luxury, the reason being that he seeks his pleasure in things outside him. Like one whose health and strength are gone, he tries to regain by the use of jellies and drugs, instead of by developing his own vital power, the true source of what he has lost. Before proceeding to the opposite, let us compare with this common type the man who comes midway between the two, endowed, it may be, not exactly with distinguished powers of mind, but with somewhat more than the ordinary amount of intellect. He will take a dilettante interest in art, or devote his attention to some branch of science — botany, for example, or physics, astronomy, history, and find a great deal of pleasure in such studies, and amuse himself with them when external sources of happiness are exhausted or fail to satisfy him any more. Of a man like this it may be said that his centre of gravity is partly in himself. But a dilettante interest in art is a very different thing from creative activity; and an amateur pursuit of science is apt to be superficial and not to penetrate to the heart of the matter. A man cannot entirely identify himself with such pursuits, or have his whole existence so completely filled and permeated with them that he loses all interest in everything else. It is only the highest intellectual power, what we call GENIUS, that attains to this degree of intensity, making all time and existence its theme, and striving to express its peculiar conception of the world, whether it contemplates life as the subject of poetry or of philosophy. Hence, undisturbed occupation with himself, his own thoughts and works, is a matter of urgent necessity to such a man; solitude is welcome, leisure is the highest good, and everything else is unnecessary, nay, even burdensome.

This is the only type of man of whom it can be said that his centre of gravity is entirely in himself; which explains why it is that people of this sort — and they are very rare — no matter how excellent their character may be, do not show that warm and unlimited interest in friends, family, and the community in general, of which others are so often capable; for if they have only themselves they are not inconsolable for the loss of everything else. This gives an isolation to their character, which is all the more effective since other people never really quite satisfy them, as being, on the whole, of a different nature; nay more, since this difference is constantly forcing itself upon their notice, they get accustomed to move about among mankind as alien beings, and in thinking of humanity in general, to say THEY instead of WE.

So the conclusion we come to is that the man whom nature has endowed with intellectual wealth is the happiest; so true it is that the subjective concerns us more

than the objective; for whatever the latter may be, it
can work only indirectly, secondarily, and through the
medium of the former — a truth finely expressed by
Lucian : —

Πλοῦτος δ τῆς ψυχῆς πλοῦτος μόνος ἐστὶν ἀληθής
Τἆλλα δ᾽ ἔχει ἄτην πλείονα τῶν κτεάνων.

— the wealth of the soul is the only true wealth, for with
all other riches comes a bane even greater than they.
The man of inner wealth wants nothing from outside but
the negative gift of undisturbed leisure, to develop and
mature his intellectual faculties, that is, to enjoy his
wealth; in short, he wants permission to be himself, his
whole life long, every day and every hour. If he is destined to impress the character of his mind upon a whole
race, he has only one measure of happiness or unhappiness — to succeed or fail in perfecting his powers and
completing his work. All else is of small consequence.
Accordingly, the greatest minds of all ages have set the
highest value upon undisturbed leisure, as worth exactly
as much as the man himself. HAPPINESS APPEARS TO CON-
SIST IN LEISURE, says Aristotle; and Diogenes Laertius re-
ports that SOCRATES PRAISED LEISURE AS THE FAIREST OF
ALL POSSESSIONS. So, in the "Nichomachean Ethics,"
Aristotle concludes that a life devoted to philosophy is
the happiest; or, as he says in the "Politics," THE FREE
EXERCISE OF ANY POWER, WHATEVER IT MAY BE, IS HAPPI-
NESS. This, again, tallies with what Goethe says in
"Wilhelm Meister:" THE MAN WHO IS BORN WITH A TALENT
WHICH HE IS MEANT TO USE, FINDS HIS GREATEST HAPPINESS
IN USING IT.

But to be in possession of undisturbed leisure is far
from being the common lot; nay, it is something alien to
human nature, for the ordinary man's destiny is to spend
life in procuring what is necessary for the subsistence of
himself and his family; he is a son of struggle and need,
not a free intelligence. So people as a rule soon get
tired of undisturbed leisure, and it becomes burdensome
if there are no fictitious and forced aims to occupy it,
play, pastime and hobbies of every kind. For this very
reason it is full of possible danger, and *difficilis in otio
quies* is a true saying, — it is difficult to keep quiet if you

have nothing to do. On the other hand, a measure of intellect far surpassing the ordinary is as unnatural as it is abnormal. But if it exists, and the man endowed with it is to be happy, he will want precisely that undisturbed leisure which the others find burdensome or pernicious; for without it he is a Pegasus in harness, and consequently unhappy. If these two unnatural circumstances, external and internal, undisturbed leisure and great intellect, happen to coincide in the same person, it is a great piece of fortune; and if fate is so far favorable, a man can lead the higher life, the life protected from the two opposite sources of human suffering, pain and boredom, from the painful struggle for existence, and the incapacity for enduring leisure (which is free existence itself) — evils which may be escaped only by being mutually neutralized.

But there is something to be said in opposition to this view. Great intellectual gifts mean an activity preeminently nervous in its character, and consequently a very high degree of susceptibility to pain in every form. Further, such gifts imply an intense temperament, larger and more vivid ideas, which, as the inseparable accompaniment of great intellectual power, entail on its possessor a corresponding intensity of the emotions, making them incomparably more violent than those to which the ordinary man is a prey. Now, there are more things in the world productive of pain than of pleasure. Again, a large endowment of intellect tends to estrange the man who has it from other people and their doings; for the more a man has in himself, the less he will be able to find in them; and the hundred things in which they take delight, he will think shallow and insipid. Here, then, perhaps, is another instance of that law of compensation which makes itself felt everywhere. How often one hears it said, and said, too, with some plausibility, that the narrow-minded man is at bottom the happiest, even though his fortune is unenviable. I shall make no attempt to forestall the reader's own judgment on this point; more especially as Sophocles himself has given utterance to two diametrically opposite opinions:

Πολλῶ τὸ φρονεῖν εὐδαιμονίας
πρῶτον ὑπάρχει.

he says in one place — wisdom is the greatest part of happiness; and again in another passage, he declares that the life of the thoughtless is the most pleasant of all —

'Εν τᾶ φρονεῖν γὰρ μηδὲν ἥδιστος βίος.

The philosophers of the OLD TESTAMENT find themselves in a like contradiction.

The life of a fool is worse than death.

And —

In much wisdom is much grief;
And he that increaseth knowledge increaseth sorrow.

I may remark, however, that a man who has no mental needs, because his intellect is of the narrow and normal amount, is, in the strict sense of the word, what is called a PHILISTINE — an expression at first peculiar to the German language, a kind of slang term at the universities, afterward used, by analogy, in a higher sense, though still in its original meaning, as denoting one who is not A SON OF THE MUSES. A philistine is and remains ἄμουσος ἀνήρ. I should prefer to take a higher point of view, and apply the term PHILISTINE to people who are always seriously occupied with realities which are no realities; but as such a definition would be a transcendental one, and therefore not generally intelligible, it would hardly be in place in the present treatise, which aims at being popular. The other definition can be more easily elucidated, indicating, as it does, satisfactorily enough, the essential nature of all those qualities which distinguish the philistine. He is defined to be A MAN WITHOUT MENTAL NEEDS. From this it follows, firstly, IN RELATION TO HIMSELF, that he has NO INTELLECTUAL PLEASURES; for, as was remarked before, there are no real pleasures without real needs. The philistine's life is animated by no desire to gain knowledge and insight for their own sake, or to experience that true æsthetic pleasure which is so nearly akin to them. If pleasures of this kind are fashionable, and the philistine finds himself compelled to pay attention to them, he will force himself to do so, but he will take as little interest in them as possible. His only real pleasures are of a sensual kind, and he thinks that these in-

3

demnify him for the loss of the others. To him oysters
and champagne are the height of existence; the aim of
his life is to procure what will contribute to his bodily
welfare, and he is indeed in a happy way if this causes
him some trouble. If the luxuries of life are heaped
upon him, he will inevitably be bored, and against boredom he has a great many fancied remedies, balls, theatres,
parties, cards, gambling, horses, women, drinking, traveling and so on; all of which cannot protect a man from
being bored, for where there are no intellectual needs, no
intellectual pleasures are possible. The peculiar characteristic of the philistine is a dull, dry kind of gravity,
akin to that of animals. Nothing really pleases, or excites, or interests him, for sensual pleasure is quickly
exhausted, and the society of philistines soon becomes
burdensome, and one may even get tired of playing cards.
True, the pleasures of vanity are left, pleasures which he
enjoys in his own way, either by feeling himself superior
in point of wealth, or rank, or influence and power to
other people, who thereupon pay him honor; or, at any
rate, by going about with those who have a superfluity of
these blessings, sunning himself in the reflection of their
splendor — what the English call A SNOB.

From the essential nature of the philistine it follows,
secondly, IN REGARD TO OTHERS, that, as he possesses no
intellectual, but only physical needs, he will seek the
society of those who can satisfy the latter, but not the
former. The last thing he will expect from his friends is
the possession of any sort of intellectual capacity; nay, if
he chances to meet with it, it will rouse his antipathy and
even hatred; simply because in addition to an unpleasant
sense of inferiority, he experiences, in his heart, a dull
kind of envy, which has to be carefully concealed even
from himself. Nevertheless, it sometimes grows into a
secret feeling of rancor. But for all that, it will never
occur to him to make his own ideas of worth or value
conform to the standard of such qualities; he will continue
to give the preference to rank and riches, power and
influence, which in his eyes seem to be the only genuine
advantages in the world; and his wish will be to excel in
them himself. All this is the consequence of his being

a man WITHOUT INTELLECTUAL NEEDS.   The great affliction
of all philistines is that they have no interest in IDEAS,
and that, to escape being bored, they are in constant need
of REALITIES.   Now realities are either unsatisfactory or
dangerous; when they lose their interest, they become
fatiguing.   But the ideal world is illimitable and calm,

> something afar
> From the sphere of our sorrow.

NOTE.— In these remarks on the personal qualities
which go to make happiness, I have been mainly concerned with the physical and intellectual nature of man.
For an account of the direct and immediate influence of
MORALITY upon happiness, let me refer to my prize essay
on " The Foundation of Morals " (Sec. 22.)

CHAPTER III.

PROPERTY, OR WHAT A MAN HAS.

EPICURUS divides the needs of mankind into three classes, and the division made by this great professor of happiness is a true and a fine one. First come natural and necessary needs, such as, when not satisfied, produce pain, —food and clothing, *victus et amictus*, needs which can easily be satisfied. Secondly, there are those needs which, though natural, are not necessary, such as the gratification of certain of the senses. I may add, however, that in the report given by Diogenes Laertius, Epicurus does not mention which of the senses he means; so that on this point my account of his doctrine is somewhat more definite and exact than the original. These are needs rather more difficult to satisfy. The third class consists of needs which are neither natural nor necessary, the need of luxury and prodigality, show and splendor, which never come to an end, and are very hard to satisfy.

It is difficult, if not impossible, to define the limits which reason should impose on the desire for wealth; for there is no absolute or definite amount of wealth which will satisfy a man. The amount is always relative, that is to say, just so much as will maintain the proportion between what he wants and what he gets; for to measure a man's happiness only by what he gets, and not also by what he expects to get, is as futile as to try to express a fraction which shall have a numerator but no denominator. A man never feels the loss of things which it never occurs to him to ask for; he is just as happy without them; while another, who may have a hundred times as much, feels miserable because he has not got the one thing which he wants. In fact, here too, every man has an horizon of his own, and he will expect just as much as he thinks it possible for him to get. If an object within his horizon looks as though he could confidently reckon on getting it, he is happy; but if difficulties come

(36)

in the way, he is miserable.   What lies beyond his horizon
has no effect at all upon him.   So it is that the vast
possessions of the rich do not agitate the poor, and conversely, that a wealthy man is not consoled by all his
wealth for the failure of his hopes.   Riches, one may say,
are like sea-water: the more you drink, the more thirsty you
become; and the same is true of fame.   The loss of wealth
and prosperity leaves a man, as soon as the first pangs of
grief are over, in very much the same habitual temper as
before; and the reason of this is, that as soon as fate
diminishes the amount of his possessions, he himself immediately reduces the amount of his claims.   But when
misfortune comes upon us, to reduce the amount of our
claims is just what is most painful; when once we have
done so, the pain becomes less and less, and is felt no
more; like an old wound which has healed.   Conversely,
when a piece of good fortune befalls us, our claims mount
higher and higher, as there is nothing to regulate them.
It is in this feeling of expansion that the delight of it lies.
But it lasts no longer than the process itself, and when
the expansion is complete, the delight ceases: we have
become accustomed to the increase in our claims, and
consequently indifferent to the amount of wealth which
satisfies them.   There is a passage in the " Odyssey "
illustrating this truth, of which I may quote the last two
lines:

Τοῖος γὰρ νόος ἐστὶν ἐπιχθονίων ἀνθρώπων
Οἷον ἐφ᾽ ἦμαρ ἄγει πατὴρ ἀνδρῶν τε θεῶν τε.

—the thoughts of man that dwells on the earth are as
the day granted him by the father of gods and men.
Discontent springs from a constant endeavor to increase
the amount of our claims, when we are powerless to increase the amount which will satisfy them.

When we consider how full of needs the human race
is, how its whole existence is based upon them, it is not
a matter for surprise that WEALTH is held in more sincere esteem, nay, in greater honor, than anything else in
the world; nor ought we to wonder that gain is made the
only goal of life, and everything that does not lead to it
pushed aside or thrown overboard — philosophy, for in-

stance, by those who profess it. People are often reproached for wishing for money above all things, and for
loving it more than anything else; but it is natural and
even inevitable for people to love that which, like an un-
wearied Proteus, is always ready to turn itself into whatever object their wandering wishes or manifold desires
may for the moment fix upon. Everything else can satisfy only ONE wish, ONE need: food is good only if you
are hungry; wine, if you are able to enjoy it; drugs, if
you are sick; fur for the winter; love for youth, and so
on. These are all only relatively good, ἀγαθὰ πρός τι
Money alone is absolutely good, because it is not only a
concrete satisfaction of one need in particular; it is an
abstract satisfaction of all.

If a man has an independent fortune, he should regard it as a bulwark against the many evils and misfortunes which he may encounter; he should not look
upon it as giving him leave to get what pleasure he can
out of the world, or as rendering it incumbent upon
him to spend it in this way. People who are not born
with a fortune, but end by making a large one through
the exercise of whatever talents they possess, almost
always come to think that their talents are their capital,
and that the money they have gained is merely the
interest upon it; they do not lay by a part of their earnings to form permanent capital, but spend their money
much as they have earned it. Accordingly, they often
fall into poverty; their earnings decrease, or come to an
end altogether, either because their talent is exhausted
by becoming antiquated, as, for instance, very often happens in the case of fine art — or else it was valid only
under a special conjunction of circumstances which has
now passed away. There is nothing to prevent those
who live on the common labor of their hands from treating their earnings in that way if they like; because their
kind of skill is not likely to disappear, or, if it does, it
can be replaced by that of their fellow-workmen; moreover, the kind of work they do is always in demand; so
that what the proverb says is quite true, A USEFUL TRADE
IS A MINE OF GOLD. But with artists and professionals of
every kind the case is quite different, and that is the

reason why they are well paid. They ought to build up a capital out of their earnings; but they recklessly look upon them as merely interest, and end in ruin. On the other hand, people who inherit money know, at least, how to distinguish between capital and interest, and most of them try to make their capital secure and not encroach upon it; nay, if they can, they put by at least an eighth of their interest in order to meet future contingencies. So most of them maintain their position. These few remarks about capital and interest are not applicable to commercial life, for merchants look upon money only as a means of further gain, just as a workman regards his tools; so even if their capital has been entirely the result of their own efforts, they try to preserve and increase it by using it. Accordingly, wealth is nowhere so much at home as in the merchant class.

It will generally be found that those who know what it is to have been in need and destitution are very much less afraid of it, and consequently more inclined to extravagance, than those who know poverty only by hearsay. People who have been born and bred in good circumstances are as a rule much more careful about the future, more economical, in fact, than those who by a piece of good luck, have suddenly passed from poverty to wealth. This looks as if poverty were not really such a very wretched thing as it appears from a distance. The true reason, however, is rather the fact that the man who has been born into a position of wealth comes to look upon it as something without which he could no more live than he could live without air; he guards it as he does his very life; and so he is generally a lover of order, prudent and economical. But the man who has been born into a poor position looks upon it as the natural one, and if by any chance he comes in for a fortune, he regards it as a superfluity, something to be enjoyed or wasted, because, if it comes to an end, he can get on just as well as before, with one anxiety the less; or, as Shakespeare says in Henry VI.,

> . . . the adage must be verified
> That beggars mounted run their horse to death.

But it should be said that people of this kind have a firm

and excessive trust, partly in fate, partly in the peculiar means which have already raised them out of need and poverty,—a trust not only of the head, but of the heart also; and so they do not, like the man born rich, look upon the shallows of poverty as bottomless, but console themselves with the thought that when they have touched ground again, they can take another upward flight. It is this trait in human character which explains the fact that women who were poor before their marriage often make greater claims, and are more extravagant, than those who have brought their husbands a rich dowry; because as a rule, rich girls bring with them, not only a fortune, but also more eagerness, nay, more of the inherited instinct, to preserve it, than poor girls do. If anyone doubts the truth of this, and thinks that it is just the opposite, he will find authority for his view in Ariosto's first Satire; but, on the other hand, Dr. Johnson agrees with my opinion. A WOMAN OF FORTUNE, he says, BEING USED TO THE HANDLING OF MONEY, SPENDS IT JUDICIOUSLY; BUT A WOMAN WHO GETS THE COMMAND OF MONEY FOR THE FIRST TIME UPON HER MARRIAGE, HAS SUCH A GUSTO IN SPENDING IT, THAT SHE THROWS IT AWAY WITH GREAT PROFUSION. And in any case let me advise anyone who marries a poor girl not to leave her the capital but only the interest, and to take especial care that she has not the management of the children's fortune.

I do not by any means think that I am touching upon a subject which is not worth my while to mention when I recommend people to be careful to preserve what they have earned or inherited. For to start life with just as much as will make one independent, that is, allow one to live comfortably without having to work—even if one has only just enough for oneself, not to speak of a family—is an advantage which cannot be overestimated; for it means exemption and immunity from that chronic disease of penury, which fastens on the life of man like a plague; it is emancipation from that forced labor which is the natural lot of every mortal. Only under a favorable fate like this can a man be said to be born free, to be, in the proper sense of the word, *sui juris*, master of his own time and powers, and able to say every morning,

THIS DAY IS MY OWN. And just for the same reason the difference between the man who has a hundred a year and the man who has a thousand, is infinitely smaller than the difference between the former and a man who has nothing at all. But inherited wealth reaches its utmost value when it falls to the individual endowed with mental powers of a high order, who is resolved to pursue a line of life not compatible with the making of money; for he is then doubly endowed by fate and can live for his genius; and he will pay his debt to mankind a hundred times, by achieving what no other could achieve, by producing some work which contributes to the general good, and redounds to the honor of humanity at large. Another, again, may use his wealth to further philanthropic schemes, and make himself well-deserving of his fellow-men. But a man who does none of these things, who does not even try to do them, who never attempts to study thoroughly some one branch of knowledge so that he may at least do what he can toward promoting it — such a one, born as he is into riches, is a mere idler and thief of time, a contemptible fellow. He will not even be happy, because, in his case, exemption from need delivers him up to the other extreme of human suffering, boredom, which is such martyrdom to him, that he would have been better off if poverty had given him something to do. And as he is bored he is apt to be extravagant, and so lose the advantage of which he showed himself unworthy. Countless numbers of people find themselves in want, simply because, when they had money, they spent it only to get momentary relief from the feeling of boredom which oppressed them.

It is quite another matter if one's object is success in political life, where favor, friends and connections are all-important, in order to mount by their aid step by step on the ladder of promotion, and perhaps gain the topmost rung. In this kind of life, it is much better to be cast on the world without a penny; and if the aspirant is not of noble family, but is a man of some talent, it will redound to his advantage to be an absolute pauper. For what every one most aims at in ordinary contact with his fellows is to prove them inferior to himself; and how

much more is this the case in politics. Now, it is only
an absolute pauper who has such a thorough conviction
of his own complete, profound and positive inferiority
from every point of view, of his own utter insignificance
and worthlessness, that he can take his place quietly in
the political machine.* He is the only one who can keep
on bowing low enough, and even go right down upon his
face if necessary; he alone can submit to everything and
laugh at it; he alone knows the entire worthlessness of
merit; he alone uses his loudest voice and his boldest
type whenever he has to speak or write of those who are
placed over his head, or occupy any position of influence;
and if they do a little scribbling, he is ready to applaud
it as a masterwork. He alone understands how to beg,
and so betimes, when he is hardly out of his boyhood, he
becomes a high priest of that hidden mystery which
Goethe brings to light; —

> Ueber's Niederträchtige
> Niemand sich beklage:
> Denn es ist das Mächtige
> Was man dir auch sage:

—it is no use to complain of low aims; for, whatever
people may say, they rule the world.

On the other hand, the man who is born with enough
to live upon is generally of a somewhat independent turn
of mind; he is accustomed to keep his head up; he has
not learned all the arts of the beggar; perhaps he even
presumes a little upon the possession of talents which, as
he ought to know, can never compete with cringing mediocrity, in the long run he comes to recognize the inferiority of those who are placed over his head, and when
they try to put insults upon him, he becomes refractory
and shy. This is not the way to get on in the world.
Nay, such a man may at last incline to the opinion freely

---

* TRANSLATOR'S NOTE. — Schopenhauer is probably here making one
of his many virulent attacks upon Hegel; in this case on account of
what he thought to be the philosopher's abject servility to the government of his day. Though the Hegelian system has been the
fruitful mother of many liberal ideas, there can be no doubt that
Hegel's influence, in his own lifetime, was an effective support of
Prussian bureaucracy.

expressed by Voltaire: WE HAVE ONLY TWO DAYS TO LIVE; IT IS NOT WORTH OUR WHILE TO SPEND THEM IN CRINGING TO CONTEMPTIBLE RASCALS. But alas! let me observe by the way, that CONTEMPTIBLE RASCAL is an attribute which may be predicted of an abominable number of people. What Juvenal says—it is difficult to rise if your poverty is greater than your talent—

> Haud facile emergunt quorum virtutibus obstat
> Res angusta domi—

is more applicable to a career of art and literature than to political and social ambition.

Wife and children I have not reckoned among a man's possessions: he is rather in their possession. It would be easier to include friends under that head; but a man's friends belong to him not a whit more than he belongs to them.

CHAPTER IV.

POSITION, OR A MAN'S PLACE IN THE ESTIMATION OF OTHERS.

SECTION I.—REPUTATION.

BY A peculiar weakness of human nature, people generally think too much about the opinion which others form of them; although the slightest reflection will show that this opinion, whatever it may be, is not in itself essential to happiness. Therefore it is hard to understand why everybody feels so very pleased when he sees that other people have a good opinion of him, or say anything flattering to his vanity. If you stroke a cat, it will purr; and, as inevitably, if you praise a man, a sweet expression of delight will appear on his face; and even though the praise is a palpable lie, it will be welcome, if the matter is one on which he prides himself. If only other people will applaud him, a man may console himself for downright misfortune, or for the pittance he gets from the two sources of human happiness already discussed; and conversely, it is astonishing how infallibly a man will be annoyed, and in some cases deeply pained by any wrong done to his feeling of self-importance, whatever be the nature, degree, or circumstances of the injury, or by any depreciation, slight, or disregard.

If the feeling of honor rests upon this peculiarity of human nature, it may have a very salutary effect upon the welfare of a great many people, as a substitute for morality; but upon their happiness, more especially upon that peace of mind and independence which are so essential to happiness, its effect will be disturbing and prejudicial rather than salutary. Therefore it is advisable, from our point of view, to set limits to this weakness, and duly to consider and rightly to estimate the relative value of advantages, and thus temper, as far as possible, this great susceptibility to other people's opinion, whether the opin

(44)

ion be one flattering to our vanity, or whether it causes us pain; for in either case it is the same feeling which is touched. Otherwise, a man is the slave of what other people are pleased to think,—and how little it requires to disconcert or soothe the mind that is greedy of praise:—

Sic leve, sic parvum est, animum quod laudis avarum
Subruit ac reficit.

Therefore it will very much conduce to our happiness if we duly compare the value of what a man is in and for himself with what he is in the eyes of others. Under the former comes everything that fills up the span of our existence and makes it what it is, in short, all the advantages already considered and summed up under the heads of personality and property; and the sphere in which all this takes place is the man's own consciousness. On the other hand, the sphere of what we are for other people is their consciousness, not ours; it is the kind of figure we make in their eyes, together with the thoughts which this arouses. * But this is something which has no direct and immediate existence for us, but can affect us only mediately and indirectly, so far, that is, as other people's behavior toward us is directed by it; and even then it ought to affect us only in so far as it can move us to modify WHAT WE ARE IN AND FOR OURSELVES. Apart from this, what goes on in other people's consciousness is, as such, a matter of indifference to us: and in time we get really indifferent to it, when we come to see how superficial and futile are most people's thoughts, how narrow their ideas, how mean their sentiments, how perverse their opinions, and how much of error there is in most of them; when we learn by experience with what depreciation a man will speak of his fellow, when he is not obliged to fear him, or thinks that what he says will not come to his ears. And if ever we have had an opportunity of seeing how the greatest of men will meet with nothing but slight from half-a-dozen blockheads, we

* Let me remark that people in the highest positions in life, with all their brilliance, pomp, display, magnificence and general show, may well say: our happiness lies entirely outside us, for it exists only in the heads of others.

shall understand that to lay great value upon what other people say is to pay them too much honor.

At all events, a man is in a very bad way, who finds no source of happiness in the first two classes of blessings already treated of, but has to seek it in the third, in other words, not in what he is in himself, but in what he is in the opinion of others. For, after all, the foundation of our whole nature, and, therefore, of our happiness, is our physique, and the most essential factor in happiness is health, and, next in importance after health, the ability to maintain ourselves in independence and freedom from care. There can be no competition or compensation between these essential factors on the one side, and honor, pomp, rank and reputation on the other, however much value we may set upon the latter. No one would hesitate to sacrifice the latter for the former, if it were necessary. We should add very much to our happiness by a timely recognition of the simple truth that every man's chief and real existence is in his own skin, and not in other people's opinions; and, consequently, that the actual conditions of our personal life,— health, temperament, capacity, income, wife, children, friends, home, are a hundred times more important for our happiness than what other people are pleased to think of us; otherwise we shall be miserable. And if people insist that honor is dearer than life itself, what they really mean is that existence and well-being are as nothing compared with other people's opinions. Of course, this may be only an exaggerated way of stating the prosaic truth that reputation, that is, the opinion others have of us, is indispensable if we are to make any progress in the world; but I shall come back to that presently. When we see that almost everything men devote their lives to attain, sparing no effort and encountering a thousand toils and dangers in the process, has, in the end, no further object than to raise themselves in the estimation of others; when we see that not only offices, titles, decorations, but also wealth, nay, even knowledge and art, are striven for only to obtain, as the ultimate goal of all effort, greater respect from one's fellow-men,— is not this a lamentable proof of the extent to which human folly can go? To set much too high a value on other people's opinion is a common error everywhere; an error, it may be, rooted in human nature itself, or the result of civilization and social arrangements generally; but, whatever its source, it exercises a very immoderate influence on all we do, and is very prejudicial to our happiness. We can trace it from a timorous and slavish regard for what other people will say, up to the feeling which made Virginius plunge the dagger into his daughter's heart, or induces many a man to sacrifice quiet, riches, health and even life itself, for posthumous glory. Undoubtedly this feeling is a very convenient instrument in the hands of those who have the control or direction of their fellow-men; and accordingly we find that in every scheme for training up humanity in the way it should go, the maintenance and strengthening of the feeling of honor occupies an important place. But it is quite a different matter in its effect on human happiness, of which it is here our object to treat; and we should rather be careful to dissuade people from setting too much store by what others think of them. Daily experience shows us, however, that this is just the mistake people persist in making; most men set the utmost value precisely on what other people think, and are more concerned about it than about what goes on in their own consciousness, which is the thing most immediately and directly present to them. They reverse the natural order, regarding the opinions of others as real existence and their own consciousness as something shadowy; making the derivative and secondary into the principal, and considering the picture they present to the world of more importance than their own selves. By thus trying to get a direct and immediate result out of what has no really direct or immediate existence, they fall into the kind of folly which is called VANITY — the appropriate term for that which has no solid or intrinsic value. Like a miser, such people forget the end in their eagerness to obtain the means.

The truth is that the value we set upon the opinion of others, and our constant endeavor in respect of it, are each quite out of proportion to any result we may reasonably hope to attain; so that this attention to other people's attitude may be regarded as a kind of universal mania which

everyone inherits. In all we do, almost the first thing we
think about is: what will people say; and nearly half
the troubles and bothers of life may be traced to our anxiety on this score; it is the anxiety which is at the bottom
of all that feeling of self-importance, which is so often
mortified because it is so very morbidly sensitive. It is
solicitude about what others will say that underlies all our
vanity and pretension, yes, and all our show and swagger
too. Without it, there would not be a tenth part of the
luxury which exists. Pride in every form, *point d'honneur*
and *punctilio*, however varied their kind or sphere, are at
bottom nothing but this — anxiety about what others will
say — and what sacrifices it often costs! One can see it
even in a child; and though it exists at every period of
life, it is strongest in age; because, when the capacity for
sensual pleasure fails, vanity and pride have only avarice
to share their dominion. Frenchmen, perhaps, afford the
best example of this feeling, and among them it is a
regular epidemic, appearing sometimes in the most absurd
ambition, or in a ridiculous kind of national vanity and
the most shameless boasting. However, they frustrate
their own aims, for other people make fun of them and
call them *la grande nation*.

By way of specially illustrating this perverse and exu·
berant respect for other people's opinion, let me take a
passage from the "TIMES" of March 31st, 1846, giving a detailed account of the execution of one Thomas Wix, an
apprentice who, from motives of vengeance, had murdered
his master. Here we have very unusual circumstances
and an extraordinary character, though one very suitable
for our purpose; and these combine to give a striking
picture of this folly, which is so deeply rooted in human
nature, and allow us to form an accurate notion of the
extent to which it will go. On the morning of the execution, says the report, THE REV. ORDINARY WAS EARLY IN
ATTENDANCE UPON HIM, BUT WIX, BEYOND A QUIET DE-
MEANOR, BETRAYED NO INTEREST IN HIS MINISTRATIONS, AP-
PEARING TO FEEL ANXIOUS ONLY TO ACQUIT HIMSELF "BRAVE-
LY" BEFORE THE SPECTATORS OF HIS IGNOMINIOUS END. . . .
IN THE PROCESSION WIX FELL INTO HIS PROPER PLACE WITH
ALACRITY, AND, AS HE ENTERED THE CHAPEL-YARD, RE-

MARKED, SUFFICIENTLY LOUD TO BE HEARD BY SEVERAL PER-
SONS NEAR HIM, "NOW, THEN, AS DR. DODD SAID, I SHALL
SOON KNOW THE GRAND SECRET." ON REACHING THE SCAF-
FOLD, THE MISERABLE WRETCH MOUNTED THE DROP WITHOUT
THE SLIGHTEST ASSISTANCE, AND WHEN HE GOT TO THE CEN-
TRE, HE BOWED TO THE SPECTATORS TWICE, A PROCEEDING
WHICH CALLED FORTH A TREMENDOUS CHEER FROM THE DE-
GRADED CROWD BENEATH.

This is an admirable example of the way in which a
man, with death in the most dreadful form before his
very eyes, and eternity beyond it, will care for nothing
but the impression he makes upon a crowd of gapers, and
the opinion he leaves behind him in their heads. There
was much the same kind of thing in the case of Le-
comte, who was executed at Frankfurt, also in 1846, for
an attempt on the king's life. At the trial he was very
much annoyed that he was not allowed to appear in
decent attire, before the Upper House; and on the day of
the execution it was a special grief to him that he was
not permitted to shave. It is not only in recent times
that this kind of thing has been known to happen. Mateo
Aleman tells us, in the introduction to his celebrated
romance, "Guzman de Alfarache," that many infatuated
criminals, instead of devoting their last hours to the welfare of their souls, as they ought to have done, neglect
this duty for the purpose of preparing and committing to
memory a speech to be made from the scaffold.

I take these extreme cases as being the best illustrations
of what I mean; for they give us a magnified reflection
of our own nature. The anxieties of all of us, our worries,
vexations, bothers, troubles, uneasy apprehensions and
strenuous efforts are due, in perhaps the large majority
of instances, to what other people will say; and we are
just as foolish in this respect as those miserable criminals.
Envy and hatred are very often traceable to a similar
source.

Now, it is obvious that happiness, which consists for
the most part in peace of mind and contentment, would
be served by nothing so much as by reducing this impulse
of human nature within reasonable limits,—which would
perhaps make it one-fiftieth part of what it is now. By

doing so, we should get rid of a thorn in the flesh which is always causing us pain. But it is a very difficult task, because the impulse in question is a natural and innate perversity of human nature. Tacitus says, THE LUST OF FAME IS THE LAST THAT A WISE MAN SHAKES OFF. The only way of putting an end to this universal folly is to see clearly that it is a folly; and this may be done by recognizing the fact that most of the opinions in men's heads are apt to be false, perverse, erroneous and absurd, and so in themselves unworthy of any attention; further, that other people's opinions can have very little real and positive influence upon us in most of the circumstances and affairs of life. Again, this opinion is generally of such an unfavorable character that it would worry a man to death to hear everything that was said of him, or the tone in which he was spoken of. And finally, among other things, we should be clear about the fact that honor itself has no really direct, but only an indirect, value. If people were generally converted from this universal folly, the result would be such an addition to our peace of mind and cheerfulness as at present seems inconceivable; people would present a firmer and more confident front to the world, and generally behave with less embarrassment and restraint. It is observable that a retired mode of life has an exceedingly beneficial influence on our peace of mind, and this is mainly because we thus escape having to live constantly in the sight of others, and pay everlasting regard to their casual opinions; in a word, we are able to return upon ourselves. At the same time a good deal of positive misfortune might be avoided, which we are now drawn into by striving after shadows, or, to speak more correctly, by indulging a mischievous piece of folly; and we should consequently have more attention to give to solid realities and enjoy them with less interruption than at present. But χαλεπὰ τὰ καλά — what is worth doing is hard to do.

Section 2. — Pride.

The folly of our nature which we are discussing puts forth three shoots, ambition, vanity and pride. The difference between the last two is this: PRIDE is an established conviction of one's own paramount worth in some particular respect; while VANITY is the desire of rousing such a conviction in others, and it is generally accompanied by the secret hope of ultimately coming to the same conviction oneself. Pride works FROM WITHIN; it is the direct appreciation of oneself. Vanity is the desire to arrive at this appreciation indirectly, FROM WITHOUT. So we find that vain people are talkative, and proud, taciturn. But the vain person ought to be aware that the good opinion of others, which he strives for, may be obtained much more easily and certainly by persistent silence than by speech, even though he has very good things to say. Anyone who wishes to affect pride is not therefore a proud man; but he will soon have to drop this, as every other, assumed character.

It is only a firm, unshakeable conviction of pre-eminent worth and special value which makes a man proud in the true sense of the word, — a conviction which may, no doubt, be a mistaken one or rest on advantages which are of an adventitious and conventional character; still pride is not the less pride for all that, so long as it be present in real earnest. And since pride is thus rooted in conviction, it resembles every other form of knowledge in not being within our own arbitrament. Pride's worst foe, I mean its greatest obstacle, is vanity, which courts the applause of the world in order to gain the necessary foundation for a high opinion of one's own worth, while pride is based upon a pre-existing conviction of it.

It is quite true that pride is something which is generally found fault with, and cried down; but usually, I imagine, by those who have nothing upon which they can pride themselves. In view of the impudence and foolhardiness of most people, anyone who possesses any kind of superiority or merit will do well to keep his eyes fixed on it, if he does not want it to be entirely forgotten; for if a man is good-natured enough to ignore his own privileges, and hobnob with the generality of other people, as if he were quite on their level, they will be sure to treat him, frankly and candidly, as one of themselves. This is a piece of advice I would specially offer to those whose superiority is of the highest kind — real superiority, I mean, of a purely personal nature — which cannot, like orders and titles, appeal to the eye or ear at every moment; as, otherwise, they will find that familiarity breeds contempt, or, as the Romans used to say, *sus Minervam*. JOKE WITH A SLAVE, AND HE'LL SOON SHOW HIS HEELS, is an excellent Arabian proverb; nor ought we to despise what Horace says,

Sume superbiam
Quæsitam meritis.

—usurp the fame you have deserved. No doubt, when modesty was made a virtue, it was a very advantageous thing for the fools; for everybody is expected to speak of himself as if he were one. This is leveling down indeed: for it comes to look as if there were nothing but fools in the world.

The cheapest sort of pride is national pride; for if a man is proud of his own nation, it argues that he has no qualities of his own of which he can be proud; otherwise, he would not have recourse to those which he shares with so many millions of his fellow-men. The man who is endowed with important personal qualities will be only too ready to see clearly in what respect his own nation falls short, since their failings will be constantly before his eyes. But every miserable fool who has nothing at all of which he can be proud adopts, as a last resource, pride in the nation to which he belongs; he is ready and glad to defend all its faults and follies tooth and nail, thus reimbursing himself for his own inferiority. For example, if you speak of the stupid and degrading bigotry of the English nation with the contempt it deserves, you will hardly find one Englishman in fifty to agree with you; but if there should be one, he will generally happen to be an intelligent man.

The Germans have no national pride, which shows how honest they are, as everybody knows! and how dishonest are those who, by a piece of ridiculous affectation, pretend that they are proud of their country — the "Deutsche Bruder" and the demagogues who flatter the mob in order to mislead it. I have heard it said that gunpowder was invented by a German. I doubt it. Lichtenberg asks, WHY IS IT THAT A MAN WHO IS NOT A GERMAN DOES NOT CARE ABOUT PRETENDING THAT HE IS ONE; AND THAT IF HE MAKES ANY PRETENSE AT ALL, IT IS TO BE A FRENCHMAN OR AN ENGLISHMAN ?*

However that may be, individuality is a far more important thing than nationality, and in any given man deserves a thousandfold more consideration. And since you cannot speak of national character without referring to large masses of people, it is impossible to be loud in your praises and at the same time honest. National character is only another name for the particular form which the littleness, perversity and baseness of mankind take in every country. If we become disgusted with one, we praise another, until we get disgusted with this too. Every nation mocks at other nations, and all are right.

The contents of this chapter, which treats, as I have said, of what we represent in the world, or what we are in the eyes of others, may be further distributed under three heads: honor, rank and fame.

SECTION 3. — RANK.

Let us take rank first, as it may be dismissed in a few words, although it plays an important part in the eyes of the masses and of the philistines, and is a most useful wheel in the machinery of the State.

It has a purely conventional value. Strictly speaking, it is a sham; its method is to exact an artificial respect, and, as a matter of fact, the whole thing is a mere farce.

Orders, it may be said, are bills of exchange drawn on

* TRANSLATOR'S NOTE.—It should be remembered that these remarks were written in the earlier part of the past century, and that a German philosopher nowadays, even though he were as apt to say bitter things as Schopenhauer, could hardly write in a similar strain.

public opinion, and the measure of their value is the credit of the drawer. Of course, as a substitute for pensions, they save the State a good deal of money; and, besides, they serve a very useful purpose, if they are distributed with discrimination and judgment. For people in general have eyes and ears, it is true; but not much else, very little judgment indeed, or even memory. There are many services to the State quite beyond the range of their understanding; others, again, are appreciated and made much of for a time, and then soon forgotten. It seems to me, therefore, very proper, that a cross or a star should proclaim to the mass of people always and everywhere, THIS MAN IS NOT LIKE YOU; HE HAS DONE SOMETHING. But orders lose their value when they are distributed unjustly, or without due selection, or in too great numbers: a prince should be as careful in conferring them as a man of business is in signing a bill. It is a pleonasm to inscribe on any order FOR DISTINGUISHED SERVICE; for every order ought to be for distinguished service. That stands to reason.

SECTION 4. — HONOR.

Honor is a much larger question than rank, and more difficult to discuss. Let us begin by trying to define it.

If I were to say HONOR IS EXTERNAL CONSCIENCE, AND CONSCIENCE IS INWARD HONOR, no doubt a good many people would assent; but there would be more show than reality about such a definition, and it would hardly go to the root of the matter. I prefer to say, HONOR IS, ON ITS OBJECTIVE SIDE, OTHER PEOPLE'S OPINION OF WHAT WE ARE WORTH; ON ITS SUBJECTIVE SIDE, IT IS THE RESPECT WE PAY TO THIS OPINION. From the latter point of view, to be A MAN OF HONOR is to exercise what is often a very wholesome, but by no means a purely moral, influence.

The feelings of honor and shame exist in every man who is not utterly depraved, and honor is everywhere recognized as something particularly valuable. The reason of this is as follows. By and in himself a man can accomplish very little; he is like Robinson Crusoe on a desert island. It is only in society that a man's powers can be called into full activity. He very soon finds this out when his consciousness begins to develop, and their arises in him the desire to be looked upon as a useful member of society, as one, that is, who is capable of playing his part as a man — *pro parte virili* — thereby acquiring a right to the benefits of social life. Now, to be a useful member of society, one must do two things: firstly, what everyone is expected to do everywhere; and, secondly, what one's own particular position in the world demands and requires.

But a man soon discovers that everything depends upon his being useful, not in his own opinion, but in the opinion of others; and so he tries his best to make that favorable impression upon the world, to which he attaches such a high value. Hence, this primitive and innate characteristic of human nature, which is called the feeling of honor, or, under another aspect, the feeling of shame — *verecundia*. It is this which brings a blush to his cheek at the thought of having suddenly to fall in the estimation of others, even when he knows that he is innocent, nay, even if his remissness extends to no absolute obligation, but only to one which he has taken upon himself of his own free will. Conversely, nothing in life gives a man so much courage as the attainment or renewal of the conviction that other people regard him with favor; because it means that everyone joins to give him help and protection, which is an infinitely stronger bulwark against the ills of life than anything he can do himself.

The variety of relations in which a man can stand to other people so as to obtain their confidence, that is, their good opinion, gives rise to a distinction between several kinds of honor, resting chiefly on the different bearings that *meum* may take to *tuum;* or, again, on the performance of various pledges; or finally, on the relation of the sexes. Hence, there are three main kinds of honor, each of which takes various forms — civic honor, official honor, and sexual honor.

CIVIC HONOR has the widest sphere of all. It consists in the assumption that we shall pay unconditional respect to the rights of others, and, therefore, never use any unjust or unlawful means of getting what we want. It is the condition of all peaceable intercourse between man and man; and it is destroyed by anything that openly and manifestly militates against this peaceable intercourse, anything, accordingly, which entails punishment at the hands of the law, always supposing that the punishment is a just one.

The ultimate foundation of honor is the conviction that moral character is unalterable: a single bad action implies that future actions of the same kind will, under similar circumstances, also be bad. This is well expressed by the English use of the word CHARACTER as meaning credit, reputation, honor. Hence honor, once lost, can never be recovered, unless the loss rested on some mistake, such as may occur if a man is slandered or his actions viewed in a false light. So the law provides remedies against slander, libel, and even insult; for insult, though it amount to no more than mere abuse, is a kind of summary slander with a suppression of the reasons. What I mean may be well put in the Greek phrase — not quoted from any author — ἔστιν ἡ λοιδορία διαβολὴ σύντομος. It is true that if a man abuses another, he is simply showing that he has no real or true causes of complaint against him; as, otherwise, he would bring these forward as the premises, and rely upon his hearers to draw the conclusion themselves; instead of which, he gives the conclusion and leaves out the premises, trusting that people will suppose that he has done so only for the sake of being brief.

Civic honor draws its existence and name from the middle classes; but it applies equally to all, not excepting the highest. No man can disregard it, and it is a very serious thing, of which everyone should be careful not to make light. The man who breaks confidence has forever forfeited confidence, whatever he may do, and whoever he may be; and the bitter consequences of the loss of confidence can never be averted.

There is a sense in which honor may be said to have a NEGATIVE character in opposition to the POSITIVE character of fame. For honor is not the opinion people have of particular qualities which a man may happen to possess exclusively: it is rather the opinion they have of the qualities which a man may be expected to exhibit, and to which he should not prove false. Honor, therefore, means that a man is not exceptional; fame, that he is. Fame is something which must be won; honor, only something which must not be lost. The absence of fame is obscurity, which is only a negative; but loss of honor is shame, which is a positive quality. This negative character of honor must not be confused with anything PASSIVE; for honor is above all things active in its working. It is the only quality which proceeds DIRECTLY from the man who exhibits it: it is concerned entirely with what he does and leaves undone, and has nothing to do with the actions of others or the obstacles they place in his way. It is something entirely in our own power — τῶν ἐφ᾽ἡμῶν. This distinction, as we shall see presently, marks off true honor from the sham honor of chivalry.

Slander is the only weapon by which honor can be attacked from without; and the only way to repel the attack is to confute the slander with the proper amount of publicity, and a due unmasking of him who utters it.

The reason why respect is paid to age is that old people have necessarily shown in the course of their lives whether or not they have been able to maintain their honor unblemished; while that of young people has not yet been put to the proof, though they are credited with the possession of it. For neither length of years, equaled as it is, and even excelled, in the case of some of the lower animals, nor, again, experience, which is only a closer knowledge of the world's ways, can be any sufficient reason for the respect which the young are everywhere required to show toward the old: for if it were merely a matter of years, the weakness which attends on age would call rather for consideration than for respect. It is, however, a remarkable fact that white hair always commands reverence — a reverence really innate and instinctive. Wrinkles — a much surer sign of old age — command no reverence at all: you never hear any one speak of VENERABLE WRINKLES; but VENERABLE WHITE HAIR is a common expression.

Honor has only an indirect value. For, as I explained at the beginning of this chapter, what other people think

of us, if it affects us at all, can affect us only in so far
as it governs their behavior toward us, and only just so
long as we live with, or have to do with, them. But it
is to society alone that we owe that safety which we and
our possessions enjoy in a state of civilization; in all we
do we need the help of others, and they, in their turn,
must have confidence in us before they can have anything to do with us. Accordingly, their opinion of us is,
indirectly, a matter of great importance; though I cannot see how it can have a direct or immediate value.
This is an opinion also held by Cicero. I QUITE AGREE,
he writes, WITH WHAT CHRYSIPPUS AND DIOGENES USED
TO SAY, THAT A GOOD REPUTATION IS NOT WORTH RAIS-
ING A FINGER TO OBTAIN, IF IT WERE NOT THAT IT IS
SO USEFUL. This truth has been insisted upon at great
length by Helvetius in his chief work "De l' Esprit,"
the conclusion of which is that WE LOVE ESTEEM NOT FOR
ITS OWN SAKE, BUT SOLELY FOR THE ADVANTAGES WHICH IT
BRINGS. And as the means can never be more than the
end, that saying, of which so much is made, HONOR IS
DEARER THAN LIFE ITSELF, is, as I have remarked, a
very exaggerated statement. So much, then, for civic honor.

OFFICIAL HONOR is the general opinion of other people
that a man who fills any office really has the necessary
qualities for the proper discharge of all the duties which
appertain to it. The greater and more important the
duties a man has to discharge in the State, and the
higher and more influential the office which he fills,
the stronger must be the opinion which people have of
the moral and intellectual qualities which render him fit
for his post. Therefore, the higher his position, the
greater must be the degree of honor paid to him, expressed, as it is, in titles, orders and the generally subservient behavior of others toward him. As a rule, a
man's official rank implies the particular degree of honor
which ought to be paid to him, however much this degree
may be modified by the capacity of the masses to form
any notion of its importance. Still, as a matter of fact,
greater honor is paid to a man who fulfills special duties
than to the common citizen, whose honor mainly consists
in keeping clear of dishonor.

Official honor demands, further, that the man who occupies an office must maintain respect for it, for the sake both of his colleagues and of those who will come after him. This respect an official can maintain by a proper observance of his duties, and by repelling any attack that may be made upon the office itself or upon its occupant: he must not, for instance, pass over unheeded any statement to the effect that the duties of the office are not properly discharged, or that the office itself does not conduce to the public welfare. He must prove the unwarrantable nature of such attacks by enforcing the legal penalty for them.

Subordinate to the honor of official personages comes that of those who serve the state in any other capacity, as doctors, lawyers, teachers, anyone, in short, who by graduating in any subject, or by any other public declaration that he is qualified to exercise some special skill, claims to practice it; in a word, the honor of all those who take any public pledges whatever. Under this head comes military honor, in the true sense of the word, the opinion that people who have bound themselves to defend their country really possess the requisite qualities which will enable them to do so, especially courage, personal bravery and strength, and that they are perfectly ready to defend their country to the death, and never and under no circumstances desert the flag to which they have once sworn allegiance. I have here taken official honor in a wider sense than that in which it is generally used, namely, the respect due by citizens to an office itself.

In treating of SEXUAL HONOR and the principles on which it rests, a little more attention and analysis are necessary; and what I shall say will support my contention that all honor really rests upon a utilitarian basis. There are two natural divisions of the subject — the honor of women and the honor of men, in either side issuing in a well-understood *esprit de corps*. The former is by far the more important of the two, because the most essential feature in woman's life is her relation to man.

Female honor is the general opinion in regard to a girl that she is pure, and in regard to a wife that she is faithful. The importance of this opinion rests upon the following considerations. Women depend upon men in all the relations of life; men upon women, it might be said, in one only. So an arrangement is made for mutual interdependence — man undertaking responsibility for all woman's needs and also for the children that spring from their union — an arrangement on which is based the welfare of the whole female race. To carry out this plan, women have to band together with a show of *esprit de corps*, and present one undivided front to their common enemy, man — who possesses all the good things of the earth, in virtue of his superior physical and intellectual power — in order to lay siege to and conquer him, and so get possession of him and a share of those good things. To this end the honor of all women depends upon the enforcement of the rule that no woman should give herself to a man except in marriage, in order that every man may be forced, as it were, to surrender and ally himself with a woman; by this arrangement provision is made for the whole of the female race. This is a result, however, which can be obtained only by a strict observance of the rule; and accordingly, women everywhere show true *esprit de corps* in carefully insisting upon its maintenance. Any girl who commits a breach of the rule betrays the whole female race, because its welfare would be destroyed if every woman were to do likewise; so she is cast out with shame as one who has lost her honor. No woman will have anything more to do with her; she is avoided like the plague. The same doom is awarded to a woman who breaks the marriage tie; for in so doing she is false to the terms upon which the man capitulated; and as her conduct is such as to frighten other men from making a similar surrender, it imperils the welfare of all her sisters. Nay more; this deception and coarse breach of troth is a crime punishable by the loss, not only of personal, but also of civic honor. This is why we minimize the shame of a girl, but not of a wife; because in the former case, marriage can restore honor, while in the latter, no atonement can be made for the breach of contract.

Once this *esprit de corps* is acknowledged to be the foundation of female honor, and is seen to be a wholesome, nay, a necessary arrangement, as at bottom a matter of prudence and interest, its extreme importance for the welfare of women will be recognized. But it does not possess anything more than a relative value. It is no absolute end, lying beyond all other aims of existence and valued above life itself. In this view, there will be nothing to applaud in the forced and extravagant conduct of a Lucretia or a Virginius — conduct which can easily degenerate into tragic farce, and produce a terrible feeling of revulsion. The conclusion of " Emelia Galotti," for instance, makes one leave the theatre completely ill at ease; and, on the other hand, all the rules of female honor cannot prevent a certain sympathy with Clara in " Egmont." To carry this principle of female honor too far is to forget the end in thinking of the means — and this is just what people often do; for such exaggeration suggests that the value of sexual honor is absolute; while the truth is that it is more relative than any other kind. One might go so far as to say that its value is purely conventional, when one sees from Thomasius how in all ages and countries, up to the time of the Reformation, irregularities were permitted and recognized by law, with no derogation to female honor — not to speak of the temple of Mylitta at Babylon.

There are also, of course, certain circumstances in civil life which make external forms of marriage impossible, especially in Catholic countries, where there is no such thing as divorce. Ruling princes everywhere, would, in my opinion, do much better, from a moral point of view, to dispense with forms altogether rather than contract a morganatic marriage, the descendants of which might raise claims to the throne if the legitimate stock happened to die out; so that there is a possibility, though, perhaps, a remote one, that a morganatic marriage might produce a civil war. And, besides, such a marriage, concluded in defiance of all outward ceremony, is a concession made to women and priests — two classes of persons to whom one should be most careful to give as little tether as possible. It is further to be remarked that

every man in a country can marry the woman of his
choice, except one poor individual, namely, the prince.
His hand belongs to his country, and can be given in
marriage only for reasons of State, that is, for the good
of the country. Still, for all that, he is a man; and, as
a man, he likes to follow whither his heart leads. It is
an unjust, ungrateful, and priggish thing to forbid, or to
desire to forbid, a prince from following his inclinations
in this matter; of course, as long as the lady has no influence upon the Government of the country. From her
point of view she occupies an exceptional position, and
does not come under the ordinary rules of sexual honor;
for she has merely given herself to a man who loves
her, and whom she loves but cannot marry. And in
general, the fact that the principle of female honor has
no origin in nature, is shown by the many bloody sacrifices which have been offered to it—the murder of
children and the mother's suicide. No doubt a girl who
contravenes the code commits a breach of faith against
her whole sex; but this faith is one which is only secretly
taken for granted, and not sworn to. And since, in most
cases, her own prospects suffer most immediately, her
folly is infinitely greater than her crime.

The corresponding virtue in men is a product of the
one I have been discussing. It is their *esprit de corps*,
which demands that, when a man has made that surrender of himself in marriage which is so advantageous to
his conqueror, he shall take care that the terms of the
treaty are maintained; both in order that the agreement
itself may lose none of its force by the permission of any
laxity in its observance, and that men, having given up
everything, may, at least, be assured of their bargain,
namely, exclusive possession. Accordingly, it is part of
a man's honor to resent a breach of the marriage tie on
the part of his wife, and to punish it, at the very least
by separating from her. If he condones the offense, his
fellow-men cry shame upon him; but the shame in this
case is not nearly so foul as that of the woman who has
lost her honor; the stain is by no means of so deep a
dye—*levioris notae macula;*—because a man's relation to
woman is subordinate to many other and more important

affairs in his life. The two great dramatic poets of modern times have each taken man's honor as the theme of two plays; Shakespeare in « Othello » and « The Winter's Tale, » and Calderon in « El Medico de su Honra » (the Physician of his Honor), and « A Secreto Agravio Secreta Venganza » (for Secret Insult Secret Vengeance). It should be said, however, that honor demands the punishment of the wife only; to punish her paramour too, is a work of supererogation. This confirms the view I have taken, that a man's honor originates in *esprit de corps*.

The kind of honor which I have been discussing hitherto has always existed in its various forms and principles among all nations and at all times; although the history of female honor shows that its principles have undergone certain local modifications at different periods. But there is another species of honor which differs from this entirely, a species of honor of which the Greeks and Romans had no conception, and up to this day it is perfectly unknown among Chinese, Hindoos or Mohammedans. It is a kind of honor which arose only in the Middle Ages, and is indigenous only to Christian Europe, nay, only to an extremely small portion of the population, that is to say, the higher classes of society, and those who ape them. It is KNIGHTLY HONOR, or *point d'honneur*. Its principles are quite different from those which underlie the kind of honor I have been treating until now, and in some respects are even opposed to them. The sort I am referring to produces the CAVALIER; while the other kind creates the MAN OF HONOR. As this is so, I shall proceed to give an explanation of its principles, as a kind of code or mirror of knightly courtesy.

(1.) To begin with, honor of this sort consists, not in other people's opinion of what we are worth, but wholly and entirely in whether they express it or not, no matter whether they really have any opinion at all, let alone whether they know of reasons for having one. Other people may entertain the worst opinion of us in consequence of what we do, and may despise us as much as they like; so long as no one dares to give expression to his opinion, our honor remains untarnished. So if our actions and qualities compel the highest respect from other people, and they have no option but to give this respect,— as soon as any one, no matter how wicked or foolish he may be, utters something depreciatory of us, our honor is offended, nay, gone forever, unless we can manage to restore it. A superfluous proof of what I say, namely, that knightly honor depends, not upon what people think, but upon what they say, is furnished by the fact that insults can be withdrawn, or, if necessary, form the subject of an apology, which makes them as though they had never been uttered. Whether the opinion which underlay the expression has also been rectified, and why the expression should ever have been used, are questions which are perfectly unimportant: so long as the statement is withdrawn, all is well. The truth is that conduct of this kind aims, not at earning respect, but at extorting it.

(2.) In the second place, this sort of honor rests, not on what a man does, but on what he suffers, the obstacles he encounters; differing from the honor which prevails in all else, in consisting, not in what he says or does himself, but in what another man says or does. His honor is thus at the mercy of every man who can talk it away on the tip of his tongue; and if he attacks it, in a moment it is gone forever,— unless the man who is attacked manages to wrest it back again by a process which I shall mention presently, a process which involves danger to his life, health, freedom, property and peace of mind. A man's whole conduct may be in accordance with the most righteous and noble principles, his spirit may be the purest that ever breathed, his intellect of the very highest order; and yet his honor may disappear the moment that anyone is pleased to insult him, anyone at all who has not offended against this code of honor himself, let him be the most worthless rascal or the most stupid beast, an idler, gambler; debtor, a man, in short, of no account at all. It is usually this sort of fellow who likes to insult people; for, as Seneca rightly remarks, *ut quisque contemtissimus et ludibrio est, ita solutissimæ linguæ est* —the more contemptible and ridiculous a man is, the readier he is with his tongue. **His** insults are most likely to be directed against the very kind of man I have described, because people of different tastes can never be friends, and the sight of pre-eminent merit is apt to raise the secret ire of a ne'er-do-well. What Goethe says in the "Westöstlicher Divan" is quite true, that it is useless to complain against your enemies; for they can never become your friends, if your whole being is a standing reproach to them:—

> Was klagst du über Feinde?
> Solten Solche je werden Freunde
> Denen das Wesen wie du bist,
> Im stillen ein ewiger Vorwurf ist?

It is obvious that people of this worthless description have good cause to be thankful to the principle of honor, because it puts them on a level with people who in every other respect stand far above them. If a fellow likes to insult anyone, attribute to him, for example, some bad quality, this is taken *prima facie* as a well-founded opinion, true in fact; a decree, as it were, with all the force of law; nay, if it is not at once wiped out in blood, it is a judgment which holds good and valid to all time. In other words, the man who is insulted remains — in the eyes of all HONORABLE PEOPLE — what the man who uttered the insult — even though he were the greatest wretch on earth — was pleased to call him; for he has PUT UP WITH the insult — the technical term, I believe. Accordingly, all HONORABLE PEOPLE will have nothing more to do with him, and treat him like a leper, and, it may be, refuse to go into any company where he may be found, and so on.

This wise proceeding may, I think, be traced back to the fact that in the Middle Ages, up to the fifteenth century, it was not the accuser in any criminal process who had to prove the guilt of the accused, but the accused who had to prove his innocence. This he could do by swearing he was not guilty; and his backers — CONSACRA-MENTALES — had to come and swear that in their opinion he was incapable of perjury. If he could find no one to help him in this way, or the accuser took objection to his backers, recourse was had to trial by THE JUDGMENT OF GOD, which generally meant a duel. For the accused

5

was now IN DISGRACE,* and had to clear himself. Here, then, is the origin of the notion of disgrace, and of that whole system which prevails now-a-days among HONORABLE PEOPLE — only that the oath is omitted. This is also the explanation of that deep feeling of indignation which HONORABLE PEOPLE are called upon to show if they are given the lie; it is a reproach which they say must be wiped out in blood. It seldom comes to this pass, however, though lies are of common occurrence; but in England, more than elsewhere, it is a superstition which has taken very deep root. As a matter of order, a man who threatens to kill another for telling a lie should never have told one himself. The fact is, that the criminal trial of the Middle Ages also admitted of a shorter form. In reply to the charge, the accused answered: THAT IS A LIE; whereupon it was left to be decided by THE JUDGMENT OF GOD. Hence, the code of knightly honor prescribes that, when the lie is given, an appeal to arms follows as a matter of course. So much, then, for the theory of insult.

But there is something even worse than insult, something so dreadful that I must beg pardon of all HONORABLE PEOPLE for so much as mentioning it in this code of knightly honor; for I know they will shiver, and their hair will stand on end, at the very thought of it — the *summum malum*, the greatest evil on earth, worse than death and damnation. A man may give another — *horribile dictu!* — a slap or a blow. This is such an awful thing, and so utterly fatal to all honor, that, while any other species of insult may be healed by blood-letting, this can be cured only by the *coup de grâce*.

(3.) In the third place, this kind of honor has absolutely nothing to do with what a man may be in and for himself; or, again, with the question whether his moral character can ever become better or worse, and all such pedantic inquiries. If your honor happens to be attacked, or to all appearances gone, it can very soon be restored

---

*TRANSLATOR'S NOTE.—It is true that this expression has another and special meaning in the technical terminology of Chivalry, but it is the nearest English equivalent which I can find for the German — *ein Bescholtener.*

in its entirety if you are only quick enough in having recourse to the one universal remedy — A DUEL. But if the aggressor does not belong to the classes which recognize the code of knightly honor, or has himself once offended against it, there is a safer way of meeting any attack upon your honor, whether it consists in blows, or merely in words. If you are armed you can strike down your opponent on the spot, or perhaps an hour later. This will restore your honor.

But if you wish to avoid such an extreme step, from fear of any unpleasant consequences arising therefrom, or from uncertainty as to whether the aggressor is subject to the laws of knightly honor or not, there is another means of making your position good, namely, the "Avantage." This consists in returning rudeness with still greater rudeness; and if insults are no use, you can try a blow, which forms a sort of climax in the redemption of your honor; for instance, a box on the ear may be cured by a blow with a stick, and a blow with a stick by a thrashing with a horsewhip; and, as the approved remedy for this last, some people recommend you to spit at your opponent.* If all these means are of no avail, you must not shrink from drawing blood. And the reason for these methods of wiping out insult is, in this code, as follows:

(4.) To receive an insult is disgraceful; to give one, honorable. Let me take an example. My opponent has truth, right, and reason on his side. Very well. I insult him. Thereupon right and honor leave him and come to me, and, for the time being, he has lost them — until he gets them back, not by the exercise of right or reason, but by shooting and sticking me. Accordingly, rudeness is a quality which, in point of honor, is a substitute for any other and outweighs them all. The rudest is always right. What more do you want? However stupid, bad, or wicked a man may have been, if he is only rude into the bargain, he condones and legitimizes all his faults. If in any discussion or conversation, another man shows

*TRANSLATOR'S NOTE.—It must be remembered that Schopenhauer is here describing or perhaps caricaturing, the manners and customs of the German aristocracy of half a century ago.

more knowledge, greater love of truth, a sounder judgment, better understanding than we, or generally exhibits intellectual qualities which cast ours into the shade, we can at once annul his superiority and our own shallowness, and in our turn be superior to him, by being insulting and offensive. For rudeness is better than any argument; it totally eclipses intellect. If our opponent does not care for our mode of attack, and will not answer still more rudely, so as to plunge us into the ignoble rivalry of the "Avantage," we are the victors and honor is on our side. Truth, knowledge, understanding, intellect, wit, must beat a retreat and leave the field to this almighty insolence.

HONORABLE PEOPLE immediately make a show of mounting their war horse, if anyone utters an opinion adverse to theirs, or shows more intelligence than they can muster; and if in any controversy they are at a loss for a reply, they look about for some weapon of rudeness, which will serve as well and come readier to hand; so they retire masters of the position. It must now be obvious that people are quite right in applauding this principle of honor as having ennobled the tone of society. This principle springs from another, which forms the heart and soul of the entire code.

(5.) Fifthly, the code implies that the highest court to which a man can appeal in any differences he may have with another on a point of honor is the court of physical force, that is, of brutality. Every piece of rudeness is, strictly speaking, an appeal to brutality; for it is a declaration that intellectual strength and moral insight are incompetent to decide, and that the battle must be fought out by physical force — a struggle which, in the case of man, whom Franklin defines as A TOOL-MAKING ANIMAL, is decided by the weapons peculiar to the species; and the decision is irrevocable. This is the well-known principle of THE RIGHT OF MIGHT — irony, of course, like THE WIT OF A FOOL, a parallel phrase. The honor of a knight may be called the glory of might.

(6.) Lastly, if, as we saw above, civic honor is very scrupulous in the matter of *meum* and *tuum*, paying great respect to obligations and a promise once made, the code we are here discussing displays, on the other hand, the noblest liberality. There is only one word which may not be broken, THE WORD OF HONOR — upon my HONOR, as people say — the presumption being, of course, that every other form of promise may be broken. Nay, if the worst comes to the worst, it is easy to break even one's word of honor, and still remain honorable — again by adopting that universal remedy, the duel, and fighting with those who maintain that we pledged our word. Further, there is one debt, and one alone, that under no circumstances must be left unpaid — a gambling debt, which has accordingly been called A DEBT OF HONOR. In all other kinds of debt you may cheat Jews and Christians as much as you like; and your knightly honor remains without a stain.

The unprejudiced reader will see at once that such a strange, savage, and ridiculous code of honor as this has no foundation in human nature, nor any warrant in a healthy view of human affairs. The extremely narrow sphere of its operation serves only to intensify the feeling, which is exclusively confined to Europe since the Middle Ages, and then only to the upper classes, officers, and soldiers, and people who imitate them. Neither Greeks nor Romans knew anything of this code of honor or of its principles; nor the highly civilized nations of Asia, ancient or modern. Among them no other kind of honor is recognized but that which I discussed first, in virtue of which a man is what he shows himself to be by his actions, not what any wagging tongue is pleased to say of him. They thought that what a man said or did might perhaps affect his own honor, but not any other man's. To them, a blow was but a blow — and any horse or donkey could give a harder one — a blow which under certain circumstances might make a man angry and demand immediate vengeance; but it had nothing to do with honor. No one kept account of blows or insulting words, or of the SATISFACTION which was demanded or omitted to be demanded. Yet in personal bravery and contempt of death, the ancients were certainly not inferior to the nations of Christian Europe. The Greeks and Romans were thorough heroes, if you like; but they knew nothing about *point d'honneur*. If they had any idea of a duel, it was totally unconnected with the life of the nobles; it was merely the exhibition of mercenary gladiators, slaves devoted to slaughter, condemned criminals, who, alternately with wild beasts, were set to butcher one another to make a Roman holiday. When Christianity was introduced, gladiatorial shows were done away with, and their place taken, in Christian times, by the duel, which was a way of settling difficulties by THE JUDGMENT OF GOD. If the gladiatorial fight was a cruel sacrifice to the prevailing desire for great spectacles, dueling is a cruel sacrifice to existing prejudices — a sacrifice, not of criminals, slaves, and prisoners, but of the noble and the free.*

There are a great many traits in the character of the ancients which show that they were entirely free from these prejudices. When, for instance, Marius was summoned to a duel by a Teutonic chief, he returned answer to the effect that, if the chief were tired of his life, he might go and hang himself; at the same time he offered him a veteran gladiator for a round or two. Plutarch relates in his life of Themistocles that Eurybiades, who was in command of the fleet, once raised his stick to strike him; whereupon Themistocles, instead of drawing his sword, simply said: STRIKE, BUT HEAR ME. How sorry the reader must be, if he is an HONORABLE man, to find that we have no information that the Athenian officers refused in a body to serve any longer under Themistocles, if he acted like that! There is a modern French writer who declares that if anyone considers Demosthenes a man of honor, his ignorance will excite a smile of pity; and that Cicero was not a man of honor either! In a certain passage in Plato's "Laws," the philosopher speaks at length of αἰκία or ASSAULT, showing us clearly enough that the ancients had no notion of any feeling of honor in connection with such matters. Socrates's frequent discussions were often followed by his being severely handled, and he bore it all mildly. Once, for instance, when

---

* TRANSLATOR'S NOTE.—These and other remarks on dueling will no doubt wear a belated look to English readers; but they are hardly yet antiquated for most parts of the Continent.

somebody kicked him, the patience with which he took
the insult surprised one of his friends. Do YOU THINK,
said Socrates, THAT IF AN ASS HAPPENED TO KICK ME,
I SHOULD RESENT IT? On another occasion, when he was
asked, HAS NOT THAT FELLOW ABUSED AND INSULTED YOU?
No, was his answer, WHAT HE SAYS IS NOT ADDRESSED TO
ME. Stobæus has preserved a long passage from Mu-
sonius, from which we can see how the ancients treated
insults. They knew no other form of satisfaction than
that which the law provided, and wise people despised
even this. If a Greek received a box on the ear, he
could get satisfaction by the aid of the law; as is evident
from Plato's "Gorgias," where Socrates's opinion may be
found. The same thing may be seen in the account
given by Gellius of one Lucius Veratius, who had the
audacity to give some Roman citizens whom he met on
the road a box on the ear, without any provocation whatever; but to avoid any ulterior consequences, he told a
slave to bring a bag of small money, and on the spot
paid the trivial legal penalty to the men whom he had
astonished by his conduct.

Crates, the celebrated Cynic philosopher, got such a
box on the ear from Nicodromus, the musician, that his
face swelled up and became black and blue; whereupon
he put a label on his forehead, with the inscription,
Nicodromus fecit, which brought much disgrace to the
fluteplayer who had committed such a piece of brutality
upon the man whom all Athens honored as a household
god. And in a letter to Melesippus, Diogenes of Sinope
tells us that he got a beating from the drunken sons of
the Athenians; but he adds that it was a matter of no
importance. And Seneca devotes the last few chapters
of his "De Constantia" to a lengthy discussion on insult —
contumelia; in order to show that a wise man will take
no notice of it. In Chapter XIV. he says, WHAT SHALL
A WISE MAN DO, IF HE IS GIVEN A BLOW? WHAT CATO DID,
WHEN SOME ONE STRUCK HIM ON THE MOUTH; — NOT FIRE
UP OR AVENGE THE INSULT, OR EVEN RETURN THE BLOW,
BUT SIMPLY IGNORE IT.

YES, you say, BUT THESE MEN WERE PHILOSOPHERS. — And
you are fools, eh? Precisely.

It is clear that the whole code of knightly honor was utterly unknown to the ancients; for the simple reason that they always took a natural and unprejudiced view of human affairs, and did not allow themselves to be influenced by any such vicious and abominable folly. A blow in the face was to them a blow and nothing more, a trivial physical injury; whereas the moderns make a catastrophe out of it, a theme for a tragedy; as, for instance, in the "Cid" of Corneille, or in a recent German comedy of middle-class life, called "The Power of Circumstance," which should have been entitled "The Power of Prejudice." If a member of the National Assembly at Paris got a blow on the ear, it would resound from one end of Europe to the other. The examples which I have given of the way in which such an occurrence would have been treated in classic times may not suit the ideas of HONORABLE PEOPLE, so let me recommend to their notice, as a kind of antidote, the story of Monsieur Desglands in Diderot's masterpiece, "Jacques le Fataliste." It is an excellent specimen of modern knightly honor, which, no doubt, they will find enjoyable and edifying.*

From what I have said it must be quite evident that the principle of knightly honor has no essential and spontaneous origin in human nature. It is an artificial product, and its source is not hard to find. Its existence obviously dates from the time when people used their fists more than their heads, when priestcraft had enchained the human intellect, the much bepraised Middle Age, with its system of chivalry. That was the time when people let the Almighty not only care for them

---

* TRANSLATOR'S NOTE.— The story to which Schopenhauer here refers is briefly as follows: Two gentlemen, one of whom was named Desglands, were paying court to the same lady. As they sat at table side by side, with the lady opposite, Desglands did his best to charm her with his conversation; but she pretended not to hear him, and kept looking at his rival. In the agony of jealousy, Desglands, as he was holding a fresh egg in his hand, involuntarily crushed it; the shell broke and its contents bespattered his rival's face. Seeing him raise his hand, Desglands seized it and whispered: SIR, I TAKE IT AS GIVEN. The next day Desglands appeared with a large piece of black sticking plaster upon his right cheek. In the duel which followed, Desglands severely

but judge for them too; when difficult cases were decided by an ordeal, a JUDGMENT OF GOD; which, with few exceptions, meant a duel, not only where nobles were concerned, but in the case of ordinary citizens as well. There is a neat illustration of this in Shakespeare's Henry VI. * Every judicial sentence was subject to an appeal to arms — a court, as it were, of higher instance, namely, THE JUDGMENT OF GOD: and this really meant that physical strength and activity, that is, our animal nature, usurped the place of reason on the judgment seat, deciding in matters of right and wrong, not by what a man had done, but by the force with which he was opposed, the same system, in fact, as prevails to-day under the principles of knightly honor. If anyone doubts that such is really the origin of our modern duel, let him read an excellent work by J. B. Millingen, "The History of Duelling." † Nay, you may still find among the supporters of the system, — who, by the way, are not usually the most educated or thoughtful of men, — some who look upon the result of a duel as really constituting a divine judgment in the matter in dispute; no doubt in consequence of the traditional feeling on the subject.

But leaving aside the question of origin, it must now be clear to us that the main tendency of the principle is to use physical menace for the purpose of extorting an appearance of respect which is deemed too difficult or superfluous to acquire in reality; a proceeding which comes to much the same thing as if you were to prove the warmth of your room by holding your hand on the thermometer and so make it rise. In fact, the kernel of the matter is this: whereas civic honor aims at peaceable intercourse, and consists in the opinion of other people that WE DESERVE FULL CONFIDENCE, because we pay unconditional respect to their rights, knightly honor on the other

---

wounded his rival; upon which he reduced the size of the plaster. When his rival recovered, they had another duel; Desglands drew blood again, and again made his plaster a little smaller; and so on for five or six times. After every duel Desglands's plaster grew less and less, until at last his rival was killed.

* Part II., Act 2, Sc. 3.

† Published in 1849.

hand, lays down that WE ARE TO BE FEARED, as being determined at all costs to maintain our own.

As not much reliance can be placed upon human integrity, the principle that it is more essential to arouse fear than to invite confidence would not, perhaps, be a false one, if we were living in a state of nature, where every man would have to protect himself and directly maintain his own rights. But in civilized life, where the State undertakes the protection of our person and property, the principle is no longer applicable: it stands, like the castles and watch-towers of the age when might was right, a useless and forlorn object, amidst well-tilled fields and frequented roads or even railways.

Accordingly, the application of knightly honor, which still recognizes this principle, is confined to those small cases of personal assault which meet with but slight punishment at the hands of the law, or even none at all, for *de minimis non*, mere trivial wrongs, committed sometimes only in jest. The consequence of this limited application of the principle is that it has forced itself into an exaggerated respect for the value of the person, a respect utterly alien to the nature, constitution or destiny of man —which it has elevated into a species of sanctity: and as it considers that the State has imposed a very insufficient penalty on the commission of such trivial injuries, it takes upon itself to punish them by attacking the aggressor in life or limb. The whole thing manifestly rests upon an excessive degree of arrogant pride, which, completely forgetting what man really is, claims that he shall be absolutely free from all attack or even censure. Those who determine to carry out this principle by main force, and announce, as their rule of action, WHOEVER INSULTS OR STRIKES ME SHALL DIE! ought for their pains to be banished the country.*

* Knightly honor is the child of pride and folly, and it is NEED, not pride, which is the heritage of the human race. It is a very remarkable fact that this extreme form of pride should be found exclusively among the adherents of the religion which teaches the deepest humility. Still, this pride must not be put down to religion, but, rather, to the feudal system, which made every nobleman a petty sovereign who recognized no human judge, and learned to regard his person as sacred and inviolable, and any attack upon it, or any blow

As a palliative to this rash arrogance, people are in the habit of giving way on everything. If two intrepid persons meet, and neither will give way, the slightest difference may cause a shower of abuse, then fisticuffs, and, finally, a fatal blow; so that it would really be a more decorous proceeding to omit the intermediate steps and appeal to arms at once. An appeal to arms has its own special formalities; and these have developed into a rigid and precise system of laws and regulations, together forming the most solemn farce there is, a regular temple of honor dedicated to folly! For if two intrepid persons dispute over some trivial matter (more important affairs are dealt with by law), one of them, the cleverer of the two, will of course yield; and they will agree to differ. That this is so is proved by the fact that common people, —or, rather, the numerous classes of the community who do not acknowledge the principle of knightly honor, let any dispute run its natural course. Among these classes homicide is a hundredfold rarer than among those — and they amount, perhaps, in all, to hardly one in a thousand, who pay homage to the principle: and even blows are of no very frequent occurrence.

Then it has been said that the manners and tone of good society are ultimately based upon this principle of honor, which, with its system of duels, is made out to be a bulwark against the assaults of savagery and rudeness. But Athens, Corinth and Rome could assuredly boast of good, nay excellent society, and manners and tone of a high order, without any support from the bogey of a knightly honor. It is true that women did not occupy that prominent place in ancient society which they hold

or insulting word, as an offense punishable by death. The principle of knightly honor and of the duel was at first confined to the nobles. and, later on, also to officers in the army, who, enjoying a kind of off-and-on relationship with the upper classes, though they were never incorporated with them, were anxious not to be behind them. It is true that duels were the product of the old ordeals; but the latter are not the foundation, but rather the consequence and application of the principle of honor: the man who recognized no human judge appealed to the divine. Ordeals, however, are not peculiar to Christendom: they may be found in great force among the Hindoos, especially of ancient times; and there are traces of them even now.

now, when conversation has taken on a frivolous and trifling character, to the exclusion of that weighty discourse which distinguished the ancients. This change has certainly contributed a great deal to bring about the tendency which is observable in good society nowadays, to prefer personal courage to the possession of any other quality. The fact is that personal courage is really a very subordinate virtue, merely the distinguishing mark of a subaltern, a virtue, indeed, in which we are surpassed by the lower animals; or else you would not hear people say, AS BRAVE AS A LION. Far from being the pillar of society, knightly honor affords a sure asylum, in general for dishonesty and wickedness, and also for small incivilities, want of consideration and unmannerliness. Rude behavior is often passed over in silence because no one cares to risk his neck in correcting it.

After what I have said, it will not appear strange that the dueling system is carried to the highest pitch of sanguinary zeal precisely in that nation whose political and financial records show that they are not too honorable. What that nation is like in its private and domestic life, is a question which may be best put to those who are experienced in the matter. Their urbanity and social culture have long been conspicuous by their absence.

There is no truth, then, in such pretexts. It can be urged with more justice that as, when you snarl at a dog, he snarls in return, and when you pet him, he fawns; so it lies in the nature of men to return hostility by hostility, and to be embittered and irritated at any signs of depreciatory treatment or hatred: and, as Cicero says, THERE IS SOMETHING SO PENETRATING IN THE SHAFT OF ENVY THAT EVEN MEN OF WISDOM AND WORTH FIND ITS WOUND A PAINFUL ONE; and nowhere in the world, except, perhaps, in a few religious sects, is an insult or a blow taken with equanimity. And yet a natural view of either would in no case demand anything more than a requital proportionate to the offense, and would never go the length of assigning DEATH as the proper penalty for anyone who accuses another of lying or stupidity or cowardice. The old German theory of BLOOD FOR A BLOW is a revolting superstition of the age of chivalry. And in any case the return or requital of an insult is dictated by anger, and not by any such obligation of honor and duty as the advocates of chivalry seek to attach to it. The fact is that, the greater the truth, the greater the slander; and it is clear that the slightest hint of some real delinquency will give much greater offense than a most terrible accusation which is perfectly baseless: so that a man who is quite sure that he has done nothing to deserve a reproach may treat it with contempt and will be safe in doing so. The theory of honor demands that he shall show a susceptibility which he does not possess, and take bloody vengeance for insults which he cannot feel. A man must himself have but a poor opinion of his own worth who hastens to prevent the utterance of an unfavorable opinion by giving his enemy a black eye.

True appreciation of his own value will make a man really indifferent to insult; but if he cannot help resenting it, a little shrewdness and culture will enable him to save appearances and dissemble his anger. If we could only get rid of this superstition about honor — the idea, I mean, that it disappears when you are insulted, and can be restored by returning the insult; if we could only stop people from thinking that wrong, brutality and insolence can be legalized by expressing readiness to give satisfaction, that is, to fight in defense of it, we should all soon come to the general opinion that insult and depreciation are like a battle in which the loser wins; and that, as Vincenzo Monti says, abuse resembles a church procession, because it always returns to the point from which it set out. If we could only get people to look upon insult in this light we should no longer have to say something rude in order to prove that we are in the right. Now, unfortunately, if we want to take a serious view of any question, we have first of all to consider whether it will not give offense in some way or other to the dullard, who generally shows alarm and resentment at the merest sign of intelligence: and it may easily happen that the head which contains the intelligent view has to be pitted against the noddle which is empty of everything but narrowness and stupidity. If all this were done away with, intellectual superiority could take the leading place in society which is its due — a place now occupied, though people do not like to confess it, by excellence of physique, mere fighting pluck, in fact; and the natural effect of such a change would be that the best kind of people would have one reason the less for withdrawing from society. This would pave the way for the introduction of real courtesy and genuinely good society, such as undoubtedly existed in Athens, Corinth and Rome. If anyone wants to see a good example of what I mean, I should like him to read Xenophon's "Banquet."

The last argument in defense of knightly honor no doubt is, that, but for its existence, the world — awful thought! would be a regular bear-garden. To which I may briefly reply that nine hundred and ninety-nine people out of a thousand who do not recognize the code, have often given and received a blow without any fatal consequences; whereas among the adherents of the code a blow usually means death to one of the parties. But let me examine this argument more closely.

I have often tried to find some tenable or, at any rate, plausible basis — other than a merely conventional one — some positive reasons, that is to say, for the rooted conviction which a portion of mankind entertains, that a blow is a very dreadful thing; but I have looked for it in vain, either in the animal or in the rational side of human nature. A blow is, and always will be, a trivial physical injury which one man can do to another; proving, thereby, nothing more than his superiority in strength or skill, or that his enemy was off his guard. Analysis will carry us no further. The same knight who regards a blow from the human hand as the greatest of evils, if he gets a ten times harder blow from his horse, will give you the assurance, as he limps away in suppressed pain, that it is a matter of no consequence whatever. So I have come to think that it is the human hand which is at the bottom of the mischief. And yet in a battle the knight may get cuts and thrusts from the same hand, and still assure you that his wounds are not worth mentioning. Now, I hear that a blow from the flat of a sword is not by any means so bad as a blow with a stick; and that, a short time ago, cadets were liable to be punished by the one but not the other, and that the very greatest honor of all is the ACCOLADE. This is all the psychological or moral basis that I can find; and so there is nothing left me but to pronounce the whole thing an antiquated superstition that has taken deep root, and one more of the many examples which show the force of tradition. My view is confirmed by the well-known fact that in China a beating with a bamboo is a very frequent punishment for the common people, and even for officials of every class, which shows that human nature, even in a highly civilized state, does not run in the same groove here and in China.

On the contrary, an unprejudiced view of human nature shows that it is just as natural for man to beat as it is for savage animals to bite and rend in pieces, or for horned beasts to butt or push. Man may be said to be the animal that beats. Hence it is revolting to our sense of the fitness of things to hear, as we sometimes do, that one man has bitten another; on the other hand, it is a natural and everyday occurrence for him to get blows or give them. It is intelligible enough that, as we become educated, we are glad to dispense with blows by a system of mutual restraint. But it is a cruel thing to compel a nation or a single class to regard a blow as an awful misfortune which must have death and murder for its consequences. There are too many genuine evils in the world to allow of our increasing them by imaginary misfortunes, which bring real ones in their train; and yet this is the precise effect of the superstition, which thus proves itself at once stupid and malign.

It does not seem to me wise of governments and legislative bodies to promote any such folly by attempting to do away with flogging as a punishment in civil or military life. Their idea is that they are acting in the interests of humanity; but, in point of fact, they are doing just the opposite; for the abolition of flogging will serve only to strengthen this inhuman and abominable superstition, to which so many sacrifices have already been made. For all offenses, except the worst, a beating is the obvious and therefore the natural penalty; and a man who will not listen to reason will yield to blows. It seems to me right and proper to administer corporal punishment to the man who possesses nothing and therefore cannot be fined, or cannot be put in prison because his master's interests would suffer by the loss of his services. There are really no arguments against it; only mere talk about THE DIGNITY OF MAN — talk which proceeds, not from any clear notions on the subject, but from the pernicious superstition I have been describing. That it is a superstition which lies at the bottom of the whole business is proved by an almost laughable example. Not long ago, in the military discipline of many countries, the cat was replaced by the stick. In either case the object was to produce physical pain; but the latter method involved no disgrace, and was not derogatory to honor.

By promoting this superstition, the State is playing into the hands of the principle of knightly honor, and therefore of the duel; while at the same time it is trying, or at any rate it pretends that it is trying, to abolish the duel by legislative enactment. As a natural consequence we find that this fragment of the theory that MIGHT IS RIGHT, which has come down to us from the most savage days of the Middle Age, has still in this nineteenth century a good deal of life left in it — more shame to us! It is high time for the principle to be driven out bag and baggage. Nowadays, no one is allowed to set dogs or cocks to fight each other, at any rate, in England it is a penal offense, but men are plunged into deadly strife, against their will, by the operation of this ridiculous, superstitious and absurd principle, which imposes upon us the obligation, as its narrow-minded supporters and advocates declare, of fighting with one another like gladiators, for any little trifle. Let me recommend our purists to adopt the expression BAITING, instead of DUEL, which probably comes to us, not from the Latin *duellum*, but from the Spanish *duelo*, — meaning suffering, nuisance, annoyance.

In any case, we may well laugh at the pedantic excess to which this foolish system has been carried. It is really revolting that this principle, with its absurd code can form a power within the State — *imperium in imperio* — a power too easily put in motion, which, recognizing no right but might, tyrannizes over the classes which come within its range, by keeping up a sort of inquisition, before which any one may be haled on the most flimsy pretext, and there and then be tried on an issue of life and death between himself and his opponent. This is the lurking place from which every rascal, if he only belongs to the classes in question, may menace and even exterminate the noblest and best of men, who, as such, must of course be an object of hatred to him. Our system of justice and police protection has made it impossible in these days for any scoundrel in the street to attack us with — YOUR MONEY OR YOUR LIFE! and common sense ought now to be able to prevent rogues disturbing the peaceable intercourse of society by coming at us with — YOUR HONOR OR YOUR LIFE! An end should be put to the burden which weighs upon the higher classes — the burden, I mean, of having to be ready every moment to expose life and limb to the mercy of anyone who takes it into his rascally head to be coarse, rude, foolish or malicious. It is perfectly atrocious that a pair of silly, passionate boys should be wounded, maimed or even killed, simply because they have had a few words.

The strength of this tyrannical power within the State, and the force of the superstition, may be measured by the fact that people who are prevented from restoring their knightly honor by the superior or inferior rank of their aggressor, or anything else that puts the persons on a different level, often come to a tragic-comic end by committing suicide in sheer despair. You may generally know a thing to be false and ridiculous by finding that, if it is carried to its logical conclusion, it results in a contradiction; and here, too, we have a very glaring absurdity. For an officer is forbidden to take part in a duel; but if he is challenged and declines to come out, he is punished by being dismissed the service.

As I am on the matter, let me be more frank still. The important distinction which is often insisted upon, between killing your enemy in a fair fight with equal weapons, and lying in ambush for him, is entirely a corollary of the fact that the power within the State, of

6

which I have spoken, recognizes no other right than might, that is, the right of the stronger, and appeals to a JUDGMENT OF GOD as the basis of the whole code. For to kill a man in a fair fight, is to prove that you are superior to him in strength or skill; and to justify the deed, YOU MUST ASSUME THAT THE RIGHT OF THE STRONGER IS REALLY A RIGHT.

But the truth is that, if my opponent is unable to defend himself, it gives me the possibility, but not by any means the right, of killing him. The RIGHT, the MORAL JUSTIFICATION, must depend entirely upon the MOTIVES which I have for taking his life. Even supposing that I have sufficient motive for taking a man's life, there is no reason why I should make his death depend upon whether I can shoot or fence better than he. In such a case, it is immaterial in what way I kill him, whether I attack him from the front or the rear. From a moral point of view the right of the stronger is no more convincing than the right of the more skillful; and it is skill which is employed if you murder a man treacherously. Might and skill are in this case equally right: in a duel, for instance, both the one and the other come into play; for a feint is only another name for treachery. If I consider myself morally justified in taking a man's life, it is stupid of me to try first of all whether he can shoot or fence better than I; as, if he can, he will not only have wronged me, but have taken my life into the bargain.

It is Rousseau's opinion that the proper way to avenge an insult is, not to fight a duel with your aggressor, but to assassinate him,—an opinion, however, which he is cautious enough only just to indicate in a mysterious note to one of the books of his " Emile." This shows the philosopher so completely under the influence of the mediæval superstition of knightly honor that he considers it justifiable to murder a man who accuses you of lying; while he must have known that every man, and himself especially, deserves to have the lie given him times without number.

The prejudice which justifies the killing of your adversary, so long as it is done in an open contest and with equal weapons, obviously looks upon might as really right, and a duel as the interference of God. The Italian who, in a fit of rage, falls upon his aggressor wherever he finds him, and dispatches him without any ceremony, acts, at any rate, consistently and naturally: he may be cleverer, but he is not worse, than the duelist. If you say, I am justified in killing my adversary in a duel, because he is at the moment doing his best to kill me, I can reply that it is your challenge which has placed him under the necessity of defending himself; and that by mutually putting it on the ground of self-defense, the combatants are seeking a plausible pretext for committing murder. I should rather justify the deed by the legal maxim *Volenti non fit injuria;* because the parties mutually agree to set their life upon the issue. This argument may, however, be rebutted by showing that the injured party is not injured *volens;* because it is this tyrannical principle of knightly honor, with its absurd code, which forcibly drags one at least of the combatants before a bloody inquisition.

I have been rather prolix on the subject of knightly honor, but I had good reasons for being so, because the Augean stable of moral and intellectual enormity in this world can be cleaned out only with the besom of philosophy. There are two things which more than all else serve to make the social arrangements of modern life compare unfavorably with those of antiquity, by giving our age a gloomy, dark, and sinister aspect, from which antiquity, fresh, natural, and, as it were, in the morning of life, is completely free; I mean modern honor and modern disease,—*par nobile fratrum!*—which have combined to poison all the relations of life, whether public or private. The second of this noble pair extends its influence much farther than at first appears to be the case, as being not merely a physical, but also a moral disease. From the time that poisoned arrows have been found in Cupid's quiver, an estranging, hostile, nay, devilish element has entered into the relations of men and women, like a sinister thread of fear and mistrust in the warp and woof of their intercourse; indirectly shaking the foundations of human fellowship, and so more or less affecting the whole tenor of existence. But it would be beside my present purpose to pursue the subject further.

An influence analogous to this, though working on other lines, is exerted by the principle of knightly honor, —that solemn farce, unknown to the ancient world, which makes modern society stiff, gloomy, and timid, forcing us to keep to the strictest watch on every word that falls. Nor is this all. The principle is a universal Minotaur; and the goodly company of the sons of noble houses which it demands in yearly tribute, comes, not from one country alone, as of old, but from every land in Europe. It is high time to make a regular attack upon this foolish system; and this is what I am trying to do now. Would that these two monsters of the modern world might disappear before the end of the century!

Let us hope that medicine may be able to find some means of preventing the one, and that, by clearing our ideas, philosophy may put an end to the other; for it is only by clearing our ideas that the evil can be eradicated. Governments have tried to do so by legislation, and failed.

Still, if they are really concerned to suppress the dueling system; and if the small success that has attended their efforts is really due only to their inability to cope with the evil, I do not mind proposing a law the success of which I am prepared to guarantee. It will involve no sanguinary measures, and can be put into operation without recourse either to the scaffold or the gallows, or to imprisonment for life. It is a small homœopathic *pilule*, with no serious after effects. If any man send or accept a challenge, let the corporal take him before the guardhouse, and there give him, in broad daylight, twelve strokes with a stick *à la Chinoise;* a non-commissioned officer or a private to receive six. If a duel has actually taken place, the usual criminal proceedings should be instituted.

A person with knightly notions might, perhaps, object that, if such a punishment were carried out, a man of honor w̧uld possibly shoot himself; to which I should answer that it is better for a fool like that to shoot himself rather than other people. However, I know very

well that governments are not really in earnest about
putting down dueling. Civil officials, and much more so,
officers in the army (except those in the highest positions), are paid most inadequately for the services they
perform; and the deficiency is made up by honor, which
is represented by titles and orders, and, in general, by
the system of rank and distinction. The duel is, so to
speak, a very serviceable extra-horse for people of rank:
so they are trained in the knowledge of it at the universities. The accidents which happen to those who use
it make up in blood for the deficiency of the pay.

Just to complete the discussion, let me here mention
the subject of NATIONAL HONOR. It is the honor of a nation
as a unit in the aggregate of nations. And as there is
no court to appeal to but the court of force; and as every
nation must be prepared to defend its own interests, the
honor of a nation consists in establishing the opinion,
not only that it may be trusted (its credit), but also that
it is to be feared. An attack upon its rights must never
be allowed to pass unheeded. It is a combination of
civic and of knightly honor.

SECTION 5.— FAME.

Under the heading of place in the estimation of the
world we have put FAME; and this we must now proceed
to consider.

Fame and honor are twins; and twins, too, like Castor
and Pollux, of whom the one was mortal and the other
was not. Fame is the undying brother of ephemeral
honor. I speak, of course, of the highest kind of fame,
that is, of fame in the true and genuine sense of the
word; for, to be sure, there are many sorts of fame,
some of which last but a day. Honor is concerned
merely with such qualities as everyone may be expected
to show under similar circumstances; fame only with
those which cannot be required of any man. Honor is
of qualities which everyone has a right to attribute to

himself; fame only of those which should be left to others to attribute. While our honor extends as far as people have knowledge of us; fame runs in advance, and makes us known wherever it finds its way. Everyone can make a claim to honor; very few to fame, as being attainable only in virtue of extraordinary achievements.

These achievements may be of two kinds, either ACTIONS or WORKS; and so to fame there are two paths open. On the path of actions, a great heart is the chief recommendation; on that of works, a great head. Each of the two paths has its own peculiar advantages and detriments; and the chief difference between them is that actions are fleeting, while works remain. The influence of an action, be it never so noble, can last but a short time; but a work of genius is a living influence, beneficial and ennobling throughout the ages. All that can remain of actions is a memory, and that becomes weak and disfigured by time — a matter of indifference to us, until at last it is extinguished altogether; unless, indeed, history takes it up, and presents it, fossilized, to posterity. Works are immortal in themselves, and once committed to writing, may live forever. Of Alexander the Great we have but the name and the record: but Plato and Aristotle, Homer and Horace are alive, and as directly at work to-day as they were in their own lifetime. The "Vedas," and their "Upanishads," are still with us; but of all contemporaneous actions not a trace has come down to us.*

* Accordingly it is a poor compliment, though sometimes a fashionable one, to try to pay honor to a work by calling it an action. For a work is something essentially higher in its nature. An action is always something based on motive, and, therefore, fragmentary and fleeting — a part, in fact, of that Will which is the universal and original element in the constitution of the world. But a great and beautiful work has a permanent character, as being of universal significance, and sprung from the Intellect, which rises, like a perfume, above the faults and follies of the world of Will.

The fame of a great action has this advantage, that it generally starts with a loud explosion, so loud, indeed, as to be heard all over Europe, whereas the fame of a great work is slow and gradual in its beginnings; the noise it makes is at first slight, but it goes on growing greater, until at last, after a hundred years perhaps, it attains its full force; but then

Another disadvantage under which actions labor is that they depend upon chance for the possibility of coming into existence; and hence, the fame they win does not flow entirely from their intrinsic value, but also from the circumstances which happened to lend them importance and lustre. Again, the fame of actions, if, as in war, they are purely personal, depends upon the testimony of fewer witnesses; and these are not always present, and even if present, are not always just or unbiased observers. This disadvantage, however, is counterbalanced by the fact that actions have the advantage of being of a practical character, and, therefore, within the range of general human intelligence; so that when the facts have been correctly reported, justice is immediately done; unless, indeed, the motive underlying the action is not at first properly understood or appreciated. No action can be really understood apart from the motive which prompted it.

It is just the contrary with works. Their inception does not depend upon chance, but wholly and entirely upon their author; and whatever they are in and for themselves, that they remain as long as they live. Further, there is a difficulty in properly judging them, which becomes all the harder, the higher their character; often there are no persons competent to understand the work, and often no unbiased or honest critics. Their fame, however, does not depend upon one judge only; they can enter an appeal to another. In the case of actions, as I have said, it is only their memory which comes down to posterity, and then only in the traditional form; but works are handed down themselves, and, except when parts of them have been lost, in the form in which they first appeared. In this case there is no room for any disfigurement of the facts; and any circumstances which may have prejudiced them in their origin, fall away with the lapse of time. Nay, it is often

it remains, because the works remain, for thousands of years. But in the other case, when the first explosion is over, the noise it makes grows less and less, and is heard by fewer and fewer persons; until it ends by the action having only a shadowy existence in the pages of history.

only after the lapse of time that the persons really competent to judge them appear—exceptional critics sitting
in judgment on exceptional works, and giving their
weighty verdicts in succession. These collectively form
a perfectly just appreciation; and though there are cases
where it has taken some hundreds of years to form it,
no further lapse of time is able to reverse the verdict;
so secure and inevitable is the fame of a great work.

Whether authors ever live to see the dawn of their
fame depends upon the chance of circumstance; and the
higher and more important their works are, the less likeli-
hood there is of their doing so. That was an incomparably fine saying of Seneca's, that fame follows merit as
surely as the body casts a shadow; sometimes falling in
front, and sometimes behind. And he goes on to remark
that THOUGH THE ENVY OF CONTEMPORARIES BE SHOWN BY
UNIVERSAL SILENCE, THERE WILL COME THOSE WHO WILL
JUDGE WITHOUT ENMITY OR FAVOR. From this remark it
is manifest that even in Seneca's age there were rascals
who understood the art of suppressing merit by mali-
ciously ignoring its existence, and of concealing good work
from the public in order to favor the bad. It is an art
well understood in our day, too, manifesting itself, both
then and now, in AN ENVIOUS CONSPIRACY OF SILENCE.

As a general rule, the longer a man's fame is likely
to last, the later it will be in coming; for all excellent
products require time for their development. The fame
which lasts to posterity is like an oak, of very slow
growth; and that which endures but a little while, like
plants which spring up in a year and then die; while
false fame is like a fungus, shooting up in a night and
perishing as soon.

And why? For this reason: the more a man belongs
to posterity, in other words, to humanity in general, the
more of an alien he is to his contemporaries; since his
work is not meant for them as such, but only for them
in so far as they form part of mankind at large; there
is none of that familiar local color about his productions
which would appeal to them; and so what he does, fails
of recognition because it is strange. People are more
likely to appreciate the man who serves the circumstances

of his own brief hour, or the temper of the moment,—belonging to it, and living and dying with it.

The general history of art and literature shows that the highest achievements of the human mind are, as a rule, not favorably received at first; but remain in obscurity until they win notice from intelligence of a higher order, by whose influence they are brought into a position which they then maintain, in virtue of the authority thus given them.

If the reason of this should be asked, it will be found that ultimately, a man can really understand and appreciate those things only which are of like nature with himself. The dull person will like what is dull, and the common person what is common; a man whose ideas are mixed will be attracted by confusion of thought; and folly will appeal to him who has no brains at all; but best of all, a man will like his own works, as being of a character thoroughly at one with himself. This is a truth as old as Epicharmus of fabulous memory—

> Θαυμαστὸν οὐδὲν ἐστί με ταῦθ' οὕτω λέγειν
> Καὶ ἀνδάνειν αὐτοῖσιν αὐτούς, καὶ δοκεῖν
> Καλῶς πεφυκέναι· καὶ γὰρ ὁ κύων κυνί
> Κάλλιστον εἶμεν φάίνεται, καὶ βοῦς βοΐ
> Ὄνος δ' ὄνῳ κάλλιστόν [ἐστιν], ὗς δ' ὑΐ.

The sense of this passage — for it should not be lost — is that we should not be surprised if people are pleased with themselves, and fancy that they are in good case; for to a dog the best thing in the world is a dog; to an ox, an ox; to an ass, an ass; and to a sow, a sow.

The strongest arm is unavailing to give impetus to a feather weight; for, instead of speeding on its way and hitting its mark with effect, it will soon fall to the ground, having expended what little energy was given to it, and possessing no mass of its own to be the vehicle of momentum. So it is with great and noble thoughts, nay, with the very masterpieces of genius, when there are none but little, weak, and perverse minds to appreciate them,— a fact which has been deplored by a chorus of the wise in all ages. Jesus, the son of Sirach, for instance, declares that HE THAT TELLETH A TALE TO A FOOL,

SPEAKETH TO ONE IN SLUMBER, WHEN HE HATH TOLD HIS TALE, HE WILL SAY, WHAT IS THE MATTER? And Hamlet says, A KNAVISH SPEECH SLEEPS IN A FOOL'S EAR. And Goethe is of the same opinion, that a dull ear mocks at the wisest word,

> Das glücklichste Wort es wird verhöhnt,
> Wenn der Hörer ein Schiefohr ist:

and again, that we should not be discouraged if people are stupid, for you can make no rings if you throw your stone into a marsh:—

> Du wirkest nicht, Alles bleibt so stumpf:
> Sei guter Dinge !
> Der Stein in Sumpf
> Macht keine Ringe.

Lichtenberg asks: WHEN A HEAD AND A BOOK COME INTO COLLISION, AND ONE SOUNDS HOLLOW, IS IT ALWAYS THE BOOK? And in another place: WORKS LIKE THIS ARE AS A MIRROR: IF AN ASS LOOKS IN, YOU CANNOT EXPECT AN APOSTLE TO LOOK OUT. We should do well to remember old Gellert's fine and touching lament, that the best gifts of all find the fewest admirers, and that most men mistake the bad for the good,—a daily evil that nothing can prevent, like a plague which no remedy can cure. There is but one thing to be done, though how difficult! the foolish must become wise, and that they can never be. The value of life they never know; they see with the outer eye but never with the mind, and praise the trivial because the good is strange to them:—

> Nie kennen sie den Werth der Dinge,
> Ihr Auge schliesst, nicht ihr Verstand;
> Sie loben ewig das Geringe
> Weil sie das Gute nie gekannt.

To the intellectual incapacity which, as Goethe says, fails to recognize and appreciate the good which exists, must be added something which comes into play everywhere, the moral baseness of mankind, here taking the form of envy. The new fame that a man wins raises him afresh over the heads of his fellows, who are thus degraded in proportion. All conspicuous merit is obtained at the cost of those who possess none; or as

Goethe has it in the "Westöstlicher Divan," another's praise is one's own depreciation:—

> Wenn wir Andern Ehre geben
> Müssen wir uns selbst entadeln.

We see, then, how it is that whatever be the form which excellence takes, mediocrity, the common lot of by far the greatest number, is leagued against it in a conspiracy to resist, and if possible, to suppress it. The password of this league is *À bas le mérite*. Nay more; those who have done something themselves, and enjoy a certain amount of fame, do not care about the appearance of a new reputation, because its success is apt to throw theirs into the shade. Hence, Goethe declares that if we had to depend for our life upon the favor of others, we would never have lived at all; from their desire to appear important themselves, people gladly ignore our very existence:—

> Hätte ich gezaudert zu werden,
> Bis man mir's Leben gegönnt,
> Ich wäre noch nicht auf Erden,
> Wie ihr begreifen könnt,
> Wenn ihr seht, wie sie sich geberden,
> Die, um etwas zu scheinen,
> Mich gerne möchten verneinen.

Honor, on the contrary, generally meets with fair appreciation, and is not exposed to the onslaught of envy; nay, every man is credited with the possession of it until the contrary is proved. But fame has to be won in despite of envy, and the tribunal which awards the laurel is composed of judges biased against the applicant from the very first. Honor is something which we are able and ready to share with everyone; fame suffers encroachment and is rendered more unattainable in proportion as more people come by it. Further, the difficulty of winning fame by any given work stands in inverse ratio to the number of people who are likely to read it; and hence it is so much harder to become famous as the author of a learned work than as a writer who aspires only to amuse. It is hardest of all in the case of philosophical works, because the result at which they aim is rather vague, and,

at the same time, useless from a material point of view.
They appeal chiefly to readers who are working on the
same lines themselves.

It is clear, then, from what I have said as to the difficulty of winning fame, that those who labor, not out of
love for their subject, nor from pleasure in pursuing it,
but under the stimulus of ambition, rarely or never leave
mankind a legacy of immortal works. The man who seeks
to do what is good and genuine, must avoid what is bad,
and be ready to defy the opinions of the mob, nay, even
to despise it and its misleaders. Hence the truth of
the remark (especially insisted upon by Osorius "de
Gloria") that fame shuns those who seek it, and seeks
those who shun it; for the one adapt themselves to the
taste of their contemporaries, and the others work in
defiance of it.

But difficult though it be to acquire fame, it is an
easy thing to keep it when once acquired. Here, again,
fame is in direct opposition to honor, with which everyone is presumably to be accredited. Honor has not to
be won; it must only not be lost. But there lies the
difficulty! For by a single unworthy action, it is gone
irretrievably. But fame, in the proper sense of the word,
can never disappear; for the action or work by which it
was acquired can never be undone; and fame attaches to
its author even though he does nothing to deserve it
anew. The fame which vanishes, or is outlived, proves
itself thereby to have been spurious, in other words,
unmerited, and due to a momentary over-estimate of a
man's work; not to speak of the kind of fame which
Hegel enjoyed, and which Lichtenberg describes as
TRUMPETED FORTH BY A CLIQUE OF ADMIRING UNDER-GRAD-
UATES — THE RESOUNDING ECHO OF EMPTY HEADS; — SUCH A
FAME AS WILL MAKE POSTERITY SMILE WHEN IT LIGHTS UPON
A GROTESQUE ARCHITECTURE OF WORDS, A FINE NEST WITH
THE BIRDS LONG AGO FLOWN; IT WILL KNOCK AT THE DOOR
OF THIS DECAYED STRUCTURE OF CONVENTIONALITIES AND
FIND IT UTTERLY EMPTY! — NOT EVEN A TRACE OF THOUGHT
THERE TO INVITE THE PASSER-BY.

The truth is that fame means nothing but what a man
is in comparison with others. It is essentially relative

in character, and therefore only indirectly valuable; for
it vanishes the moment other people become what the
famous man is. Absolute value can be predicated only
of what a man possesses under any and all circumstances,—
here, what a man is directly and in himself. It is the
possession of a great heart or a great head, and not the
mere fame of it, which is worth having, and conducive
to happiness. Not fame, but that which deserves to be
famous, is what a man should hold in esteem. This is,
as it were, the true underlying substance, and fame is
only an accident, affecting its subject chiefly as a kind
of external symptom, which serves to confirm his own
opinion of himself. Light is not visible unless it meets
with something to reflect it; and talent is sure of itself
only when its fame is noised abroad. But fame is not a
certain symptom of merit; because you can have the one
without the other; or, as Lessing nicely puts it, SOME
PEOPLE OBTAIN FAME, AND OTHERS DESERVE IT.

It would be a miserable existence which should make
its value or want of value depend upon what other people think; but such would be the life of a hero or a
genius if its worth consisted in fame, that is, in the
applause of the world. Every man lives and exists on
his own account, and, therefore, mainly in and for himself; and what he is and the whole manner of his being
concern himself more than anyone else; so if he is not
worth much in this respect, he cannot be worth much
otherwise. The idea which other people form of his
existence is something secondary, derivative, exposed to
all the chances of fate, and in the end affecting him but
very indirectly. Besides, other people's heads are a
wretched place to be the home of a man's true happiness
—a fanciful happiness perhaps, but not a real one.

And what a mixed company inhabits the Temple of
Universal Fame!—generals, ministers, charlatans, jug-
glers, dancers, singers, millionaires and Jews! It is a
temple in which more sincere recognition, more genuine
esteem, is given to the several excellences of such folk,
than to superiority of mind, even of a high order, which
obtains from the great majority only a verbal acknowledg-
ment.

From the point of view of human happiness, fame is, surely, nothing but a very rare and delicate morsel for the appetite that feeds on pride and vanity — an appetite which, however carefully concealed, exists to an immoderate degree in every man, and is, perhaps, strongest of all in those who set their hearts on becoming famous at any cost. Such people generally have to wait some time in uncertainty as to their own value, before the opportunity comes which will put it to the proof and let other people see what they are made of; but until then, they feel as if they were suffering secret injustice.*

But, as I explained at the beginning of this chapter, an unreasonable value is set upon other people's opinion, and one quite disproportionate to its real worth. Hobbes has some strong remarks on this subject; and no doubt he is quite right. MENTAL PLEASURE, he writes, AND EC-STASY OF ANY KIND, ARISE WHEN, ON COMPARING OURSELVES WITH OTHERS, WE COME TO THE CONCLUSION THAT WE MAY THINK WELL OF OURSELVES. So we can easily understand the great value which is always attached to fame, as worth any sacrifices if there is the slightest hope of attaining it.

> Fame is the spur that the clear spirit doth raise
> (That last infirmity of noble mind)
> To scorn delights and live laborious days.

And again:

> How hard it is to climb
> The heights where Fame's proud temple shines afar!

We can thus understand how it is that the vainest people in the world are always talking about *la gloire*, with the most implicit faith in it as a stimulus to great actions and great works. But there can be no doubt that fame is something secondary in its character, a mere echo or reflection — as it were, a shadow or symptom — of merit; and, in any case, what excites admiration must

---

* Our greatest pleasure consists in being admired; but those who admire us, even if they have every reason to do so, are slow to express their sentiments. Hence he is the happiest man who, no matter how, manages sincerely to admire himself — so long as other people leave him alone.

be of more value than the admiration itself. The truth
is that a man is made happy, not by fame, but by that
which brings him fame, by his merits, or to speak more
correctly, by the disposition and capacity from which his
merits proceed, whether they be moral or intellectual.
The best side of a man's nature must of necessity be
more important for him than for anyone else: the reflection of it, the opinion which exists in the heads of
others, is a matter that can affect him only in a very
subordinate degree. He who deserves fame without getting it possesses by far the more important element of
happiness, which should console him for the loss of the
other. It is not that a man is thought to be great by
masses of incompetent and often infatuated people, but
that he really is great, which should move us to envy his
position; and his happiness lies, not in the fact that posterity will hear of him, but that he is the creator of
thoughts worthy to be treasured up and studied for hundreds of years.

Besides, if a man has done this, he possesses something
which cannot be wrested from him; and, unlike fame, it
is a possession dependent entirely upon himself. If admiration were his chief aim, there would be nothing in
ḥim to admire. This is just what happens in the case of
false, that is, unmerited, fame; for its recipient lives
upon it without actually possessing the solid substratum
of which fame is the outward and visible sign. False
fame must often put its possessor out of conceit with
himself; for the time may come when, in spite of the
illusions born of self-love, he will feel giddy on the
heights which he was never meant to climb, or look
upon himself as spurious coin; and in the anguish of
threatened discovery and well-merited degradation, he
will read the sentence of posterity on the foreheads of
the wise — like a man who owes his property to a forged
will.

The truest fame, the fame that comes after death, is
never heard of by its recipient; and yet he is called a
happy man. His happiness lay both in the possession of
those great qualities which won him fame, and in the
opportunity that was granted him of developing them —

the leisure he had to act as he pleased, to dedicate himself to his favorite pursuits. It is only work done from the heart that ever gains the laurel.

Greatness of soul, or wealth of intellect, is what makes a man happy—intellect, such as, when stamped on its productions, will receive the admiration of centuries to come,—thoughts which made him happy at the time, and will in their turn be a source of study and delight to the noblest minds of the most remote posterity. The value of posthumous fame lies in deserving it; and this is its own reward. Whether works destined to fame attain it in the lifetime of their author is a chance affair, of no very great importance. For the average man has no critical power of his own, and is absolutely incapable of appreciating the difficulty of a great work. People are always swayed by authority; and where fame is widespread, it means that ninety-nine out of a hundred take it on faith alone. If a man is famed far and wide in his own lifetime, he will, if he is wise, not set too much value upon it, because it is no more than the echo of a few voices, which the chance of a day has touched in his favor.

Would a musician feel flattered by the loud applause of an audience if he knew that they were nearly all deaf, and that, to conceal their infirmity, they set to work to clap vigorously as soon as ever they saw one or two persons applauding? And what would he say if he got to know that those one or two persons had often taken bribes to secure the loudest applause for the poorest player!

It is easy to see why contemporary praise so seldom develops into posthumous fame. D'Alembert, in an extremely fine description of the temple of literary fame, remarks that the sanctuary of the temple is inhabited by the great dead, who during their life had no place there, and by a very few living persons, who are nearly all ejected on their death. Let me remark, in passing, that to erect a monument to a man in his lifetime is as much as declaring that posterity is not to be trusted in its judgment of him. If a man does happen to see his own true fame, it can very rarely be before he is old, though there have been artists and musicians who have been exceptions to this rule, but very few philosophers. This is confirmed by the portraits of people celebrated by their works; for most of them are taken only after their subjects have attained celebrity, generally depicting them as old and gray; more especially if philosophy has been the work of their lives. From a eudæmonistic standpoint, this is a very proper arrangement; as fame and youth are too much for mortal at one and the same time. Life is such a poor business that the strictest economy must be exercised in its good things. Youth has enough and to spare in itself, and must rest content with what it has. But when the delights and joys of life fall away in old age, as the leaves from a tree in autumn, fame buds forth opportunely, like a plant that is green in winter. Fame is, as it were, the fruit that must grow all the summer before it can be enjoyed at Yule. There is no greater consolation in age than the feeling of having put the whole force of one's youth into works which still remain young.

Finally, let us examine a little more closely the kinds of fame which attach to various intellectual pursuits; for it is with fame of this sort that my remarks are more immediately concerned.

I think it may be said broadly that the intellectual superiority it denotes consists in forming theories, that is, new combinations of certain facts. These facts may be of very different kinds; but the better they are known, and the more they come within everyday experience, the greater and wider will be the fame which is to be won by theorizing about them. For instance, if the facts in question are numbers or lines or special branches of science, such as physics, zoology, botany, anatomy, or corrupt passages in ancient authors, or undecipherable inscriptions, written, it may be, in some unknown alphabet, or obscure points in history; the kind of fame which may be obtained by correctly manipulating such facts will not extend much beyond those who make a study of them —a small number of persons, most of whom live retired lives and are envious of others who become famous in their special branch of knowledge.

7

But if the facts be such as are known to everyone, for example, the fundamental characteristics of the human mind or the human heart, which are shared by all alike, or the great physical agencies which are constantly in operation before our eyes, or the general course of natural laws, the kind of fame which is to be won by spreading the light of a new and manifestly true theory in regard to them, is such as in time will extend almost all over the civilized world: for if the facts be such as everyone can grasp, the theory also will be generally intelligible. But the extent of the fame will depend upon the difficulties overcome; and the more generally known the facts are, the harder it will be to form a theory that shall be both new and true; because a great many heads will have been occupied with them, and there will be little or no possibility of saying anything that has not been said before.

On the other hand, facts which are not accessible to everybody, and can be got at only after much difficulty and labor, nearly always admit of new combinations and theories; so that, if sound understanding and judgment are brought to bear upon them — qualities which do not involve very high intellectual power — a man may easily be so fortunate as to light upon some new theory in regard to them which shall be also true. But fame won on such paths does not extend much beyond those who possess a knowledge of the facts in question. To solve problems of this sort requires, no doubt, a great deal of study and labor, if only to get at the facts; while on the path where the greatest and most widespread fame is to be won, the facts may be grasped without any labor at all. But just in proportion as less labor is necessary, more talent or genius is required; and between such qualities and the drudgery of research no comparison is possible, in respect either of their intrinsic value, or of the estimation in which they are held.

And so people who feel that they possess solid intellectual capacity and a sound judgment, and yet cannot claim the highest mental powers, should not be afraid of laborious study; for by its aid they may work themselves

above the great mob of humanity who have the facts
constantly before their eyes, and reach those secluded
spots which are accessible to learned toil. For this is a
sphere where there are infinitely fewer rivals, and a man
of only moderate capacity may soon find an opportunity
of proclaiming a theory that shall be both new and true;
nay, the merit of his discovery will partly rest upon the
difficulty of coming at the facts. But applause from
one's fellow-students, who are the only persons with a
knowledge of the subject, sounds very faint to the far-off
multitude. And if we follow up this sort of fame far
enough, we shall at last come to a point where facts
very difficult to get at are in themselves sufficient to lay
a foundation of fame, without any necessity for forming
a theory; — travels, for instance, in remote and little-
known countries, which make a man famous by what he
has seen, not by what he has thought. The great advantage of this kind of fame is that to relate what one
has seen, is much easier than to impart one's thoughts,
and people are apt to understand descriptions better than
ideas, reading the one more readily than the other; for, as
Asmus says,

> When one goes forth a-voyaging
> He has a tale to tell.

And yet, for all that, a personal acquaintance with
celebrated travelers often reminds us of a line from
Horace — new scenes do not always mean new ideas —

Coelum non animum mutant qui trans mare currunt.

But if a man finds himself in possession of great mental faculties, such as alone should venture on the solution
of the hardest of all problems — those which concern
nature as a whole and humanity in its widest range, he
will do well to extend his view equally in all directions,
without ever straying too far amid the intricacies of
various bypaths, or invading regions little known; in
other words, without occupying himself with special
branches of knowledge, to say nothing of their petty
details. There is no necessity for him to seek out subjects difficult of access, in order to escape a crowd of

rivals; the common objects of life will give him material for new theories at once serious and true; and the service he renders will be appreciated by all those — and they form a great part of mankind — who know the facts of which he treats. What a vast distinction there is between students of physics, chemistry, anatomy, mineralogy, zoology, philology, history, and the men who deal with the great facts of human life, the poet, and the philosopher!

SKETCH OF A HISTORY OF THE DOCTRINE OF THE IDEAL AND REAL.

DESCARTES is rightly deemed the father of modern philosophy, and this in a special, as well as a general sense, inasmuch as he placed the reason on its own feet by teaching men to use their own brains, in the place of which the Bible had previously served on the one hand, and Aristotle on the other. But in a more special and a narrower sense he was this also; since he was the first to bring the problem upon which philosophy has mainly turned to consciousness — the problem of the Ideal and Real — *i. e.*, the question as to what in our knowledge is objective, and what is subjective; in other words, what might be ascribed by us to other things, and what we must ascribe to ourselves. Images do not arise in our brain as it were arbitrarily from within, nor do they proceed from the connection of our own thoughts — hence they must spring from an external cause. But these images are immediately known to us — THEY ARE GIVEN. Now what relation do they have to things existing completely separate from, and independent of us, and which are in some way the cause of these images? Have we any certainty at all that such things exist? or even if this be so, that the images afford us any clue to their nature? This is the problem, and in consequence the main endeavor of philosophers has been for the two past hundred years to separate by a correctly-drawn line of cleavage — the Ideal, *i. e.*, that which belongs solely to our knowledge as such, from the Real, *i. e.*, that which exists independently of it, and thus to determine the relation of each to the other.

Certainly neither the philosophers of antiquity, nor yet the schoolmen seem to have arrived at a clear consciousness of this fundamental problem of philosophy, although we find a trace of it, as Idealism, and even as the doctrine of the Ideality of time, in Plotinus, in Enneas III.,

Lib. VII., cx., where he teaches that the soul has made
the world by its transition from eternity into time. He
there says, for instance, οὐ γάρ τις αὐτοῦ τούτου τοῦ πάντος
τόπος, ἢ ψυχή. (*Neque datur alius hujus universi locus,
quam anima*) also δεῖ δὲ οὐχ ἔξωθεν τῆς ψυχῆς λαμβάνειν τὸν
χρόνον ὥσπερ οὐδὲ τὸν αἰῶνα ἔχει ἔξω τοῦ ὄντος. (*Oportet autem
nequaquam extra animam tempus accipere, quemadmodum
neque aeternitatem ibi extra id, quod ens appellatur.*)
Here it will be seen we have a distinct statement even
of Kant's ideality of time. And in the following chapter οὗτος ὁ βίος τὸν χρόνον γεννᾷ· διὸ καὶ εἴρηται ἅμα τῷδε τῷ
πάντι γεγονέναι, ᾗτι ψυχὴ αὐτὸν μετὰ τοῦδε τοῦ πάντος ἐγέννησεν.
(*Haec vita nostra tempus gignit: quamobrem dictum
est, tempus simul cum hoc universo factum esse: quia
anima tempus una cum hoc universo progenuit.*) Nevertheless, this problem clearly recognized, became the
specially characteristic subject of MODERN philosophy
after the necessary reflection had been awakened in Descartes, who was impressed with the truth that we are
immediately limited to our own consciousness, and that
the world is given us merely as presentment (*Vorstellung.*) With his well-known *dubito, cogito, ergo sum,*
he sought to accentuate the sole certainty of the subjective consciousness in contradistinction to the problem-
atical nature of everything else, and to declare the great
truth that the only real, and unconditionally GIVEN, is
self-consciousness. Strictly considered, his celebrated
proposition is the equivalent of that from which I started.
"The world is my presentment." The only difference is,
that his proposition accentuates the immediateness of the
subject; mine, the mediateness of the object. Both
propositions express the same thing from two sides.
They are the "reverses" of each other, standing in much
the same relation as the law of inertia and that of
causality, as expounded by me in the preface to my
"Ethics." (The two ground problems of "Ethics,"
treated in two academical prize essays by Dr. Arthur
Schopenhauer. Frankfurt-am-Main, 1841, p. xxiv; 2d
edition, Liepzig, 1860, p. xxiv.) Certainly, since his time,
Descartes's proposition has been often enough repeated,
owing to the mere feeling of its importance, and with-

out a clear understanding of its special sense and purport. (See Descartes's "Meditationes," Med. ii. p. 14.) He it was, then, who discovered the chasm which lies between the Subjective or Ideal, and the Objective or Real. This insight he clothed in the form of a doubt as to the existence of the outer world; but by his inadequate solution of this doubt—to wit, that the good God would not deceive us—he showed how deep and difficult to solve the problem was. Meantime, this scruple had been introduced into philosophy by him, and could not fail to continue to work disturbingly till its final settlement. The consciousness that without thorough knowledge and understanding of the distinction which had been discovered, no certain and sufficient system would be possible, has been from that time ever present, and the question could no longer be shirked.

In order to solve it, Malebranche invented his system of occasional causes. He grasped the problem in its whole range more clearly, seriously, and deeply than Descartes ("Recherche de la Vérité," *Livre* III. *seconde partie*). The latter had accepted the reality of the outer world on the credit of God; and it was curious enough that while the other theistic philosophers sought to demonstrate the existence of God from the existence of the world, Descartes, on the contrary, determines the existence of the world from the existence and trustworthiness of God—it is the cosmological demonstration turned round. Even here, going a step farther, Malebranche teaches that we see all things immediately in God. This is certainly to explain an unknown by a still more unknown. Moreover, according to him, we not only see all things in God, but God is the sole activity therein, so that physical causes are only apparently such—they are mere *causes occasionnelles*. ("Rech. d. l. Vér.," *Livre* VI., *seconde partie*, ch. iii.) We have here, therefore, in all essentials, the Pantheism of Spinoza, who seems to have learned more from Malebranche than he did from Descartes.

Altogether, one might wonder that Pantheism did not gain a complete victory over Theism even in the seventeenth century, seeing that the most original, the most

beautiful, and the most thorough-going European pre-
sentations of it (for assuredly none of them will bear
comparison with the Upanishads of the Vedas) all saw
the light in that age, to wit, Bruno, Malebranche, Spinoza, and Scotus Erigena, the last of whom, after he had
remained for many centuries lost and forgotten, was recovered at Oxford, and in 1681, four years, that is, after
Spinoza's death, for the first time saw the light in print.
This seems to prove that the insight of individuals cannot produce its effect, so long as the spirit of the time
is unripe for its acceptance, for in our days Pantheism,
although only presented in the eclectic and confused
rechauffé of Schelling, has become the dominant mode
of thought with scholars, and even with persons of ordinary
culture.   This is because Kant had preceded, and with his
overthrow of theistic dogmatism, had prepared the ground,
in consequence of which the spirit of the time was ready
for it, as a plowed field is ready for the seed.   In the
seventeenth century, on the other hand, philosophy forsook this path, and arrived accordingly on the one side,
at Locke, for whom Bacon and Hobbes had prepared the
way, and on the other at Christian Wolff, through Lieb-
nitz.   These two were dominant therefore in the eight-
eenth century, especially in Germany, although latterly
only in so far as they had been absorbed by syncretistic
eclecticism.

The profound conception of Malebranche gave the immediate occasion to Leibnitz's system of *harmonia praestabilita*, the widely extended fame and high consideration
of which in his time, affords a confirmation of the fact
that it is the absurd which makes the easiest success in
the world.   Although I cannot pretend to have a clear
notion of the monads of Leibnitz, which are at once
mathematical points, corporate atoms, and souls, yet it
seems to me unquestionable that such an assumption
once decided upon might serve to spare us all further
hypothesis for the explanation of the connection between
Ideal and Real, and to settle the question in the sense
that both are already fully identified in the monads (for
which reason, in our days, Schelling, as originator of the
system of identity, has displayed a particular relish for

it). Nevertheless, it did not please the eminent philosophizing mathematician, polyhistor, and politician to use it for the purpose; but he saw fit to specially formulate a pre-established harmony to this end. The latter furnishes us with two totally distinct worlds, each incapable of acting in any way on the other ("Principia Philos," § 84, and "Examen du Sentiment du P. Malebranche," p. 500, *sq.* of the "Œuvres de Leibnitz," published P. Kaspe), each the entirely superfluous duplicate of the other, but both of which, once for all there, run exactly parallel, and keep time with each other to a hair; the originator of both having from the first established the exactest harmony between them, so that they proceed thenceforward in the most beautiful manner. We may observe, by the way, that the *harmonia praestabilita* may perhaps be best made comprehensible by a comparison with the stage, where very often the *influxus physicus* is only apparently present, since cause and effect are connected simply by means of a pre-established harmony of the stage manager; as, for instance, when the one shoots and the other falls *a tempo*. Leibnitz has presented the matter in its monstrous absurdity in the crassest manner, and in brief, §§ 62, 63 of his "Theodicy." And yet with the whole dogma he does not even have the merit of originality, since Spinoza had already clearly enough presented the *harmonia praestabilita* in the second part of his "Ethics," *i. e.,* in the 6th and 7th propositions, together with their corollaries, and again in P. V., prop. 1, after he had in the 5th proposition of P. II., stated in his own manner the so very cognate doctrine of Malebranche, that we see all in God.

Malebranche is, therefore, alone the originator of this whole line of thought which Spinoza as well as Leibnitz, each in his own way, has utilized and modified. Leibnitz, indeed, might very well have dispensed with it altogether, since he has already forsaken the simple fact which constitutes the problem, *i. e.,* that the world is given us immediately as our presentment, in order to substitute for it the dogma of a corporeal world and a spiritual world, between which no bridge is possible; at the same time interweaving the question of the relation of our

presentment to the things in themselves with that of the
possibility of the motion of the body by the will, and
then solving both together by means of his *harmonia
praestabilita*. ("Système nouveau de la Nature," in Leibnitz; "Opp. ed. Edmann," p. 123; Brucker, "Hist. Ph.,"
tom. iv., p. ii. 425.) The monstrous absurdity of his
assumption was placed in the clearest light even by his
own contemporaries, particularly by Bayle, who showed
the consequences which flowed from it (see also in Leibnitz's smaller writings, translated by Huth, *anno* 1740,
the observation on page 79, where even Leibnitz himself
is obliged to expose the preposterous consequences of his
own doctrine). Nevertheless, the very absurdity of the
assumption to which a thinking head was driven by the
problem in hand, proves the magnitude, the difficulty,
the perplexity of it, and how little it can be got rid of,
and the knot be cut, by its mere repudiation, such as has
been ventured upon in our days.

Spinoza again starts immediately from Descartes, hence,
at first in his character of Cartesian he even retains the
dualism of his teacher and assumes accordingly a *substantia cogitans* and a *substantia extensa*, the one as subject the other as object of knowledge. But later, when
he stood on his own feet, he found that both were one
and the same substance viewed from different sides; on
the one side conceived as a *substantia extensa* on the other as a *substantia cogitans*. This is as much as to say
that the distinction of the thinking and extended, or soul
and body, is an unfounded one and therefore inadmissible; so that nothing more ought to be said about it. He
nevertheless retains it, since he is untiring in repeating
that both are one. To this he adds, as it were by a
mere *sic etiam* that *Modus extensionis et idea illius modi una
eademque est res* ("Eth." P. II., prop. 7, schol.); by which
he means that our presentment of bodies and these bodies
themselves are one and the same. The *sic etiam*, however, is an insufficient transition to this, since it does not
by any means follow from the fact that the distinction
between mind and body or between the presenting and
the presented is unfounded, that the distinction between
our presentment and an objective and real, existing out-

side the same — the main problem, that is, that was started by Descartes — is also unfounded. The presenting and the presented may be perfectly well homogeneous, and yet still the question remains how I am with certainty to infer from presentments in my head as to the existence of beings in themselves that are independent of the former. The difficulty is not that on which Leibnitz (*e. g.*, "Theodic," Part I. § 59) would make it mainly turn, to wit, that between the assumed souls and the corporeal world as between two wholly heterogeneous kinds of substances no sort of reciprocal action could take place — for which reason he denied physical influence; for this difficulty is merely a consequence of rational psychology and only requires to be discarded as a fiction, as is done by Spinoza; and besides this, there is the *argumentum ad hominem* against the maintainers of this doctrine, that their own dogma that God, who is a spirit, has created and continuously governs the corporeal world implies that spirit can act immediately on bodies. The abiding difficulty is rather the Cartesian, that the world, which is only given us immediately, is simply an ideal world, a world, that is, consisting of presentments in our brain; while we, over and above this, undertake to judge of a real world existing independently of our presentment. Spinoza then, in so far as he abolishes the distinction between *substantia cogitans* and *substantia extensa* has not solved the problem but, at most, rendered physical influence again admissible. But this is insufficient to solve the difficulty for the law of causality is demonstratively of subjective origin. But even if it sprang from external experience it would still merely appertain to the ideally given world that is in question. Hence, in no case can it furnish a bridge between the absolutely objective and the subjective, but it is rather, merely the band which connects phenomena with one another (see "Welt als Wille und Vorstellung," vol. ii. p. 12). And nevertheless, in order more nearly to explain the above adduced identity of extension and presentment, Spinoza postulates something which is contained alike in the view of Malebranche and Leibnitz. In accordance with Malebranche, namely, we see all things in God;

rerum singularium ideae non ipsa ideata, sive res perceptas, pro causa agnoscunt, sed ipsum Deum, quatenus est res cogitans ("Eth." P. II., pr. 5); and this God is also at the same time the real and active principle therein, even with Malebranche. The mere fact, however, of Spinoza affixing to the world the name Deus explains nothing, in the last resort. But at the same time there is with him, as with Leibnitz, an exact parallelism between the extended and the presented world: *ordo et connexio idearum idem est ac ordo et connexio rerum* (P. II. pr. 7), and other similar passages. This is the *harmonia praestabilita* of Leibnitz; only that here the objectively existing world and the presented world are not entirely separated as with the last mentioned, merely corresponding to one another by virtue of a *harmonia* regulated in advance and from outside, but they are really one and the same. We have here, therefore, in the first place, a thorough-going Realism in so far as the existence of the things exactly corresponds to their presentment in us, both being one; we cognize accordingly the things in themselves — they are in themselves *extensa* as they appear as *cogitata;* in other words, in our presentment of them, they appear as *extensa* (here, too, it may be remarked, by the way, is the origin of Schelling's identity of the Real and Ideal). All this is, properly speaking, based on mere assertion. The exposition is already rendered unclear by the ambiguity of the word Deus which is used in a wholly improper sense; hence, it loses itself in obscurity and comes in the end to *nec impraesentiarum haec clarius possum explicare.* But the want of clearness in the exposition arises always from a want of clearness in the understanding and thinking out of the philosopher. Vauvenargues said very truly, *la clarté est la bonne foi des philosophes* (see "Révue des deux Mondes," 1853, 15 Aout, p. 635). What in music is the "pure section" is in philosophy complete clearness, which is the *conditio sine qua non* without the fulfilling of which everything loses its value, and we are compelled to say *quodcumque ostendis mihi sic incredulus odi.* If, in the ordinary affairs of practical life, one has to carefully avoid misunderstanding by clearness, how much the less ought one to express oneself incomprehensibly in the very abstruse, difficult, and wellnigh impenetrable subjects of thought, which constitute the problems of philosophy? The obscurity complained of in the doctrine of Spinoza, is owing to his not proceeding in a straightforward manner from the nature of things as he finds them; but from Cartesianism, and accordingly from all sorts of traditional conceptions, such as *Deus*, *substantia*, *perfectio*, etc., which he was concerned to bring in a roundabout way into harmony with truth. He often expresses the best ideas only indirectly, continually speaking *per ambages* and almost allegorically, as in the second part of the "Ethics." On the other hand, Spinoza expresses an unmistakable TRANSCENDENTAL IDEALISM amounting to, at least, a general recognition of the truth clearly expounded by Locke and still more by Kant, as to the real distinction between the phenomenon and the thing itself, and the recognition that only the first is knowable by us. As instances of this may be consulted, "Eth.," P. II. prop. 16, with the second corollary; prop. 17, schol.; prop. 18, schol.; prop. 19; prop. 23, where it is extended to self-knowledge; prop. 25, which expresses it clearly, and finally as *résumé*, the corollary to prop. 29, which distinctly says that we can neither know ourselves nor the things, as they are in themselves, but only as they appear. The demonstration of prop. 27, P. III., expresses the matter the clearest, at least in the beginning. Respecting the relation of the doctrines of Spinoza to those of Descartes I may recall here what I have said on the subject in the "World as Will and Presentment": vol. ii., p. 639 (3d ed. p. 739). The fact of his starting from the conceptions of the Cartesian philosophy, has not only been the occasion of much obscurity and misunderstanding in the exposition of Spinoza, but he has thereby been led into many flagrant paradoxes, obvious fallacies, and indeed absurdities and contradictions. In this way his doctrine, which contains so much that is true and excellent has acquired a highly undesirable addition of simply indigestible matter, so that the reader is divided within himself between admiration and vexation. But, in the aspect considered here, the chief fault of Spinoza is that he has drawn his line of cleavage between the Ideal

and Real, or the Subjective and Objective world, from a
false standpoint. EXTENSION, namely, is in no wise the
opposite of PRESENTMENT, but lies wholly within the latter.

We perceive things as extended, and, in so far as they
are extended, they are our presentment. But whether,
independently of our presentment, anything is extended,
or indeed, whether anything exists at all is the question
and the original problem. This was solved later by Kant,
and in so far, with indisputable accuracy, in the sense
that extension or space lies entirely in the presentment;
in other words, that it depends on the latter, inasmuch as
the whole of space is its mere form; and therefore, independently of our presentment, no extended can exist, and
most certainly does not exist.

Spinoza's line of cleavage is accordingly drawn wholly
on the ideal side; he has taken his stand on the PRESENTED
world, regarding the latter, indicated by its form of extension, as the Real, and therefore as existing independently of its possibility of presentment, i. e., in itself. He
is on this ground, therefore, quite right in saying, that
that which is extended and that which is presented — i. e.,
our presentment of bodies and these bodies themselves
— are one and the same (P. II., prop. 7, schol.). For
assuredly the things are presented as extended and are
only as extended, presentable — the world as presentment
and the world in space is *una eademque res;* this we can
fully admit. But were the extension, quality of the things-
in-themselves, our perception would then be a knowledge
of things-in-themselves, which is what he assumes, and in
which consists his realism. Since, however, he does not
ground or prove this, to wit, that our perception of a
spacial world involves a spacial world independent of this
perception, the fundamental problem remains unsolved.
This arises, however, from the fact, that the line of cleavage between the Real and Ideal, the Objective and the
Subjective, the Thing-in-itself and the Phenomenon, is
not correctly drawn. On the contrary as has been said,
the cleavage, being in the middle of the Ideal, Subjective,
Phenomenal side of the world — that is, drawn through
the world as presentment — splits the latter into the extended or spacial and our presentment of the same, where-

upon much trouble is taken to show that both are only one; as indeed they are.

Just because Spinoza holds entirely by the Ideal side of the world, inasmuch as he thought to find the Real in the extended belonging thereto, and as, in consequence, the perceivable is the only Real WITHOUT us, and the knowing (*cogitans*) is the only Real WITHIN us, so he, from another side, casts the only true Real, the Will, into the Ideal, which he makes a mere *modus cogitandi*, even identifying it with the judgment. As to this consult "Eth." P. II., the proofs of the props. 48 *et* 49, where we read: *Per voluntatem intelligo affirmandi et negandi facultatem;* and again: *Concipiamus singularem aliquam volitionem, nempe modum cogitandi, quo mens affirmat, tres angulos trianguli æquales esse duobus rectis*, whereupon the corollary follows: *Voluntas et intellectus unum et idem sunt.*

Spinoza has, generally, the great fault of purposely misusing words for the designation of conceptions which throughout all the world bear other names, and of taking from these the meaning which they everywhere have. Thus he calls "God" what is everywhere termed "World"; "Justice" what is everywhere termed "Power," and "Will" what is everywhere termed "Judgment." We are fully justified as regards this, in recalling the Hetman of the Cossacks in Kotzebue's "Benjowskij."

Berkeley, although certainly later, and with the knowledge of Locke, went logically farther in this problem than the Cartesians, and was thereby the originator of the proper and true Idealism, that is, of the knowledge, that that in space which is extended and which fills it, in short, the perceivable world generally, can only have an existence as such, in our presentment; and that it is absurd, and even contradictory, to attribute to it a further existence outside of all presentment, and independently of the knowing subject, and thereby to assume a matter existing in itself.*

---

* With laymen in philosophy, to whom many doctors of the same belong, one ought never to use the word "Idealism," because they do not know what it means, and carry on with it all sorts of nonsense. They understand by "Idealism" at times "Spiritualism," and at times something or other which is opposed to Philistinism, and are confirmed and

This is, indeed, a true and deep insight, but his whole philosophy consists in nothing else. He hit upon the Ideal and separated it completely; but he did not know where to find the Real, about which he troubled himself but little, expressing himself respecting it only occasionally, piecemeal, and inadequately. God's Will and Omnipotence is with him the immediate cause of the phenomena of the perceivable world, *i.e.*, of all our presentments. Real existence only accrues to knowing and willing beings, such as we ourselves are; hence these constitute, together with God, the Real. They are spirits, that is, knowing and willing beings, for willing and knowing he regarded as inseparable. He has this also in common with his predecessors, that he regards God as better known than the present world, and deems a reduction to him an explanation. His clerical, and, indeed, episcopal position laid altogether too heavy chains on him, and limited him to a narrow circle of thought with which he could never come into conflict. Hence he could go no farther, but true and false had to learn to mutually accommodate themselves in his head as well as they could. This remark, indeed, may be extended to the works of all these philosophers, with the exception of Spinoza. The Jewish Theism, unamenable to any test, dead to all research, and hence appearing really as a fixed idea, planting itself in the way of truth at every step, vitiates them all; so that the evil which it produces here in the theoretical sphere, may be taken as a pendant to that which it has produced throughout a thousand years in the practical — I mean in the shape of religious wars, inquisitions, and conversions of nations by the sword. The closest affinity between Malebranche, Spinoza, and Berkeley is unmistakable. We see them all proceeding from Descartes, in so far as they retain and

strengthened in this view by ordinary men of letters. The words "Idealism" and "Realism" are not anything and everything, but have their fixed philosophical meaning. Those who mean something else should employ another word.

The opposition of "Idealism" and "Realism" concerns the Known, the Object, while that between Spiritualism and Materialism, concerns the knowing, the Subject. (Modern ignorant muddlers confound Idealism and Spiritualism).

seek to solve the fundamental problem presented by him in the form of a doubt as to the existence of the outer world; concerned as they are to investigate the separation and connection of the world which is Ideal, subjective or given solely in our presentment, and the Real or objective, which is independent of it, and, therefore, existing in itself. As we have said, therefore, this problem is the axis on which the whole of modern philosophy turns. Locke distinguishes himself from these philosophers in that probably because he stands under the influence of Hobbes and Bacon, he attaches himself as closely as possible to experience and the common understanding, avoiding as far as may be hyperphysical hypotheses. The REAL is for him MATTER, and without turning his attention to the Leibnitzean scruple as to the impossibility of a casual connection between the immaterial, thinking, and the material, extended substance, he at once assumes physical influence between matter and the knowing subject. In this he proceeds with rare deliberation and honesty so far as to confess that possibly knowing and thinking substance itself might also be matter ("On the Human Understanding," L. IV., c. 3, § 6). This it was, which procured for him later the repeated ·praise of the great Voltaire, and in his own time, on the other hand, the malicious attacks of a cunning Anglican priest, the Bishop of Worcester. With him the Real, *i. e.*, Matter generates in the knowing subject by "Impulse," that is, contact, presentments, or the Ideal (*Ibid.*, L. I., c. 8, § 11). We have here, therefore, a thoroughly massive Realism, calling forth contradiction by its very exorbitance, and giving occasion to the Berkeleyan Idealism, whose special origination is, perhaps, to be found when Locke at the end of § 2 of the 31st chapter of the 2nd book with such a surprising absence of reflection, says, among other things: "Solidity, Extension, Figure, Motion and Rest, would be really in the world as they are, whether there were any sensible being to receive them or not." For as soon as one considers the matter one must recognize the above as false, in which case the Berkeleyan Idealism stands there and is undeniable. In the meantime Locke does not

8

overlook the chasm between the presentments in us and the things existing independently of us, in short, the distinction of Ideal and Real; in the end, however, he disposes of it by arguments of sound but rough common sense, and by appealing to the sufficiency of our knowledge of things for practical purposes (*Ibid.*, L. IV., c. 4 and 9), which obviously has nothing to do with the question, and only shows how very inadequate to the problem Empiricism remains. But even his Realism leads him to limit that in our knowledge which involves the Real, to the qualities inhering in the things as they are IN THEMSELVES, and to distinguish these from our mere knowledge of them or from that which merely pertains to the Ideal — terming the latter accordingly SECONDARY, but the former PRIMARY qualities. This is the origin of the distinction between thing in itself and phenomenon, which becomes so important later on in the Kantian philosophy. In Locke, then, we have the true genetic point of connection between the Kantian doctrines and the earlier philosophy. The former were stimulated and more immediately occasioned by Hume's sceptical criticisms of Locke's doctrines; while, on the other hand, they have only a polemical relation to the Leibnitz-Wolffian philosophy.

The above PRIMARY qualities, which are exclusively the determinations in the things in themselves, and which hence appertain to these outside and independently of our presentment, resolve themselves entirely into such as cannot be thought away, namely, extension, impenetrability, figure, motion, or rest, and number. All the remainder are recognized as SECONDARY, that is, as creations of the actions of those primary qualities on our organs of sense, and consequently as mere feelings in these; such are color, tone, taste, smell, hardness, softness, smoothness, roughness, etc. These therefore, have no similarity whatever with the quality in the thing in itself which excites them, but are reducible to the primary qualities as their causes such alone being purely objective and really part of the existing things (*Ibid.*, L. I., c. 8, § 7, *seq.* .). Our conceptions of these latter are therefore really true copies, which accurately reproduce

the qualities that are present in the things in themselves
(l.c. § 15). I wish the reader joy who really feels here
the *reductio ad absurdum* of Realism. We see then that
Locke deduces from the nature of the things in themselves, whose presentments we receive from without, that
which accrues to the action of the nerves of the sense-
organs, an easy, comprehensible, and indisputable consideration. But Kant later on made the immeasurably
greater step of also deducing what belongs to the action
of our brain (that incomparably greater nervous mass);
whereby all the above pretended primary qualities sink
into secondary ones, and the assumed things themselves
into mere phenomena, but the real thing in itself, now
stripped of these qualities, remains over as an entirely
unknown quantity, a mere x. This assuredly requires a
difficult and deep analysis, and one which has long to be
defended against the attacks alike of misunderstanding
and lack of understanding.

Locke does not deduce his primary qualities of things,
and does not give any further ground why only these
and no others are purely objective, except that they are
indestructible. Now if we investigate for ourselves why
he declares some qualities of things which work immediately on the sensibility, and consequently come
directly from without, not to be present objectively,
while he concedes objectivity to those which, as has since
been recognized, proceed from the special functions of
our intellect, we find the reason to be that the objec-
tively-preceiving consciousness (the consciousness of other
things) necessarily requires a complex apparatus, as the
function of which it appears, and consequently that its
most essential ground-determinations are fixed from within. In this way the univeral form or mode of perception
from which alone the *à priori* knowable can proceed,
presents itself as the warp of the perceived world, and
accordingly appears as that which is absolutely necessary,
unexceptional, and in no way to be got rid of; so that
it stands as the condition of everything else in its manifold variety. This is admitted to be, immediately, time
and space, and that which follows from them, and is
only possible through them. In themselves time and

space are empty. If anything is to come within them, it must appear as matter, that is, as an activity; in other words, as causality, for matter is through and through simply causality; its being consists in its action, and *vice versâ;* it is but the objectively-conceived form of the understanding for causality itself. ("On the Four-fold Root of the Principle of Cause," 2d ed., p. 77; 3d ed., p. 82; as also "World as Will and Present-ment," 2d ed., vol. i., p. 9, and vol. ii., pp. 48, 49; 3d ed., vol. i., p. 10, and vol. ii., p. 52.) Hence it comes that Locke's primary qualities are merely such as cannot be thought away — a fact which itself clearly enough indicates their subjective origin, as proceeding immedi-ately from the construction of the perceiving apparatus — and he therefore holds for absolutely objective pre-cisely that which, as function of the brain, is much more subjective than the sense-feeling, which is occasioned, or at least more directly determined, from without.

In the meantime it is interesting to see how through all these various conceptions and explanations, the prob-lem started by Descartes respecting the relation between the Ideal and the Real becomes ever more developed and clarified, and the truth thus promoted. It is true this was favored by the circumstances of the time, or, more correctly, of nature, which, in the short space of two cen-turies, gave birth to and ripened half a dozen thinking heads in Europe. By the gift of fortune, in addition, they were enabled, in the midst of a groveling world struggling after advantage and pleasure, to follow their noble calling undisturbed by the yelping of priests, or the foolish talk and caballing of the contemporary professors of philosophy.

Now Locke, in accordance with his strict empiricism, had deduced the knowledge of the causal relation from experience, while Hume did not dispute as he ought to have done, this false assumption, but immediately over-shot the mark by the observation, correct in itself, that experience can never give us anything more than a mere sequence of things upon one another, sensibly and imme-diately, and never a proper consequence and action—*i.e.,* a necessary interconnection. It is well known how the sceptical objection of Hume was the occasion of Kant's incomparably deeper investigations into the subject, which led him to the result that space and time, no less than causality, are known by us *a priori*, that is, lie in us before all experience, and hence belong to the subjective side of knowledge. From this it follows further, that all those primary, that is, absolute qualities of things, which Locke had assigned to them, since they are all composed of pure determinations of time, of space, and of causality, cannot belong to the things in themselves, but to our mode of knowledge of the same, and consequently are to be counted to the Ideal and not to the Real. The final consequence of this is that we know the things in no respect as they are IN THEMSELVES, but solely in their PHENOMENA. The Real, the thing in itself, therefore remains something wholly unknown, a mere x, and the whole perceivable world accrues to the Ideal as a mere presentment, a phenomenon, which nevertheless, even as such, in some way involves the Real, as thing in itself.

From this standpoint I, finally, have made a step, and believe that it will be the last; because I have solved the problem upon which, since Descartes, all philosophizing turns, in that I reduce all being and knowledge to the two elements of our self-consciousness, in other words, to something beyond which there can be no further principle of explanation, since it is the most immediate and therefore ultimate. I have called to mind, what indeed results from the researches of all my predecessors, which I have here noticed, to wit, that the absolute Real or the thing in itself can never be given us directly from without, in the way of mere presentment, since it is inevitably in the nature of the latter only to furnish the Ideal; while, on the contrary, since we ourselves are indisputably Real, the knowledge of the Real must in some way or other be derivable from within our own nature. And in fact it here appears, in an immediate manner in consciousness, as WILL. The line of cleavage between the Real and the Ideal falls therefore, with me, in such wise that the whole perceivable and objectively-presented world, including every man's body, together with time, space, and causality, in other words, together with the EXTENDED of Spinoza, and the MATTER of Locke, belongs as presentment to the Ideal. But in this case the Will alone remains as the Real, and this the whole of my predecessors, thoughtlessly and without reflection, had thrown into the Ideal as a mere result of presentment and of thought, Descartes and Spinoza having even identified it with the judgment. Ethics is therefore with me directly and incomparably more closely knit to metaphysics than in any other system, and thus the moral significance of the world and of existence is more firmly fixed than ever. But Will and Presentment are fundamentally distinct, inasmuch as they constitute the ultimate and basal opposition in all things in the world and leave nothing remaining over. The presented thing and the presentment of it are the same, but only the PRESENTED thing, and not the thing IN ITSELF. The latter is always Will, it matters not in what form it may appear in presentment.

APPENDIX.

READERS who are familiar with what has passed for philosophy in Germany, in the course of the present century, may perhaps be surprised not to find mentioned in the period between Kant and myself, either the Fichtean Idealism or the system of the Absolute Identity of the Real and Ideal, since they seem specially to belong to our subject. But I have not been able to include them, simply because, in my opinion, Fichte, Schelling, and Hegel are no philosophers, inasmuch as they fail in the first requirement of the philosopher, earnestness and honesty of research. They are mere sophists; they wanted to seem and not to be, and have sought, not the truth, but their own interest and advancement in the world. Places from governments, *honoraria* from students and booksellers, and as means to this end as much sensation and effect as possible from their sham philosophy — such were the guiding stars and inspiring genii of these disciples of wisdom. Hence they have not passed the entrance-examination, and so cannot be admitted into the honorable company of the thinkers of the human race.

Meanwhile, they have excelled in one thing, and that is, in the art of turning the head of the public and of making themselves pass for what they were not, which requires talent, indeed, but not philosophical talent. That they were incapable of effecting anything solid in philosophy was owing, in the last resort, to the fact that their INTELLECT WAS NOT FREE, but remained in the service of the WILL; and in this case, though the intellect can indeed achieve much for this or that purpose, it can do nothing for philosophy any more than for art. For these lay down as their first condition, that the intellect should act on its own account, and during the time of this activity should cease to be in the service of the will, that is, to have the objects of one's own personality in view; but when it is itself active, simply of its own motion, it, in accordance with its nature, knows no other purpose than the truth. Hence it does not suffice, in order to be a philosopher, which means lover of wisdom (this being nothing else than truth), to love the truth in so far as it harmonizes with one's own interest, or with the will of superiors, or the dogmas of the church, or the prejudices or tastes of contemporaries; as long as one remains in this position, one is only a φίλαυτος and no φιλόσοφος. For this title of honor is well and wisely conceived, in that it implies that one should love the truth earnestly, and with one's whole heart, and therefore unconditionally, without reserve before everything, and in case of necessity even to the defiance of everything. The reason is to be found in the fact above indicated that the intellect has become FREE, in which case it does not even know or understand any other interest than that of truth; the consequence being, that one then acquires an irreconcilable hatred against all lying and deception, no matter what garb they may wear. In this way we are not very likely to get on well in the world, but all the more in philosophy. On the other hand, it is a bad auspice for the latter, if proceeding avowedly from the investigation of truth, we begin, thereupon, to say farewell to all uprightness, honesty, and thoroughness, and are only concerned to make ourselves appear what we are not. In this case one assumes, like the above three sophists, now a false pathos, now an artificially high earnestness, now a mien of infinite superiority, in order to dazzle where one despairs of being able to convince; one writes without consideration, because, only thinking of writing, one saves one's thought up for the purpose of writing; one seeks now to inculcate palpable sophisms as demonstrations, now to propound hollow and senseless logomachy for deep thoughts; one invokes intellectual intuition or the absolute thought and self-movement of conceptions; one challenges expressly the standpoint of "reflection," that is, of rational thought, straightforward consideration, and honest presentation, in other words, the proper and normal use of the reason generally; one expresses a boundless contempt for the "philosophy of reflection," by which name is designated every connected course of thought which

deduces consequences from principles, such as has constituted every earlier philosophy; and accordingly, if one
is only provided with sufficient audacity, and encouraged
by the pitiable spirit of the age, one expresses oneself
in some such manner as follows: "It is not difficult to
see that the mode of stating a proposition, adducing
reasons for it and refuting its opposite in the same way,
by reason, is not the form which truth can assume.
Truth is the movement of itself within itself," etc.
(Hegel, preface to the "Phenomenology of the Mind,"
p. lvii., in the complete edition, p. 36.) I think it is not
difficult to see that whoever puts forward anything like
this, is a shameless charlatan, who is anxious to befool
simpletons, and who observes that he has found his people
in the Germans of the nineteenth century.

If, accordingly, under pretense of hurrying to the temple of truth, one hands over the bridle to the interests
of one's own person, which looks sideways toward altogether different guiding stars, such, for instance, as the
tastes and foibles of contemporaries, the religion of the land,
but especially toward the purposes and hints of the gov-
erning powers — Oh, how then can one expect to reach
the high, abrupt, bald rock on which stands the temple
of truth? One may easily attach to oneself, by the sure
bond of interest, a crowd of genuinely hopeful disciples,
hopeful, that is, for protection and places, who may
apparently form a sect, but really a faction, and by
whose united stentorian voices one may be proclaimed to
all the four winds as a sage without parallel — the interest of the person is satisfied, that of truth betrayed.

All this explains the painful feeling which seizes one,
when, after the study of real thinkers, such as have
been above described, one turns to the writings of Fichte
and Schelling, or indeed to the audaciously daubed nonsense of Hegel, produced as it is with a boundless,
though justified, confidence in German folly. With the
former one had always found an honest investigation of
truth, and as honest an endeavor to communicate their
thoughts to others. Hence he who reads Locke, Kant,
Hume, Malebranche, Spinoza, Descartes, feels himself
elevated and pleasurably impressed. This is effected by

contact with a noble mind, which has thoughts and
awakens thoughts. The reverse of this takes place in
reading the above-mentioned three German sophists. A
straightforward person who opens one of their books and
then asks himself whether this is the tone of a thinker
who would teach or of a charlatan who would deceive,
cannot remain five minutes in doubt about it; so much
does everything here breathe of dishonesty. The tone
of quiet investigation characterizing all previous philosophy is exchanged for that of unshakable certainty such
as is common to charlatanry of every kind in all time,
but which in this case claims to rest on immediate intellectual intuition, or on thought which is absolute, that
is, independent of the subject and its fallibility. From
every page, from every line, speaks the endeavor to
hoodwink, to deceive, the reader, now by dazzling to
disconcert him, now by incomprehensible phrases and
flagrant nonsense to stun him, now by audacity of assertion to befool him, in short, in every possible way to
throw dust in his eyes and to mystify him. Hence
the feeling which discovers itself in the transition in
question in respect of the theoretical, may be compared with that which in respect of the practical he
has, who coming from a society of honorable men, finds
himself in a haunt of swindlers. How worthy a man,
in comparison with such, is that Christian Wolff, so
undervalued and ridiculed by these three sophists! He
had and furnished real thoughts, but they only word
images and phrases for the purpose of deceiving. The
truly distinguishing character of the philosophy of this
whole, so-called, Post-Kantian school, is dishonesty, its
element is the blue ether and personal ends its goal.
Its exponents are concerned to SEEM not to BE,—they are
therefore sophists, not philosophers. The mockery of
future generations, extending itself to their votaries, and
then oblivion, awaits them. With the tendency of these
persons, as above indicated, is connected, we may say in
passing, the scolding and abusive tone which, as an
obligato accompaniment, pervades all Schelling's writings.
If this were not so, if honesty rather than pretentious-
ness and emptiness had been at work, Schelling, who is

without doubt the most gifted of the three, might at
least have occupied the subordinate rank in philosophy
of an eclectic of passing service. The amalgam which
he prepared from the doctrines of Plotinos, of Spinoza,
of Jakob Böhme, of Kant, and of the natural science of
modern times, might for a while have filled the vacancy produced by the negative results of the Kantian
philosophy, until a really new philosophy had come forward and properly afforded the satisfaction required by
the former. He has more particularly used the natural
science of our century to revive the abstract pantheism
of Spinoza. Spinoza had, without any knowlege of nature,
philosophized out of abstract conceptions, and, without
knowing the things themselves properly, had erected the
edifice of his doctrines. To clothe this dry skeleton with
flesh and blood, and, as well as might be, to communicate life and motion to it by the application of the
natural science which has since then developed, although
often done with a false application, is the undeniable
service of Schelling in his philosophy of nature, which is
also the best of his multifarious attempts and new
departures.

Just as children play with weapons intended for serious
purposes, or other tools of grown-up persons, so the three
sophists we have under consideration have dealt with the
subject here treated of, thus furnishing the grotesque
pendant to two centuries of laborious investigations on
the part of serious philosophers. After Kant had more
than ever accentuated the great problem of the relation
between the self-existent and our presentments, and
thereby brought it much nearer its solution, Fichte
starts up with the assertion that there is nothing behind
the presentments, these being no more than products of
the knowing subjects, of the Ego. While seeking in this
way to outbid Kant, he produced a mere caricature of
the latter's philosophy, inasmuch as, by the continuous
application of the method so much vaunted by these
three pseudo-philosophers, he abolished the Real altogether, and left nothing but the Ideal remaining. Then
came Schelling, who, in his system of the absolute
identity of the Real and Ideal, declared the whole dis-

tinction of no account, and maintained the Ideal to be also the Real, that both were one. In this way he attempted to throw again into confusion what had been so carefully, and, by a process of such slow and gradually developed reflection, separated. (Schelling, "On the Relation of the Philosophy of Nature to the Fichtean," pp. 14-21.) The distinction of Ideal and Real is crudely denied, in imitation of the above criticised error of Spinoza. At the same time, even the monads of Leibnitz,—that monstrous identification of two absurdities, namely, of the atoms and of the indivisible original and essentially knowing individuals, termed souls — are again brought forward, pompously apotheosized, and pressed into the service. (Schelling, "Ideas for the Philosophy of Nature," 2d ed., pp. 38, 82.) Schelling's philosophy of nature bears the name of the philosophy of identity, because, walking in the footsteps of Spinoza, it does away with three distinctions which the latter had also done away with, to wit, that between God and the world, that between body and soul, and, finally, that between Ideal and Real, in the perceived world. The last distinction, however, as has been above shown, in the consideration of Spinoza, in no way depends on the two others. On the contrary, the more it is brought into prominence, by so much the more the two others are rendered doubtful, for while it is based on a simple act of reflection, they are based on dogmatic demonstrations, which Kant has overthrown. In accordance with all this, metaphysic was identified by Schelling with physic, and hence, to a mere physical-chemical diatribe, the high-sounding title of "concerning the world-soul" was affixed. All those properly metaphysical problems, which untiringly impress themselves upon the human consciousness, were to be silenced by a crude denial clothed in strong assertions. Nature is here just because it is, of itself and through itself; we bestow upon it the title God, and therewith it is disposed of, and he who asks for anything more is a fool. The distinction between subjective and objective is a mere invention of the schools, like the whole Kantian philosophy, whose distinction of *a priori* and *a posteriori* is also of no account, our empirical perception of itself supplying

us with the things-in-themselves, etc.   Let the reader consult "On the Relation of the Philosophy of Nature with
the Fichtean," pp. 51 and 57, as also p. 61, where ridicule
is expressly heaped on those "who are astounded to find
that not is nothing, and cannot sufficiently wonder that
anything really exists." We see, therefore, that with Herr
von Schelling everything seems to explain itself.   At
bottom, however, this sort of talk is only a veiled appeal
in pompous phraseology to the so-called sound, but more
correctly rough, understanding. For the rest, I may recall
here what I have said in the second volume of my chief
work, at the beginning of chapter xvii. Significant for
our subject and very naïve is the passage on p. 69, in the
book of Schelling's just quoted from: "Had empiricism
completely attained its object, its opposition to philosophy, and therewith philosophy itself, as special sphere or
kind of science, would disappear; all abstractions would
dissolve themselves in the direct, 'friendly,' perception;
the highest would be the sport of pleasure and innocence,
the most difficult easy, the most senseless sensible, and
man might read joyfully and freely in the book of nature."
This would certainly be very nice! but it is not the case
with us. Thought does not let itself be shown the door
in this manner. The serious old Sphinx with its riddle
lies immovably there, and does not dash itself off the rock
because you explain that it is a spectre. As, therefore,
Schelling himself observed later that the metaphysical
problem cannot be got rid of by dictatorial assertions, he
gives us a genuinely metaphysical essay in his treatise on
freedom, which is, however, a mere piece of imagination,
a *conte bleu*, whence it comes that the style, whenever it
assumes the tone of demonstration, has a decidedly comical
effect.

By his doctrine of the identity of the Ideal and the
Real, Schelling has accordingly sought to solve the problem, set going by Descartes, dealt with by all great
thinkers, and finally accentuated in the strongest manner by Kant, by cutting the knot, that is, by denying
the opposition between the two. With Kant, from whom
he professed to start, he came in consequence into direct
contradiction. Meanwhile he had at least held fast the

original and special sense of the problem, which concerns the relation between our PERCEPTION and the being and essence in themselves of the things which present themselves in the former. But because he got his doctrines chiefly out of Spinoza, he adopted from the latter the expressions THOUGHT and BEING, which designated the problem very badly, and gave occasion later to the maddest monstrosities. Spinoza had attempted, with his doctrine, that *substantia cogitans et substantia extensa una eademque est substantia, quæ jam sub hoc jam sub illo attributo comprehenditur* (ii. 7, Sch.), or, *scilicet mens et corpus una eademque est res, quæ jam sub cogitationis, jam sub extensionis attributo concipitur* (iii. 2, Sch.), to abolish the Cartesian opposition of body and soul; he may also have recognized that the empirical object is not distinct from our presentment of it. Schelling adopted from him the expressions THOUGHT and BEING, which he gradually substituted for those of INTUITION (perception), or rather intuited (perceived), and the thing-in-itself ("New Journal of Speculative Physic," vol. i., 1st article, "Further expositions," etc.). For the relation of our perception of things to their BEING and ESSENCE in themselves is the great problem whose history I have here sketched; that of our thoughts, *i. e.*, conceptions, is a different one, for these are, quite obviously and undeniably, mere abstractions from that which is perceptibly known, having arisen through the arbitrary thinking away, or letting fall, of some qualities, and retention of others; and to doubt that this is so would ever occur to any reasonable man. These conceptions and thoughts, which constitute the class of NON-PERCEPTIVE presentments, never have therefore an immediate relation to the nature and being of the things-in-themselves, but are always mediate, that is, under the mediation of perception; it is the last-mentioned which on the one side furnishes for them the matter, and on the other stands related to the things-in-themselves, that is, to the unknown true nature of the things which is objectivized in perception.

The inexact expression borrowed by Schelling from Spinoza was used subsequently by the spiritless and tasteless charlatan Hegel, who in this respect appears as

Schelling's *hanswurst*, and distorted, so far as to make thought itself, in the narrower sense, namely, as conception, identical with the nature of the things-in-themselves. That, therefore, which is thought *in abstracto*, should, as such and immediately, be one with that which is objectively present in itself, and logic should, accordingly, be the true metaphysic; in which case we should only require to think or to let our conception have free course in order to know how the world without is absolutely constituted. As a natural consequence, every brain-phantasm would be at once true and real. Since, therefore, "the madder the better" was the motto of the philosophasters of this period, the absurdity in question was supported by a second, to wit, that it was not we who thought, but that the conception alone and without our help completed the thought process, which is therefore called the dialectical self-movement of the conception, and counts for a revelation of all things *in et extra naturam*. But this humbug was based upon another, equally resting on the misuse of words, and which was, indeed, never clearly stated, though it undoubtedly lies behind. Schelling had, according to Spinoza's procedure, entitled the world "God." Hegel took this in its literal sense. Now since this word properly signifies a personal being, embracing, together with other qualities altogether incompatible with the world, that of omniscience, this was also transferred by him to the world, in which it could naturally obtain no other place than in the empty head of men who only require to give their thoughts free play (dialectical self-movement) in order to reveal all the mysteries of heaven and earth, as in the absolute galimatias of the Hegelian dialectic. One art this Hegel has certainly understood, namely, how to lead the Germans by the nose. But that is no very great one. We see with what tricks he was able to hold the learned world of Germany for thirty years. That the professors of philosophy still treat these three sophists seriously, and hold it for important to assign them a place in the history of philosophy, happens only because it belongs to their *gagne-pain*, in that they obtain thereby material for elaborate dissertations, verbal and written, on the history of the so-called Post-Kantian philosophy, in which the opinions of the said sophists are elaborately expounded and seriously considered. From a reasonable point of view, one has no business to concern oneself at all with what these persons, in order to seem something, brought to market, unless it were that it should be deemed desirable for the scribblings of Hegel to be kept in the chemists' shops as a physically active vomitive, the disgust they excite being really quite peculiar. But enough of them and their originator, whose glorification we will leave to the Danish Academy of Sciences, which has recognized in him a *summus philosophus*, in its sense of the word, and hence requires him to be treated with respect, a fact brought out in the judgment appended to my prize essay on the foundations of morality, as a lasting memorial, and which, no less on account of its acuteness than of its memorable honesty, deserves to be rescued from oblivion, if only that it furnishes a remarkable confirmation of Labruyère's beautiful saying: "*Du même fonds, dont on néglige un homme de mérite, l'on sait encore admirer un sot.*"

FRAGMENTS OF THE HISTORY OF PHILOSOPHY.

SECTION I.

ON THE SAME.

To READ, instead of the original works of philosophers, all sorts of expositions of their doctrines, or history of philosophy generally, is as though one should get some one else to masticate one's food. Would anyone read the history of the world if it were possible for him to behold the interesting events of ancient times with his own eyes? But, as regards the history of philosophy, such an autopsy of the subject is really possible for him, to wit, the original writings of philosophers; in which he may none the less, for the sake of shortness, limit himself to well-chosen leading chapters, especially inasmuch as they all teem with repetitions, which one may just as well spare oneself. In this way, then, he will learn to know the essential in their doctrines, in an authentic and unfalsified form, while from the half-dozen histories of philosophy annually appearing he merely receives as much of it as has entered the head of a professor of philosophy, and, indeed, as it appears there. Now it is obvious of itself, that the thoughts of a great mind must shrink up considerably in order to find a place in the three-pound brain of a parasite of philosophy, from which they emerge again clothed in the contemporary jargon of the day, and accompanied by his sapient reflections. Besides this, it must be considered that the money-making history writer of philosophy can hardly have read a tenth part of the writings which he reports. Their real study demands the whole of a long and laborious life, such as formerly, in the old industrious times, the brave Brucker devoted to them. But what can such persons, who are detained by continuous lectures, official duties, vacation tours and dissipations, and who, for

9   (129)

the most part, come forward with their histories of philosophy in their earlier years, have thoroughly investigated? Add to this, that they are anxious to be pragmatical, and claim to have fathomed and to expound the necessity of the origin and the sequence of systems, and even to judge, correct, and dominate over the earnest and genuine philosophers of former times. How could it be otherwise than that they should copy the older ones, and each other, and then, in order to hide this, make matters worse by endeavoring to give them the modern tournure of the current quinquennium, pronouncing upon them, likewise, in the same spirit? On the contrary, a collection of important passages and essential chapters of all the leading philosophers, made by honest and intelligent scholars, conscientiously and in common, arranged in a chronologically-pragmatic order, much in the same way as formerly Gödicke, and, after him, Ritter and Preller, have done with the philosophy of antiquity, although much more completely — in short, a universal chrestomathy accomplished with care and a knowledge of the subject — would be very useful.

The fragments which I here give are at least not traditional, that is, copied; they are, rather, thoughts occasioned by my own study of the original works.

SECTION 2.

PRE-SOKRATIC PHILOSOPHY.

The Eleatic philosophers are the first who became conscious of the opposition between the perceived and the thought, φαινόμενα and νοούμενα. The latter alone was for them the true being, the ὄντως ὄν. Respecting this, they maintain that it is one, unchangeable and immovable; not so, however, with the φαινομένοις, that is, with the perceived, appearing empirically given, of which it would have been absurd to maintain anything of the kind — hence the so misunderstood proposition refuted by Diogenes in his well-known manner. They already distinguished, therefore, between APPEARANCE, φαινόμενον, and

THE THING-IN-ITSELF, ὄντος ὄν. The last mentioned could
not be senuously perceived, but only comprehended by
thought, and was accordingly known as νοούμενον (Arist.,
"Metaph.," i., 5, p. 986, et "Scholia," edit. Berol., pp.
429, 430, 509). In the "Scholia to Aristotle" (pp. 460,
536, 544, et 798), the work of Parmenides, τὰ κατὰ δόξαν is
mentioned. This, then, would have been the doctrine
of the phenomenon, physics, which would, without doubt,
have implied another work, τὰ κατ' ἀληθείαν, the doctrine of
the thing-in-itself, or metaphysic. Respecting Melissos,
indeed, a scholium of Philoponos says: ἐν τοῖς πρὸς ἀλήθειαν
ἐν εἶναι λέγων τὸ ὄν, ἐν τοῖς πρὸς δόξαν δύο (should be πολλὰ)
φησὶν εἶναι. The opposition to the Eleatics, and probably
called forth by them, is Herakleitos, who taught the ceaseless movement of all things, as they taught their absolute
immobility. He took his stand, therefore, on the φαινόμενον
("Arist. d. Cœlo," iii. 1, p. 298, edit. Berol.). He
called forth thereby as HIS opposite, Plato's doctrine of
Ideas, as appears from the statement of Aristotle ("Metaph.," p. 1078).

It is noteworthy that we find the comparatively few main
propositions of the Pre-Sokratic philosophers which have
been preserved, numberless times repeated in the writings of the ancients, but very little beyond them; as,
for instance, the doctrines of Anaxagoras, of the νοῦς and
of the ὁμοιομερίαι; that of Empedokles, of φιλία καὶ νεῖκος and
the four elements; that of Demokritos and Lukippos, of
the atoms, εἰδώλοις; that of Herakleitos, of the continuous
flux of all things; that of the Eleatics, as above explained;
that of the Pythagoreans, of the numbers, of metempsychosis, etc. It may well be, therefore, that this was the
sum of all their philosophizing; for we find also in the
works of the moderns, e.g., of Descartes, Spinoza, Leibnitz, and even Kant, the few fundamental propositions
of their philosophies numberless times repeated; so that
all these philosophers would seem to have adopted the
motto of Empedokles, who may also have been a lover of
the sign of repetition, δὶς καὶ τρὶς τὸ καλόν (see Sturz.,
"Empedocl. Agrigent.," p. 504).

The two dogmas Anaxagoras started stand in close
connection. πάντα ἐν πᾶσιν is, namely, a symbolical desig-

nation of the dogma of the *homoiomeroi*. In the primal chaotic mass, accordingly, the *partes similares* (in the physiological sense) of all things were present in their completeness. In order to their differentiation, and to their combination into specifically distinct things (*partes dissimilares*), it required a νοῦς to arrange and to form them, who by a selection of the elements, reduced confusion to order, since this chaos contained the most complete mixture of all substances ("Scholia in Aristot.," p. 337). Nevertheless the νοῦς had not brought the first separation to complete perfection, and therefore in everything was contained the elements of everything else, although in a lesser degree: πάλιν γὰρ πᾶν ἐν πάντι μεμίκται (*Ibid*).

Empedokles, on the other hand, instead of the numberless homoiomeroi, had only four elements, from which the things proceeded as products, not as with Anaxagoras as educts. The negating and separating, that is ordering, rôle of the νοῦς is, according to him, played by φιλία καὶ νεῖκος, love and hate. Both of these are very much better. For here not the INTELLECT (νοῦς) but the WILL (φιλία καὶ νεῖκος) has the ordering of things assigned to it, and the variety of substances are not, as with Anaxagoras, mere educts, but real products. While Anaxagoras makes them realized by a separating understanding, Empedokles does so by a blind impulse, *i.e.*, a knowledgeless will.

Empedokles is altogether a thorough man, and his φιλία καὶ νεῖκος has for its basis a deep and true *appercu*. Even in inorganic nature we see the elements unite and separate, seek or flee from each other, according to the laws of elective affinity. But those that show the strongest disposition to unite themselves chemically, which can only be effected in a state of fluidity, assume an attitude of the most decisive electrical antagonism when they come into contact with one another in a solid state—now they separate in opposed and mutually hostile polarities, now they again seek and embrace each other; and what, I ask, is that polar antagonism which appears throughout all nature in the most diverse forms, other than a continually renewed quarrel, upon which the earnestly

desired reconciliation follows? So φιλία καὶ νεῖκος is everywhere present, and, according to circumstances, first one
and then the other displays itself at different times. We
ourselves even may be immediately impressed in a
friendly or a hostile sense with any human being that
comes near us—the disposition to either is there and
waits on circumstances. It is only prudence that induces
us to tarry on the indifference point of impartiality,
which is also, be it said, the freezing point. In the same
way, the strange dog which we approach is ready at once
to adopt the friendly or the hostile key, and changes
easily from barking and growling to wagging, and *vice
versâ*. What lies at the foundation of this all penetrating phenomenon of the φιλία καὶ νεῖκος is assuredly, at
bottom, the great primal opposition between the unity of
all natures, according to their being in themselves and
their complete distinction in the phenomenon, which has
for its form the *principiuw individuationis*. Similarly,
Empedokles recognized the doctrine of atoms, already
known to him, as false, and taught on the contrary, the
infinite divisibility of bodies, as Lucretius tells us (lib. i.,
v., 747, etc.).

But above all things in the doctrines of Empedokles,
his decided pessimism is noteworthy. He has fully recognized the misery of our existence, and the world is for
him as much as for the true Christian a vale of sorrows,
Ἄτης λειμών. He compares it, indeed, like Plato later, to a
dark cavern, in which we are immured. In our earthly
existence he sees a state of banishment and misery, and
the body is the prison of the soul. These souls were
once in a state of infinite happiness, and have through
their own fault and sins reached the present wretchedness
wherein they, by sinful conduct, more and more entangle
themselves, getting involved in the circle of metempsychosis; while, on the contrary, by virtue and moral purity, to which the abstinence from animal food belongs,
and by renunciation of earthly enjoyments and wishes,
they may again attain to their previous condition. Thus
the same primal wisdom which constitutes the basal
thought of Brahmanism and Buddhism, and even of true
Christianity (by which is not to be understood the

optimistic Jewish-Protestant rationalism), was also brought
into consciousness by this ancient Greek, who completes
the *consensus gentium* on the subject. That Empedokles,
whom the ancients throughout designated a Pythagorean,
received this view from Pythagoras is probable, particularly as at bottom it is shared by Plato who was also
under the influence of Pythagoras. Empedokles declares his
adherence most distinctly to the doctrine of metempsychosis,
which is connected with this view of the world. The
passages in the ancients which, together with his own
verses, bear witness to this conception of Empedokles, are
to be found collected, with great industry in Sturzzi,
"Empedocles Agrigentinus," pp. 448-458. The opinion
that the body is a prison and life a condition of suffering
and purification from which we are released by death, if
we are but quit of the soul-wandering, is shared by
Egyptians, Pythagoreans, and Empedokles, together with
the Hindoos and Buddhists. With the exception of
metempsychosis it is also contained in Christianity.
Diodorus Siculus and Cicero also bear witness to the
above views of the ancients. (See "Wernsdorf de metemp-
sychosi veterum," p. 31, and "Cicero fragmenta," p. 299
["Somn. Scip.," 310, 319, ed. Bip.]) Cicero does not indicate in these passages to what philosophical school they
belong, but they would seem to be remains of Pythagorean
wisdom.

In the remaining doctrines of these Pre-Sokratic philosophers there is also much that is true to be pointed
out, of which I will give some illustrations.

According to the cosmogony of Kant and Laplace—
which has received a practical confirmation, *a posteriori*,
in the observations of Herschel, and which Lord Ross is
concerned, to the consolation of English clericalism, again
to render doubtful by means of his giant telescope—the
planetary systems form themselves by the condensation
of slowly coagulating and then revolving luminous neb-
ulæ, and thus, after thousands of years, Anaximenes is
justified when he declared air and vapor for the primal
elements of all things ("Schol. in Arist.," p. 514). At
the same time, also, Empedokles and Demokritos received
confirmation, for they, like Laplace, explained the origin

and constitution of the world from a vortex δίνη ("Arist. Op." ed. Berol., p. 295, *et* "Scholia," p. 351), at which Aristophanes ("Nubes," v. 820) mocks as blasphemy; just as do the English priests to-day over the Laplacian theory, they being anxious respecting their benefices, as they always are when a new truth comes to light. Our modern chemistry indeed carries us back to the Pythagorean philosophy of numbers: τὰ γὰρ πάθη καὶ αι ἕξεις τῶν ἀριθμῶν τῶν ἐν τοῖς οἶσι παθῶν τε καὶ ἕξεων αἴτια, οἶον τὸ διπλάσιον, τὸ ἐπίτριτον, τὸ ἡμιόλιον ("Schol. in Arist.," p. 543 *et* 829). That the Kopernican system was anticipated by the Pythagoreans is well known; it was even known to Kopernicus himself, who drew his chief ideas from the well-known passage on Hiketas, in Cicero's "Questionibus Acad." (ii. 39), and from Philolaos in Plutarch, "De placitis Philosophorum" (lib. iii., c. 13). This important insight was afterward rejected by Aristotle, in order that he might put his whims in the place of it, as to which, see below, § 5 (compare "World as Will and Presentment," ii., p. 342 of the 2d ed.; ii., p. 390, 3d ed.). Even Fourier's and Cordier's discoveries on the heat in the interior of the earth are confirmations of the doctrines of the ancients: ἔλεγον οἱ Πυθαγόρειοι πῦρ εἶναι δημιουργικὸν περὶ τὸ μέσον καὶ κέντρον τῆς γῆς τὸ ἀναθάλπον τὴν γῆν καὶ ζωοποιοῦν ("Schol. in Arist.," p. 504). And in consequence of these discoveries, the crust of the earth to-day is looked upon as a thin layer between two media (atmosphere and hot fluid metals and metalloids) whose contact would occasion a conflagration that would annihilate that crust, also confirming the opinion in which all the ancient philosophers agree, and which is shared even by the Hindoos ("Lettres édifiantes," *édit. de* 1819, vol. vii., p. 114) that the world will finally be consumed by fire. It is also deserving of mention that, as may be seen from Aristotle ("Metaph.," i., 5, p. 986), the Pythagoreans, under the name of δέκα ἀρχαί, had conceived the *yn* and *yang* of the Chinese.

That the metaphysics of music, as explained by me in my chief work (vol. i., § 52, and vol. ii., chap. 39) must be regarded as an exposition of the Pythagorean philosophy of numbers, I have already shortly indicated, and will here somewhat further explain — presupposing, at the same time, in the reader an acquaintance with the passages referred to. In accordance with the above, MELODY expresses all movements of the will such as are made known in human consciousness, that is, all affections, feelings, etc.; HARMONY, again, denotes the ladder of the objectivation of the will in the rest of nature. Music is, in this sense, a second reality, which runs entirely parallel with the first, although it is of quite another kind and character, so that while it has a complete analogy it has no similarity with it — music, as such, existing only in our auditory nerves and brain. Outside these, or in itself (understood in the Lockean sense) it consists in mere relations of tones directly, that is, in respect of quantity, in rhythm, and in respect of quality, in the intervals of the scales which rest on the arithmetical relation of vibrations; in other words, numerical as it is in its rhythmical element, so is it also in its harmonic element.

The whole nature of the world, therefore, as well of the microcosm as of the macrocosm, may be certainly expressed by mere numerical relations, and is, therefore, reducible to these. And in this sense Pythagoras was right in placing the proper nature of things in numbers. But what now are numbers? Relations of succession whose possibility is based on time.

When one reads what is said about the number-philosophy of the Pythagoreans in the "Scholia to Aristotle" (p. 829, ed., Berol.) one might be led to the supposition, that the use of the word λόγος in the introduction to the gospel ascribed to John, so strange and mysterious and verging on the absurd, as also the earlier and analogous passages in Philo, originate in the Pythagorean philosophy of numbers, from the signification, that is, of the word λόγος in the arithmetical sense, as numerical relation, *ratio numerica*. Such a relation constitutes, with the Pythagoreans, the innermost and indestructible essence of every being; in other words, its first and original principle ἀρχή; whence of everything might be said, ἐν ἀρχῇ ἦν ὁ λόγος. It should be noted also that Aristotle says ("De Anima," i. 1): τὰ πάθη λόγοι ἔνυλοί εἰσι, *et mox:* ὁ μὲν γὰρ λόγος εἶδος τοῦ πράγματος. One is also reminded here of the λόγος στερματικος of the Stoics, to which I shall shortly return.

According to Jamblichos' biography of Pythagoras, the latter owed his education chiefly to Egypt, where he remained from his twenty-second to his fifty-sixth year, and, indeed, to the Egyptian priests. Returning in his fifty-sixth year, he had conceived the project of founding a kind of priestly state, in imitation of the Egyptian temple hierarchies, of course, with the modifications necessary to Greeks; and though he did not succeed in this in his fatherland, Samos, he did, to a certain extent, in Krotona. Now, as Egyptian culture and religion, without doubt, came from India, as is proved by the sanctity of the cow, together with a hundred other things ("Herod.," ii., 41), this would also explain the regulation of Pythagoras respecting abstinence from animal nourishment, especially the prohibition of slaughtering oxen (Jambl., "Vit. Puith.," c. 28, § 150), as also the consideration for all animals which is enjoined; similarly, also, his doctrine of metempsychosis, his white robes, his eternal mystification, which gave rise to symbolical modes of speech, and even extended itself to mathematical theorems; yet, again, the foundation of a priestly caste, strict discipline and much ceremonial, the worship of the sun (c. 35, § 256), and many other things.* His most important astronomical principles he had also from the Egyptians. Hence the priority of his doctrine of the inclination of the ecliptic was disputed by Œnopides, who had been with him in Egypt. (Consult, as to this, the conclusion of the 24th chapter of the 1st book of the "Eklogues of Stobæos," with Heeren's note from Diodorus.) From the rest, when one looks through the elementary notions of astronomy collected by Stobæos from all the Greek philosophers (especially lib. i., c. 25),

* It may be well to remind the reader that Schopenhauer's statements as to the origin of Egyptian civilization are in no way borne out by the results of recent research. The coincidences mentioned by Schopenhauer might be extended to most early civilizations, and do not by any means give color to the farfetched hypothesis of the borrowing of the ancient Egyptian culture from India. The Egyptian civilization is undoubtedly of greater antiquity than the Indian.—Tr.

one finds that they have produced mere absurdities, with the single exception of the Pythagoreans, who, as a rule, are quite correct. That this is not their own invention, but comes from Egypt, is not to be doubted. The well-known prohibition of Pythagoras respecting beans is of purely Egyptian origin, and merely a superstition derived from thence, since Herodotus (ii., 37), relates that in Egypt the bean is considered unclean and abhorred, so that the priests will not even tolerate the sight of it.

That the doctrine of Pythagoras is a decided pantheism is proved as conclusively as briefly by a sentence of the Pythagoreans, preserved by Clement of Alexandria, contained in the "*Hortatio ad gentes,*" the Doric dialect of which points to its genuineness: Οὐκ ἀποκρύπτεον οὐδὲ τοὺς ἀμφὶ τὸν Πυθαγόραν, οι φασίν· Ὁ μὲν θεὸς εἷς· χ οὗτος δὲ οὐχ, ὥς τινες ὑπονοοῦσιν, ἐκτὸς τᾶς διακοσμήσιος, ἀλλ' ἐν αὐτα, ὅλος ἐν ὅλω τῶ κύκλω, ἐπίσκοπος πάσας γενέστος, κρᾶσις τῶν ὅλων· ἀεὶ ὤν, καὶ ἐργάτας τῶν αὐτοῦ δυνάμιων καὶ ἔργων ἁπάντων ἐν οὐράνω φωστὴρ, καὶ πάντων πατὴρ, νοῦς καὶ ψυχωσις τῶ ὅλω κύκλω, πάντων κίνασις. (See "Clem. Alex. Opera," tom. i., p. 118, in "Sanctorum Patrum Oper. Polem.," vol. iv., Wirceburgi, 1778.) It is good, namely, to convince oneself at every opportunity that, properly speaking, Theism and Judaism are exchangeable terms.

According to Apuleius, Pythagoras got as far as India, and was even instructed by the Brahmins. (See Apuleius, "Florida," p. 130, ed. Bip.) I believe, nevertheless, that the assuredly considerable wisdom and knowledge of Pythagoras consisted, not so much in what he thought, as in what he learned, was not so much his own, that is, as of foreign origin. This is confirmed by a saying of Herakleitos ("Diog. Laert.," lib. viii., c. 1, § 5). Otherwise he would have written it down in order to rescue his thoughts from oblivion; while, on the other hand, what was learned from abroad was safe enough at the fountain-head.

SECTION 3.

SOKRATES.

The wisdom of Sokrates is an article of philosophic faith. That the Platonic Sokrates was an ideal and therefore poetical person, who enunciated Platonic thoughts, is perfectly clear, but in the Xenophontic Socrates there is not precisely very much wisdom to be found. According to Lukian ("Philo. Pseudes," 24), Sokrates had a fat belly, which does not belong to the signs of genius. But it is just as doubtful as to the high mental powers of all those who have not written, and hence also of Pythagoras. A great mind must gradually recognize his calling and his position toward humanity, and consequently attain to the conviction that he does not belong to the flock, but to the shepherds—to the educators, that is, of the human race. But from this the obligation becomes clear not to limit his immediate and certain action to the few which chance brings into his neighborhood, but to extend it to humanity, in order that it may reach the exceptions, the elect, in the latter. But the only organ with which one speaks to humanity is writing; verbally one addresses only a number of individuals, and therefore anything so said, remains, as far as the human race is concerned, a private matter. For such individuals are generally a bad soil for the best seed, which either does not influence them at all, or else what it produces rapidly degenerates. The seed itself, therefore, must be preserved, and this cannot be done through tradition, which is falsified at every step, but solely through writing, the only true preserver of thoughts. Add to this, that every deep-thinking mind necessarily has the impulse, for the sake of its own satisfaction, to retain its thoughts and reduce them to the greatest possible clearness and definition, and consequently to embody them in words. But this is only perfectly attained in writing, for the written delivery is essentially different from the verbal, since it alone admits the highest precision, concision, and the most pregnant brevity, thus becoming a pure ektypos of thought. In consequence of all this, it would be a marvelous conceit in any thinker to wish to leave the most important invention of the human race unutilized. For this reason, it is hard for me to believe in the really great intellect of those who have not written. I am rather disposed to hold them to have been mainly practical heroes, who effected more by their character than by their brains. The majestic authors of the "Upanishads of the Vedas" have written, though the "Sanhita of the Vedas," consisting as it does merely of prayers, may originally have been only verbally propagated.

Between Sokrates and Kant many parallels may be drawn. Both reject all dogmatism; both profess a complete ignorance in matters of metaphysic and make their speciality the clear consciousness of this ignorance. Both maintain that the practical, that which man has to do and to forbear, is, on the other hand, perfectly certain of itself without any further theoretical foundation. Both had the fortune, that their immediate successors and declared disciples broke away from them precisely on these principles, and, elaborating a metaphysic, established thoroughly dogmatic systems; and further, that these systems turned out very diverse, and yet all agreed in maintaining that they started from the doctrines of Sokrates or Kant, as the case might be. As I am myself a Kantian, I will here notify my relation to him in one word. Kant teaches that we cannnot know anything beyond experience and its possibility. I admit this, but maintain that experience itself, in its totality, is susceptible of an explanation which I have endeavored to give by deciphering it like a writing, and not, as with all earlier philosophers, by undertaking to transcend it by means of its mere forms, a method Kant had proved to be invalid.

The advantage of the SOKRATIC METHOD, as we learn it from Plato, consists in that the foundation of the propositions, which are intended to be proved by the collocutor or opponent, are admitted singly before their consequences are seen. Since, however, in a didactic delivery in continuous speech, consequences and grounds are able to be seen at once, one would attack them if they did not please one. Meanwhile, among the things which Plato would impose upon us is this — to wit, that by means of the application of this method, the Sophists and other fools had in all innocence let Sokrates prove to them that they were such. This is incredible; it is much more likely that, at the last quarter of the way, or as soon as they noticed what he was driving at, they would, by manœuvres denying what had previously been said, intentional misunderstandings and such other tricks and dodges as are employed instinctively by dishonesty desirous of justifying itself, have spoiled the artificially-planned game of Sokrates and torn his net, or they would have become so rude and insulting, that he would have found it advisable to save his skin betimes. For why should not the Sophists have understood the method by which everyone can make himself equal to everyone else, and for the moment bring himself to the level of the greatest intellectual eminence — namely, insult? The low nature indeed feels an instinctive inclination to this as soon as it begins to detect intellectual superiority.

SECTION 4.

PLATO.

Already in Plato we find the origin of a certain false dianoialogy, which is put forward with a secret metaphysical purpose, namely, for the behoof of a rational psychology and a doctrine of immortality depending on it. It has proved itself again and again as a deceptive doctrine of the toughest vitality, dragging on its existence as it has throughout the whole of ancient, mediæval, and modern philosophy, till Kant, the all-destroyer, finally knocked it on the head. The doctrine here referred to is the rationalism of the theory of knowledge with its metaphysical purpose. It may be summed up shortly as follows: That which knows in us is an immaterial substance, fundamentally distinct from the body

called Soul; the body being a hindrance to knowledge.
Hence all knowledge through the senses is deceptive, the
only true, accurate, and certain knowledge being that
which is free and removed from all sensibility (*i.e.* from
all perception), in other words, PURE THOUGHT, or that
which functions exclusively by means of abstract conceptions. For this instructs the soul entirely by its own
methods, and consequently will work best after it is separated from the body, that is, after we are dead. In
such wise, therefore, dianoialogy plays into the hands of
rational psychology to the benefit of its doctrine of immortality. This doctrine which I have here summed up, we
find fully and clearly in the " Phædo," chap. x. It is
somewhat differently conceived in the " Timæus," from
which Sextus Empiricus expounds it very precisely and
clearly in the following words: Παλαιά τις παρὰ τοῖς φυσικοις
κυλίεται δόξα περὶ τοῦ τὰ ὁμοῖα τῶν ὁμοίων εἶναι γνωριστικά. Μοx:
Πλατὼν δὲ, ἐν τῷ Τιμαίῳ, πρὸς παραστασιν τοῦ ἀσωματον εἶναι τὴν
ψυκην, τῷ αὐτῷ γένει τῆς ἀποδείξεως κέχρηται. Εἰ γὰρ ἡ μὲν
δρασίς, φησι, φωτὸς ἀντιλαμβανομένη, εὐθύς ἐστι φωτοειδὴς, ἡ δὲ ἀκοη
ἀέρα πεπληγμένον κρίνουσα, ὅπερ ἐστι τὴν φωνὴν, εὐθὺς ἀεροειδὴς
θεωρεῖται, ἡ δὲ ὄσφρησις ἀτμοὺς γνωρίζουσα πάντως ἐστι ἀτμοειδής,
καὶ ἡ γεῦσις χυλοὺς, χυλοειδής· κατ' ἀναγκὴν καὶ ἡ ψυχὴ τάς ἀσωμάτους
ἰδέας λαμβάνουσα, καθάπερ τὰς ἐν τοῖς ἀριθμοῖς καὶ τὰς ἐν τοῖς
πέρασι τῶν σωμάτων (that is, pure mathematics) γίνεταί τις
ἀσώματος (" Adv. Math.," vii., 116 *et* 119). (*Vetus quæ-
dam, a physicis usque probata, versatur opinio, quod similia
similibus cognoscantur.—Mox: Plato, in Timæo, ad pro-
bandum, animan esse incorpoream, usus est eodem genere
demonstrationis: " nam si visio," inquit, " apprehendens lu-
cem statim est luminosa, auditus autem aërem percussum
judicans, nempe vocem, protinus cernitur ad aëris accedens
speciem, odoratus autem cognoscens vapores, est omnino va-
poris aliquam habens formam, et gustus, qui humores, hu-
moris habens speciem ; necessario et anima, ideas suscipiens
incorporeas, ut quæ sunt in numeris et in finibus corporum,
est incorporea.*")
Even Aristotle admits this argument, at least hypotheti-
cally, where, in the first book of the " De Anima " (c. i.),
he says that the separate existence of the soul would be
thereby constituted if any manifestation in which the

body had no part accrued to it, and that such a manifestation seemed above all things to be Thought. But if
even THIS is not possible without perception and imagination, it cannot obtain without the body (εἰ δέ ἐστι καὶ
τὸ νοεῖν φαντασία τις, ἢ μὴ ἄνευ φαντασίας, οὐκ ἐνδέχοιτ' ἂν οὐδὲ
τοῦτο ἄνευ σώματος εἶναι). Yet Aristotle does not even admit
the above conditions, which are the premises of the
argumentation, in so far, namely, as he teaches what was
later formulated in the proposition, *nihil est in intellectu,
quod non prius fuerit in sensibus*. (See, as to this, " De
Anima," iii., 8.) Even he saw, therefore, that all that is
purely and abstractly thought has first borrowed its entire material and content from the perceived. This also
disturbed the Schoolmen, and hence, even in the Middle
Ages, men endeavored to prove that there are pure cognitions of reason — that is, thoughts having no reference
to any images; in other words, a thought which draws
all its material from itself. The efforts and controversies
on this point are to be found collected in Pomponasius,
who derives his main argument from them. In order to
answer the requirement spoken of, the *universalia* and
the cognitions *a priori*, conceived as *æternæ veritates*, had
to serve. The development which the matter received
through Descartes and his school I have already explained
in the elaborate observation appended to section six of my
prize essay on the foundation of morals, in which I have
adduced the valuable original words of the Cartesian De la
Forge — for one finds the false doctrines of a philosopher
as a rule expressed the clearest by his disciples, since these
are not, like the master himself, concerned to keep in the
background as much as possible those sides of his system
which might betray its weakness, inasmuch as they have
no fear about it. But Spinoza opposed to the whole
Cartesian dualism his doctrine *substantia cogitans et substantia extensa una eademque est substantia, quæ jam sub
hoc, jam sub illo attributo comprehenditur*, thereby showing his great superiority. Leibnitz, on the other hand,
remained exquisitely on the path of Descartes and ortho-
doxy. But this again called out the, for philosophy, so
thoroughly healthy endeavor of the excellent Locke, who
finally plunged into the investigation of the ORIGIN OF

CONCEPTIONS, and made the phrase NO INNATE IDEAS, after
he had carefully expounded it, the foundation of his
philosophy.   The French, for whom his system was
worked out by Condillac, proceeded much farther in the
matter on the same basis, inasmuch as they put forward
and urged the proposition, *penser, c'est sentir*.   Taken
absolutely, this proposition is false, but there lies this
truth in it, that all thought in part presupposes feeling
as ingredient of the perception which furnishes for it its
material; in part it is no more than feeling conditioned
by corporeal organs.   As the latter, namely, is conditioned by the nerves of sense, so is the former by the
brain, and both consist in nervous activity.   Yet even
the French school does not hold closely by this proposition, but only with a metaphysical — in this case a materialistic — purpose, just as their Platonic, Cartesian,
Leibnitzian opponents had only held the false proposition that the only accurate knowledge of things consists
in pure thought, also with a metaphysical object, in order
thereby to prove the immateriality of the soul.   Kant
alone leads us away from both these false paths, and
from a quarrel in which neither party, properly speaking, proceeds honestly to the truth.   The two sides both
profess dianoialogy, but their attention is really turned
to metaphysic, and hence they falsify dianoialogy.   Kant
says: "Certainly there is a pure knowledge from reason,
that is, cognitions *a priori*, which precede all experience,
and consequently also a Thought, which does not owe
its material to any knowledge by means of the senses."
But even this knowledge *a priori*, although not drawn
FROM experience, has only worth and validity for the
SAKE of experience; for it is nothing else but the aware-
ness of our OWN KNOWLEDGE APPARATUS and its *modus
operandi* (brain function), or, as Kant expresses it, the
form of the knowing consciousness itself, which receives
its material primarily through the empirical knowledge,
with which it is connected by means of the sense feeling, and without which it is empty and useless; whence
his philosophy is termed the "Critique of pure Reason."
Therewith all the above metaphysical psychology falls to
the ground, and with it falls all Plato's pure activity of

the soul. For we see that knowledge without the perception which is brought about through the body has no material, and that therefore the knowing subject, as such, is nothing but a mere empty form without the presupposition of the body, even setting aside the fact that all thought is a mere physiological function of the brain as digestion is of the stomach.

If then, accordingly, Plato's doctrine of isolating knowledge and keeping it pure from all communication with the body, the senses, and perception, is shown to be purposeless, mistaken, and even impossible, we may, notwithstanding, regard my doctrine, that only the intuitive knowledge kept pure from all community with the will attains the highest objectivity, and therefore perfection, as the true analogue of the same. Respecting this I refer the reader to the third book of my chief work.

SECTION 5.

ARISTOTLE.

The main characteristic of Aristotle may be said to have been pre-eminent acuteness, combined with circumspection, power of observation, many-sidedness, and want of depth. His conception of the world is tame, although acutely worked out. Depth of thought finds its material in ourselves; acuteness has to receive it from without if it is to have any data. But at that time the empirical data were, on the one hand few, and on the other false. For this reason the study of Aristotle is nowadays not very profitable, while that of Plato remains so in the highest degree. The want of depth complained of in Aristotle is naturally most apparent in his "Metaphysic," where mere acuteness will not, as elsewhere, suffice; hence, in the latter, he is least satisfactory. His "Metaphysic" is, for the most part, a conversation as to the philosophies of his predecessors, which he criticises and refutes from his standpoint, mostly from isolated sayings, without penetrating their meaning, and somewhat like one who breaks windows from the outside.

10

He propounds few or no dogmas of his own, or at least not in a connected manner. That we are indebted to his polemic for a great part of our knowledge of the older philosophies, is an accidental service. He is most hostile to Plato precisely where Plato is entirely right. The « ideas » of the latter return like something which he cannot digest again and again into his mouth; he is resolved not to admit their validity. Acuteness suffices in the empirical sciences; hence Aristotle has a pre-eminently empirical bent. But inasmuch as, since his time, experience has made such progress as to stand to its then state in the relation of adult age to childhood, the empirical sciences cannot, to-day, be directly very much advanced by the method and the specially scientific attitude which characterized him and was started by him, though indirectly they may be. In zoology, however, he is still, at least in some respects, of direct use. His empirical bent in general gives him the disposition to continually dissipate himself. He is apt, accordingly, to spring so easily aside from the line of thought which he had begun, as to be almost incapable of following out any line of thought for long and to the end, in the capacity for which consists precisely the faculty of deep thought. On the contrary, he is always starting problems, but only touching them, and proceeding at once, without solving them or even thoroughly discussing them, to something else. Hence his reader often thinks, "Now it's coming," but it does not come; and hence it often appears, when he has stirred a problem and followed it out a short way, that the truth has been hanging upon his lips, when suddenly he is off to something else and leaves us in doubt. For he cannot keep to anything, but springs from that which he intended to something different which occurs to him at the moment, as a child lets a toy fall in order to seize another it has just seen. This is the weak side of his intellect; it is the vivacity of superficiality. It is the explanation of why, although Aristotle was a highly systematic head, since from him proceeded the separation and classification of the sciences, nevertheless his exposition is throughout deficient in systematic arrangement, and we miss therein a methodical progress, namely, the separation of the dissimilar and collocation of the similar. He deals with things as they occur to him without having previously thought them out and sketched a clear plan of them; he thinks with a pen in his hand, a method which, though it is a great facility for the writer, is a great grievance for the reader. Hence the planlessness and insufficiency of his exposition; hence the reason why he comes back a hundred times to the same thing, simply because something foreign to it had come in between; hence the reason why he cannot keep to a subject, but goes from the hundredth to the thousandth; hence it is that he leads, as above described, the reader, anxious for the solution of the problem mooted, about by the nose; hence it is that, after having devoted several pages to a subject, he begins his investigation suddenly from the beginning with λάβωμεν οὖν ἄλλην ἀρχὴν τῆς σκέψεως, and this six times in one work; hence the motto, *quid feret hic tanto dignum promissor hiatu*, applies to so many of the exordiums of his books and chapters; hence, in a word, he is so often confused and unsatisfactory. In exceptional cases he has certainly done things differently, as, for instance, the three books of "Rhetoric," which are throughout a model of scientific method, and indeed exhibit an architectonic symmetry which may well have been the original of the Kantian.

The radical antithesis of Aristotle, alike in his mode of thought as also in his exposition, is Plato. The latter holds fast to his leading thought as if with an iron hand, follows out its thread, be it never so thin, in all its ramifications, through the labyrinths of the longest dialogues, and finds it again after all episodes. One sees from this that he had fully and ripely thought out his subject, and had planned an artistic arrangement for its exposition, before he started to write. Hence, every dialogue is a planned work of art, all of whose parts have a well thought-out connection, though it is often purposely hidden for a time, and whose frequent episodes often lead back, unexpectedly and of themselves, to the leading idea, after it has been made clear by them. Plato always knew, in the full sense of the word, what he wanted and

intended; although for the most part he does not carry
through the problems to a decisive issue, but is satisfied
with their thorough-going discussion. We need not much
wonder, therefore, if some accounts, especially in Ælian
("Var. Hist.," iii., 19, iv. 9, etc.), state that between Plato
and Aristotle considerable personal want of harmony was
displayed; also that Plato now and then spoke somewhat
disparagingly of Aristotle, whose unsteadiness, flashiness,
and levity, though it was connected with his polymathy,
was quite antipathetic to Plato. Schiller's poem, "Breadth
and Depth," may be applied to the antithesis between
Aristotle and Plato.

In spite of this empirical mental attitude, Aristotle was,
nevertheless, no logical and methodical empiricist; hence
he had to be overthrown and driven out by the true
father of empiricism, Bacon of Verulam. Anyone who
wants to properly understand in what sense and why the
latter was the opponent and conqueror of Aristotle and
his method, has only to read the books of Aristotle, "De
degeneratione et corruptione." Here he will find a true
a priori treatment of nature, one which seeks to understand and explain its processes from mere conceptions;
a particularly bad instance is furnished in l. ii., c. 4,
where a chemistry is constructed *a priori*. Bacon, on
the other hand, appeared with the advice not to make
the abstract, but the perceptual experience, the source
of the knowledge of nature. The brilliant result of this
is the present high state of the natural sciences, from
which we look down, with a piteous smile, on these
Aristotelian vexations of spirit. In this respect it is very
remarkable that the above mentioned books of Aristotle
disclose, quite plainly even, the origin of scholasticism;
indeed the quibbling, word-juggling method of the latter
is already to be met with there. For the same purpose
the books "De cœlo" are also very useful, and therefore
worthy of being read. Even the first chapters are a good
sample of the method of seeking to determine and to
know the essence of nature from mere conceptions, and
the failure is here obvious. It is there proved to us in
chap. viii., from mere conception and *locis communibus*,
that there are not several worlds, and in chap. xii. it is

similarly speculated as to the course of the stars.   It is
a logical reasoning from false conceptions, a quite special
nature-dialectic, which undertakes, from certain universal
axioms, which are supposed to express what is reasonable and proper, to decide *a priori* what nature is and
how it must act.   In seeing such a great, indeed stupen-
dous, intellect such as, after all said and done, Aristotle
remains, entangled so thickly in errors of this sort,
which maintained their validity till a few hundred years
ago, it is pre-eminently plain to us how very much humanity owes to Kopernicus, Kepler, Galilei, Bacon, Rob-
ert Hook, and Newton.   In chaps. vii. and viii. of the
second book, Aristotle expounds to us his whole absurd
arrangement of the heavens: The stars cleave fast to
the revolving hollow globe; sun and planets to similar
nearer ones; the friction of revolving produces light and
heat; the earth stands, it is expressly said, still.   All
this might pass if there had not already been something
better; but when he himself, in chap. xiii., presents to
us the entirely correct views of the Pythagoreans on the
form, place, and motion of the earth in order to reject
them, it can hardly fail to arouse our indignation.   This
will rise when we see from his frequent polemic against
Empedokles, Herakleitos, and Demokritos, how all these
had much more correct insight into nature, and had even
attended to experience better, than the barren talker that
we have before us.   Empedokles had, indeed, already
taught a tangential force arising from revolution and acting in opposition to gravity (ii. 1 and 13, also the " Scholia,"
p. 491).   Far removed from being able to estimate this at
its true value, Aristotle does not even admit the correct
views of these ancients on the true significance of above
and below, but here also takes his stand on the
vulgar opinion which follows the superficial appearance
(iv., 2).   But we have further to bear in mind that these
his views found recognition and circulation, superseding
all that was earlier and better, and so became, later on
the foundation of Hipparchus, and afterward of the
Ptolemaic cosmology, with which mankind had to content
itself till the beginning of the sixteenth century, to the
great advantage, doubtless, of the Jewish-Christian reli-

gious dogmas, which are at bottom incompatible with the
Kopernican cosmology. (For how should there be a God
in heaven when there is no heaven?) Theism when
seriously meant, necessarily presupposes the division of
the world into heaven and earth; on the latter men run
about, in the former sits the God who rules them. But
if astronomy takes the heaven away, it has taken the God
with it also; it has, that is to say, so extended the world
that there is no room left for God. But a personal being,
such as every God must necessarily be, who has no place,
but is everywhere and nowhere, can merely be spoken of,
but not imagined, and therefore not believed in. To the
extent, accordingly, to which physical astronomy is
popularized, theism must wane, however much it may
have been impressed upon men by an unceasing and
pompous preaching. The Catholic Church rightly recognized this at once, and accordingly persecuted the Kopernican system; as regards which it is childish to wonder
and shriek over the crushing of Galilei, for *omnis natura
vult esse conservatrix sui.* Who knows whether a secret
knowledge, or at least presentiment, of this congeniality
of Aristotle to the doctrines of the Church, and of the
danger averted by him, did not contribute to the overweening adoration of him in the Middle Ages? Who
knows whether many a one, stimulated by his accounts
of the olden astronomical systems, had not secretly
penetrated these truths long before Kopernicus, who,
after many years of hesitation, and with the intention
of separating himself from the world finally ventured to
proclaim them?

SECTION 6.

STOICS.

A very beautiful and pregnant conception with the
Stoics, is that of the λόγος σπερματικός, although more complete accounts respecting it than those which have come
down to us might be desired ("Diog. Laert.," vii., 136;
"Plut. de Plac. Phil.," i., 7; "Stob. Ecl.," i., p. 372).

Thus much is clear, however, that what was understood thereby was that which in the successive individuals of a kind asserted and preserved its identical form, inasmuch as it passes over from the one to the other; as, for instance, the conception of the species embodied in the seed. The *Logos spermaticus* is accordingly the indestructible element in the individual, that, namely, through which it is one of a species representing and maintaining it. It is that by virtue of which the death which annihilates the individual does not touch the kind, which makes the individual continuously present in spite of death. Hence we might translate λόλος σπερματικός as the magical formula which at all times calls this form into the phenomenon. Nearly related to it is the conception of the *forma substantialis* of the Schoolmen, through which the inner principle of the complex of all the qualities of every natural being is thought; its antithesis is the *materia prima*, the pure matter, destitute of all form and quality. The soul of man is just his *forma substantialis*. What distinguishes both conceptions is, that the λόγος σπερματικός accrues solely to living and procreating beings, but the *forma substantialis* to inorganic beings also. The one refers, moreover, directly to the individual, the other directly to the kind; both, on the other hand, are obviously related to the Platonic idea. Explanations of the *forma substantialis* are to be seen in "Scotus Erigena de Divis. Nat.," lib. iii., p. 139 of the Oxford edition; in "Giordino Bruno, della Cosa," dial. 3, p. 252 *seq.*, and developed at length in the "Disputationibus Metaphsicis" of Suarez (disp. 15, sect. 1), that genuine compendium of the whole scholastic wisdom, where one should seek its acquaintance rather than in the bald placidity of soulless German professors of philosophy, the quintessence of all shallowness and tediousness.

One chief source of our knowledge of the Stoic ethics is the very complete presentation of them preserved for us by Stobæus ("Ecl. Eth.," 1. 2, c. vii.), in which one may flatter oneself that one possesses, for the most part, verbal extracts from Zeno and Chrysippus. If this be correct, it is not calculated to give us a high opinion of the spirit of these philosophers, seeing that it is a pedantic, pedagogic,

eminently bald, incredibly empty, flat and spiritless exposition of the Stoic morality, without force and life, and
without valuable, striking, or noble thoughts. Everything
in it is deduced from mere conceptions, and not drawn
from reality and experience. Mankind is accordingly
divided into σπουδαῖοι and φαῦλοι, virtuous and vicious; to
the former is attributed everything good, to the latter
everything bad, all things appearing in consequence black
and white, like a Prussian sentry-box. Assuredly these
dull school-exercises will not bear comparison with the
energetic, powerful, and well-thought-out paragraphs of
Seneca.

The dissertations of Arrian on the philosophy of Epictetus, composed some four hundred years after the origin
of the Stoa, give us no reliable information as to the
true spirit and the special principles of the Stoic ethics,
for the book is unsatisfactory both as to form and content. Firstly, as regards the form, one misses in it every
trace of method, of systematic treatment, and even of
orderly progression. In chapters tacked on to one another
without order and connection, it is untiringly repeated
that one should pay no attention to anything that is not
the expression of our own will, and that therefore everything that otherwise moves men should be regarded
completely without interest; this is the Stoic ἀταραξία.
That, namely, which is not ἐφ' ἡμῖν would also not be πρὸς
ἡμᾶς. This colossal paradox, however, is not deduced
from any principles at all, but the most extraordinary
opinion of the world is required of us without any ground
being given for it. Instead of this we find endless declamations in ceaselessly recurring phrases and turns of
expression. For the consequences of these wonderful
maxims are expounded in the most complete and vivid
manner, and we accordingly have described how the Stoics
make something from nothing at all. Meanwhile, everyone who thinks differently is unceasingly abused as a slave
and a fool. But one hopes in vain for the indication of any
clear and adequate ground for the assumption of this
remarkable mode of thought, although such would have
more effect than all the abuse and declamations of the
whole thick book. As it is, it is a true Capuchin's sermon,

with its hyperbolic descriptions of the Stoic apathy, its incessantly repeated panegyrics of the holy fathers Kleanthes, Chrysippos, Zeno, Krates, Diogenese, Sokrates, and its abuse of all who differ from them. To such a book is certainly suited the planless and desultory nature of the whole contents. What the heading of a chapter indicates is only the subject of its beginning; at the first opportunity a jump is made, and, as far as the *nexus idearum* is concerned, we pass from the hundredth to the thousandth. So much as to form.

As regards the content, it is the same; and even if we overlook the fact that the foundation is entirely wanting, it is at all events not genuine and thoroughly Stoical, but has a strong foreign admixture, which smacks of a Christian-Jewish source. The most undeniable proof of this is the theism which is to be found on every side and is also the support of the ethics; the Cynics and the Stoics act here on behalf of God, whose will is their guiding-star; they are devoted to him, hope in him, etc. The genuine, original Stoa is quite foreign to all this; God and the world are there one, and nothing is known of a God who thinks, wills, commands, and provides for men. Not alone in Arrian, however, but in most of the heathen philosophic writers of the first Christian century, we see the Jewish theism, destined ere long to become a popular creed in Christianity, already peering through, just as to-day there peers through the writings of scholars the pantheism native to India, which is also destined hereafter to pass over into the popular belief. *Ex oriente lux.*

For the reasons above given, the ethic here expounded is not purely Stoical. Many of its maxims are, indeed, mutually incompatible, hence no ground-principles common to it can be mentioned. In the same way Cynicism is entirely falsified by the doctrine that the Cynic should be such chiefly for the sake of others, namely, in order to act upon them by his example as commissioned by God, and in order by mixing in their affairs to guide them. Hence it is said, "In a city where there were only wise men, no Cynic would be necessary;" and, in the same way, that he should be healthy, strong, and cleanly, in order not to repel people. How far is this

from the self-satisfaction of the old genuine Cynics? It
is true Diogenes and Krates were the domestic friends
and advisers of many families; but that was secondary
and accidental, and in no wise the purpose of Cynicism.

Arrian has therefore entirely lost sight of the properly
fundamental idea of Cynicism as of the Stoic ethics; indeed he does not even seem to have felt the need of
them. He preaches self-renunciation because it pleases
him, and perhaps it only pleases him becuse it is difficult and opposed to human nature, while in the meantime the preaching is easy. He did not seek for the
grounds of self-renunciation; hence one thinks, now one
is listening to a Christian ascetic, now again to a Stoic.
For the maxims of both often concur, but the principles
on which they rest are quite different. I refer the reader
in this matter to my chief work (vol. i., § 16, and vol.
ii., chap. xvi.), where for the first time the true spirit
of Cynicism as of the Stoa is systematically expounded.

The inconsistency of Arrian presents itself, indeed, in
a ridiculous manner, in that he, with his countless times
repeated description of the Stoic, always says: "He
blames no one, complains neither of Gods nor of men,
scolds no one," while at the same time his whole book
is throughout conceived in a scolding tone, which often
descends to abuse.

Notwithstanding all this, there are here and there genuine Stoic thoughts to be met with in the book, which
Arrian or Epictetus had derived from the ancient Stoics;
and similarly Cynicism is in some of its features tellingly
and vividly depicted. In places there is also much sound
common sense, as well as descriptions, drawn from life,
of man and his doings. The style is easy and flowing,
but very bald.

That Epictetus' "Encheiridion" is also composed by
Arrian, as A. Wolfe assured us in his lectures, I do not
believe. It has much more spirit in fewer words than
the dissertations, is instinct throughout with sound sense,
has no empty declamations, no ostentation, is concise to
the point, and moreover written in the tone of a well-
meaning friend giving his advice; while, on the other
hand, the dissertations speak mostly in a scolding and

execrating tone. The content of both books is, on the whole, the same; only that the "Encheiridion" has very little of the theism of the dissertations. Perhaps the "Encheiridion" was Epictetus' own compendium, which he dictated to his hearers, but the dissertations the manuscript copied from the free discourse by his commentator Arrian.

SECTION 7.

NEOPLATONISTS.

The reading of the Neoplatonists requires much patience, since they fail entirely as regards form and style. Far better than the others in this respect is Porphyry. He is the only one who writes clearly and connectedly, so that one reads him without repulsion.

The worst, on the contrary, is Iamblichos, in his book "De Mysteriis Egyptiorum," which is full of crass superstition and crude demonology, besides being conceited. He has, it is true, another as it were esoteric opinion on magic and theurgy, but his statements concerning this are only flat and insignificant. On the whole, he is a bad and turgid writer, limited, distorted, grossly superstitious, confused, and unclear. One sees plainly that what he teaches has by no means arisen from his own reflection, but that they are foreign, often only half understood, but all the more strenuously asserted dogmas; hence, also, he is full of contradictions. But the book in question is now denied to be by Iamblichos, and I am inclined to agree with this opinion when I read the long extracts from his lost works preserved by Stobæus, and which are incomparably better than the book "De Mysteriis," containing as they do many good thoughts of the Neoplatonic school.

Proklos, again, is a dry, bald, insipid talker; his commentary to Plato's "Alkibiades," one of the worst of the Platonic dialogues, which, moreover, may be ungenuine, is the baldest, most diffuse piece of insipidity in the world. Over every, even the most insignificant, word of

Plato's there is endless talk, and deep meaning is sought
therein. What by Plato was said mythically and allegorically is taken in its literal sense and in a spirit of
rigid dogmatism, everything being twisted into the superstitious and the theosophical. It is, nevertheless, not to
be denied, that in the first half of this commentary some
very good ideas are to be met with, though they probably more strictly belong to the school than to Proklos
himself. It is a highly important proposition that closes
the *fasciculum primum partis primæ:* αἱ τῶν ψυχῶν ἐφέσεις τὰ
μέγιστα συντελοῦσι πρὸς τοὺς βίους, καὶ οὐ πλαττομένοις ἔξωθεν
ἐοίκαμεν, ἀλλ᾽ ἐφ᾽ ἑαυτῶν πίοβάλλομεν τὰς αἱρέσεις, καθ᾽ ἃς διάζωμεν
(*animorum appetitus* [*ante hanc vitam concepti*] *plurimam
vim habent in vitas eligendas, nec extrinsecus fictis similes
sumus, sed nostra sponte facimus electiones, secundum quas
deinde vitas transigimus*). This certainly has its root
in Plato, and approaches Plato's doctrine of intelligible
character, standing high above the dull and narrow
theories of the freedom of the individual will, that
can always do thus and otherwise, with which our
professors of philosophy—the catechism forever before
their eyes—content themselves up to the present day.
Augustine and Luther, for their part, had called in aid
election by grace. That was good enough for those God-
given times, when people were ready, if it pleased God
to go to the devil in God's name; but in our time refuge
can only be taken in aseity of the will, and it must be
acknowledged that, as Proklos has it, οὐ πλαττομένοις ἔξωθεν
ἐοίκαμεν.

Plotinos, finally, the most important of all, is very
unequal, and the various "Enneads" are of extremely diverse value and content; the fourth is excellent. Exposition and style are, however, for the most part, very
bad with him; his thoughts are not ordered nor previously considered, but he writes them down just as they
come. Porphyry in his biography tells us of the loose,
careless way in which he set to work. Hence his bald
tedious diffuseness and confusion often overcomes all patience, so that one wonders how such stuff could have
come down to the modern world. He usually has the
style of a pulpit preacher, and as the latter sets forth

the gospel, so he sets forth the Platonic doctrines. At
the same time, what Plato has said mythically or half
metaphorically, he drags down to intentional prosaic seriousness, and chews at the same thought for hours without adding anything to it from his own resources. In
this he proceeds authoritatively, and not demonstratively,
speaking throughout *ex tripode;* explains the matter as he
thinks it to be, without attempting to lay any foundation for it. And yet there are great, important, and
pregnant truths to be found in his works, and these he
certainly understood himself, for he is by no means without insight; for which reason he undoubtedly deserves to
be read, and richly rewards the patience necessary thereto.

The explanation of these characteristics of Plotinos I
find in the fact that he and the Neoplatonists generally
are not properly philosophers, are not original thinkers,
but that what they expound is an alien, traditional doctrine, notwithstanding that it has been well digested and
assimilated by them. It is, namely, Indo-Egyptian wisdom, which they sought to embody in the Greek philosophy, and as a suitable connective tissue — a conduit or
menstruum for this — they use the Platonic philosophy,
especially those parts of it which branch off into the
mystical. To the Indian origin, through Egypt, of the
Neoplatonic dogmas, the All-One doctrine of Plotinos testifies directly and unmistakably, as we find it admirably
presented in the fourth "Ennead." Even the first chapter of the first book of the latter, περὶ οὐσίας ψυχῆς, gives
in great brevity the ground doctrines of his whole philosophy of the ψυχή, which is originally one, and is only
sundered into many by means of the corporeal world.
Particularly interesting is the eighth book of this "Ennead," which shows how the ψυχή has reached this state
of multiplicity by a sinful striving. It carries, accordingly, a double guilt; firstly, that of its descent into this
world, and secondly, that of its sinful deeds in the same;
the former it expiates by its temporal existence generally,
the latter, which is the less important, by transmigration
(c. 5). This is obviously the same thought as the Christian original sin and particular sin. But above all worthy
of being read is the ninth book, where, in chap. iii., εἰ

πᾶσαι αἱ ψυχαὶ μία, from the unity of the above world
soul, among other things, the wonders of animal magnetism are explained, especially the phenomenon even
now observed, that the somnambule hears a softly spoken
word at the greatest distance, though this, of course,
requires a chain of persons standing *en rapport* with her.
With Plotinos, moreover, there appears, probably for the
first time in Western philosophy, the Idealism already
long current in the East, inasmuch as it is taught
("Enn.," iii., 1. 7, c. 10) that the soul has made the world
in its process from eternity into time with the explanation: οὐ γάρ τις αὐτοῦ τοῦδε τοῦ πάντος τόπος, ἢ ψυχὴ (*neque
est alter hujus universi locus, quam anima*), while the
ideality of time is expressed in the words: δεῖ δὲ οὐκ ἔξωθεν
τῆς ψυχῆς λαμβάνειν τὸν χρόνον, ὥσπερ οὐδὲ τὸν αἰῶνα ἐκεῖ ἔξω τοῦ
ὄντος (*oportet autem nequaquam extra animan tempus accipere*). That ἐκεῖ (hereafter) is the opposite of ἐνθάδε
(here), and a very favorite conception, with him, which
he more nearly explains by κόσμος ροητός and κόσμος αἰσθητός
mundus intelligibilis et sensibilis, also by τὰ ἄνω, καὶ τὰ κάτω.
The ideality of time receives, in chapters xi. and xii.,
very good elucidation. Attached thereto is the beautiful
explanation, that we, in our temporal condition, are not
what we ought to be and might be; hence, that we
always expect better things of the future, and look toward
the fulfillment of that which is wanting to us, whence
arises the future and its condition time (c. 2 *et* 3). A
further confirmation of the Indian origin is afforded us by
Iamblichos ("De Mysteriis," sect. 4, c. 4 *et* 5), in his exposition of the doctrine of Metempsychosis, where also
may be found (sect. 5, c. 6), the doctrine of the finite
liberation and salvation from the bonds of birth and
death, ψυχῆς καθαρσις, καὶ τελείωσις, καὶ ἡ ἀπὸ τῆς γενέσεως
ἀπαλλαγή, and (c. 12) τὸ ἐν ταῖς θυσίαις πῦρ ἡμᾶς ἀπόλυει τῶν
τῆς γενέσεως δεσμῶν, in other words, the promise contained in all Indian religious books, which is designated
in English by FINAL EMANCIPATION or salvation. In addition to this there is, lastly (a. a. o., sect. 7, c. 2), the
account of an Egyptian symbol which represents a creative God sitting on the lotus; obviously the world-creating
Brahma sitting on the lotus-flower, corresponding to the

navel of Vishnu, as he is frequently represented, *e.g.*, in Langles, "Monuments de l'Hindoustan," vol. i., ad p. 175; in Coleman's "Mythology of the Hindus," tab. 5, etc. This symbol is extremely important as a sure proof of the Hindu origin of the Egyptian religion, as, in the same respect, is the report also given by Porphyry "De Abstinentia," lib. ii., that in Egypt the cow was holy, and might not be slaughtered. Even the circumstance related by Porphyry in his life of Plotinos, that the latter, after he had been for many years the disciple of Ammonius Saccas, had intended going with the army of Gordian to Persia and India, but was prevented by the overthrow and death of Gordian, indicates that the doctrines of Ammonius were of Indian origin, and that Plotinos had intended, at last, to acquire them more purely from their source. The same Porphyry furnished a complete theory on Metempsychosis, which is conceived entirely in the Indian spirit, although impregnated with the Platonic Psychology; it is given in the Stobæos "Eclogues," 1. i., c. 52, § 54.

SECTION 8.

THE GNOSTICS.

The Cabalistic and Gnostic philosophies, with whose originators, as Jews and Christians, Monotheism stood in the forefront, are attempts to get rid of the flagrant contradiction between the production of this world by an almighty, all-good, and all-wise being, and the sadly deficient construction of the same world. They introduce, therefore, between the world and the world-cause a series of intermediate beings, by whose fault a decline, and thereby the world, has arisen; hence they roll off the fault, as it were, from the sovereign on to his ministers. This proceeding had already been indicated in the myth of the fall, which is in every way the culminating point of Judaism. These beings are, with the Gnostics, the πλήρωμα, the æons, the ϑλη, the demiurgos, etc. The series was lengthened at pleasure by each Gnostic.

The whole proceeding is analogous to that whereby, in order to modify the contradiction involved in the assumed connection and reciprocal action of a material and immaterial substance in man, physiological philosophers have sought to interpose mediate essences, such as nervous fluidity, nervous ether, vital spirits, and so forth. Both seek to hide what they are not able to abolish.

SECTION 9.

SCOTUS ERIGENA.

This remarkable man affords us the interesting spectacle of the struggle between recognized and apprehended truth and local dogmas, fixed by early indoctrination and grown beyond the reach of all doubt, or at least of all direct attack, side by side with the endeavor proceeding from a noble nature to reduce to harmony, by some means or other, the dissonance which had thus arisen. This can indeed only happen, in so far as the dogmas are turned, twisted, and where necessary distorted, until *nolentes volentes* they fit into the recognized truth, which remains the dominating principle, but is, notwithstanding, obliged to go about in a strange and uncomfortable garb. Erigena knows how to carry out this method, and his great work, "De Divisione Naturæ," is a complete success until at last he has to make up his account with the origin of evil and of sin, together with the threatened pains of hell, when he comes to grief, more particularly in the optimism which is a consequence of his Jewish Monotheism. He teaches in the fifth book the return of all things to God, and the metaphysical unity and indivisibility of all humanity, and even of all nature. The question now arises, where does sin remain? It cannot be with God. Where is hell, with its endless pains, such as have been promised? Who is to go there? Humanity is saved, and that in its entirety. The dogma here remains unconquerable. Erigena writhes miserably through diffuse sophisms, which turn in the end on words,

and is finally driven to contradiction and absurdity, especially since the question as to the origin of sin has inevitably crept in, and yet the latter can neither lie in God nor in the will created by him, since otherwise God would be the originator of sin, which last point he sees clearly (see p. 287 of the Oxford *editio princeps* of 1681). He is now driven to absurdities: sin must have neither a cause nor a subject: *malum incausale est . . . penitus incausale et insubstantiale est* (*Ibid.*). The true cause of this stumbling-block is, that the doctrine of the EMANCIPATION of humanity and the world, which is obviously of Indian origin, presupposes the Indian doctrine according to which the origin of the world (this Sansara of the Buddhists) is itself evil, proceeding, namely, from a sinful act of Brahma, which Brahma, again, we ourselves are, for the Indian mythology is everywhere transparent. On the contrary, in Christianity this doctrine of the emancipation of the world had to be based on the Jewish Theism, where the Lord not only made the world, but afterward found it very good: παντα καλὰ λίαν. *Hinc illæ lacrimæ:* hence arise those difficulties which Erigena fully recognized, although he, in his age, did not venture to attack the evil by the root. Meanwhile he has the Hindustanic mildness. He rejects the eternal damnation and punishment asserted by Christianity. All creatures rational, animal, vegetable, and lifeless must, according to their inner essence, in the necessary course of nature, attain to eternal happiness, for they have proceeded from the eternally good. But only for the saints and righteous is the complete unity with God, *Deificatio.* For the rest, Erigena is sufficiently honest as not to hide the great embarrassment in which the origin of evil places him; he expounds it clearly in the passage quoted in the fifth book. As a matter of fact, the origin of evil is the rock on which Theism, no less than Pantheism, splits, for both imply Optimism. But evil and sin, both in their fearful magnitude, are not to be explained away, while the threatened punishments for the latter only increase the former. Whence all this, now, in a world which is either itself a God, or the well-intentioned work of a God? If the theistic opponents of Pantheism exclaim against it, "What! all evil, terrible, abominable

11

entities are God?" the Pantheists may reply: "How! all these evil, terrible, abominable entities have been produced by a God *de gaieté de cœur*." We find Erigena in the same difficulty in the other work of his which has come down to us, viz, in the book, "De Predestinatione," which nevertheless is far inferior to the "De Divisione Naturæ," and where he appears, not in the character of philosopher, but of theologian. Here also he plagues himself miserably with contradictions having their ultimate ground in the fact that Christianity is founded on Judaism. But his endeavors place them only in a still clearer light. God is all, all and in all, and has made all; thus much is fixed, "consequently also sin and evil." This inevitable consequence has to be got rid of, and Erigena finds himself necessitated to put forward the most miserable word-juggles. If evil and sin are not, then nothing is—not even the devil! Or else freewill is to blame for it. God has indeed created this, but created it free, and therefore it concerns him not what it does afterward. For it was FREE, that is, it could act so and otherwise; it might therefore be just as well good as bad. Bravo! but the truth is that free being and created being are two mutually destructive and therefore contradictory qualities; hence the assumption that God has created beings, and has at the same time imparted to them freedom of will, is as much as to say that he has created them, and at the same time he has not created them. For *operari sequitur esse, i. e.*, the effects or actions of any possible thing can never be anything else than the consequences of its nature, which is only known through them. Hence a being, in order to be free in the sense here required, must have no nature, that is, must be nothing, or, in other words, must both be and not be at once. For what IS must also be SOMETHING; an existence without essence cannot even be thought. If a being is created, it is created as it is created, and therefore it is badly created if it IS badly created, and badly created if it acts badly, *i. e.*, its effects are bad. As a consequence the guilt of the world, which is just as little to be explained away as its evil, always shifts itself back on its originator, and Scotus Erigena, like Augustine before him, is pitiably occupied in endeavoring to relieve him of it.

If, on the other hand, a being is morally free, it cannot have been created, but must have aseity, that is, must be an original thing existing by virtue of his own power and completeness, and not referable to another. Its existence is then its own act of creation, which unfolds and expands itself in time, exhibiting once for all the distinct character of this being, which is, nevertheless, its own work, for all of whose manifestations the responsibility rests upon itself alone. If, now, a being is responsible for its action — if it is to be accountable— it must be free. Thus, from the responsibility and imputability which our conscience declares, it follows very certainly that the will is free, but from this, again, that it is the original thing itself, and hence, that not merely the action, but also the existence and essence of man are his own work. Respecting all this I refer the reader to my treatise on the freedom of the will, where it will be found completely and irrefutably expounded. For this reason the professors of philosophy have sought, by the most complete silence, to boycott this crowned prize essay of mine. The guilt of sin and evil necessarily falls from nature back on its author. But if the latter is Will manifesting itself in all its phenomena, the guilt has come back to the right man; if, on the contrary, it is a God, the origin of sin and evil contradict his divinity.

In reading Dionysius Areopagita, to whom Erigena so often refers, I have found that the former is in every respect his prototype. The pantheism of Erigena, as well as his theory of sin and evil, are to be found, in their main features at least, already in Dionysius, although Dionysius only indicates what Erigena has developed, expressed with boldness, and expounded with fire. Erigena had infinitely more genius than Dionysius, but Dionysius had given him the material and the direction of his reflections, and consequently prepared the way for him. That Dionysius is ungenuine does not affect the question, since it is indifferent what the author of the book "De Divinis Nominibus" was called. As he, in the meantime, probably lived in Alexandria, I believe that, in a

roundabout way unknown to us, he was the channel
through which a drop of Indian wisdom may have reached
Erigena, since, as Colebrooke has observed in his treatise
on the philosophy of the Hindus (in Colebrooke's "Miscellaneous Essays," vol. i., p. 244), the proposition III, of
the "Karika of Kapila" is to be found in Erigena.

Section 10.

SCHOLASTICISM.

I should place the properly distinctive character of
Scholasticism in that its chief criterion of truth is Scripture, to which one may always appeal from every conclusion of reason. To its specialities belongs, that its
style has throughout a polemical character. Every investigation is soon transformed into a controversy, whose
pro et contra generate new *pro et contra*, and thereby
furnish its material, which without it would soon run
dry. The hidden ultimate root of this speciality consists, however, in the antagonism between Reason and
Revelation.

The reciprocal justification between Realism and Nominalism, and thereby the possibility of the so long and
obstinately fought-out quarrel, may be rendered intelligible in the following way.

I call the most diverse things RED if they have this
color. Obviously RED is a mere name by which I designate this phenomenon, no matter where it appears. In
the same way all common notions are mere names to
designate qualities appearing in diverse things. These
things, on the contrary, are the actual and real, so that
NOMINALISM is obviously right.

On the other hand, when we observe that all those
actual things, of which alone reality can be predicated,
are temporal, and consequently pass away, while the
qualities, as red, hard, soft, life, plant, horse, man, which
these names signify, continue to exist irrespective of this,
and consequently are always there, we find that the
qualities which these names designate by means of com-

mon conceptions, are conceived through their indestructible existence, and therefore have reality, which is
consequently to be attributed to the conceptions, and
not to the particular being, whence it follows that Realism is right.

Nominalism leads directly to Materialism, for after the
removal of all qualities matter alone remains in the last
resort.   If conceptions are mere names, and the singular
things the. Real, their qualities as partaking of their
singular nature would be transient.   There remains, therefore, as that which continues, which is real, only matter.
But, strictly speaking, the justification of realism above
given does not belong to it, but to the Platonic doctrine
of ideas, of which it is the extension.   The eternal forms
and qualities of natural things, εἴδη, it is which subsist
through all change, and to which therefore a reality of
a higher kind is to be attributed than to the individuals
in which they display themselves.   On the contrary, this
cannot be conceded to the mere abstractions, which are
not perceivable.   What, for example, is the Real in such
conceptions as "relation, difference, separation, injury,
indeterminateness," etc.?

A certain relation, or at least a parallelism, of apposi-
tions is discernable when one places Plato against Aristotle, Augustine against Pelagius, the Realists against
the Nominalists.   One might even assert that there is a
certain kind of polar repulsion of thought manifested
here, which, by a most extraordinary coincidence, expressed itself for the first time, and most decisively, in
two very great men, who happened to be contemporary,
and to live near each other.

SECTION II.

BACON OF VERULAM.

In another and more specifically definite sense than
that indicated, the express and intentional antithesis to
Aristotle was Bacon of Verulam.   The former, namely,
had for the first time systematically expounded the correct

method of attaining from universal to particular truths, in other words, the way downward, which is the same as the syllogism, the *organum Aristotelis*. On the other hand, Bacon exhibited the way upward, in so far as he expounded the method of attaining from special to general truths. This is induction in contradistinction to deduction, and its exposition is the *novum organum*, which expression, chosen in opposition to Aristotle, says in effect,—"It is quite a different manner of attacking the subject." The error of Aristotle, or rather the error of the Aristotelians, lay in the assumption that they already possessed all truth—that truth, namely, is contained in their axioms, to wit, in certain *a priori* propositions, or propositions which count for such, and that, in order to gain particular truths, deduction from the former is all that is necessary. An Aristotelian instance of this is given in the books "De Cœlo." Bacon shows on the contrary, with justice, that the above axioms did not have such a content, that the truth did not lie at all in the system of human knowledge at that time in vogue, but rather outside it, and that therefore it was not to be developed from it, but had to be introduced into it, and that as a consequence universal and true propositions of a great and rich content had first to be won through INDUCTION.

The Schoolmen, led by Aristotle, thought, we will in the first place establish the universal; the particular will flow therefrom, or may afterward find a place therein as it can. We will, therefore, first of all establish what accrues to the ENS, to the thing IN GENERAL. The speciality of particular things may afterward be gradually added, and of course through experience, but the latter can never alter anything in the universal. Bacon said, rather, we will in the first instance learn to know the individual things as completely as possible, then we shall at last know what the thing in general is.

Meanwhile, Bacon is inferior to Aristotle in so far as his method, leading upward, is never so accurate, certain, and infallible as that of Aristotle, leading downward. Indeed, Bacon himself has, in his physical investigations, set aside the rules of his method as given in the "New Organon."

Bacon's attention was chiefly turned to physical science. What he did for this, to wit, beginning from the beginning, Descartes did immediately afterward for metaphysics.

Section 12.

THE PHILOSOPHY OF THE MODERNS.

In the arithmetic books the accuracy of the solution of an example is wont to be announced by the balancing of the same, that is, by the fact that no remainder is left. With the resolution of the riddle of the world it is similar. All systems are sums which do not balance; they leave a remainder, or, if a chemical simile be preferred, an unresolved deposit. This consists in that, if one draws a correct conclusion from their premises, the results do not answer to the real world lying before us, but rather that many sides of it remain on the hypothesis quite inexplicable. Thus, for example, with the materialistic systems, which make the world arise from a matter possessed of simply mechanical qualities and in accordance with their laws, neither the complete and remarkable adaptability of ends to means in nature, nor the existence of consciousness in which this same matter is first presented, agree. This then is their remainder. With the theistic systems, on the contrary, and not more so with the pantheistic, the overweening physical evils and the moral obliquity of the world cannot be brought into harmony. These, therefore, stand over as a remainder, or lie as an unresolved deposit. It is true that in such cases there is no lack of sophisms, or, where necessary, of mere words and phrases in order to cover up such remainders, but such devices will not hold water for long. Individual errors in the reckoning are then sought for, since the sum will not balance, until finally it is obliged to be confessed that the starting point has been wrong. If, again, the thorough-going consequence and harmony of all the propositions of a system be accompanied at every step by a similar thorough-going

harmony with the world of experience, without any dis-
cord being audible between the two, this is the criterion
of its truth, the required balancing of the arithmetical
sum. In the same way, if the starting point has been
false, it is as much to say that from the beginning the
matter has not been seized by the right end, whereby
one is afterward led from error to error, for in philosophy, as in many other things, everything turns on
whether one seizes it by the right end. But the phenomena of the world which have to be explained present
countless ends to us, of which one only can be the right
one; they resemble an intricate tangle of thread, with
many false end-threads hanging from it. He who finds
out the right one can disentangle the whole. But one
there is which disentangles itself easily from the others,
and from this it may be known that it is the right
end. One may also compare it to a labyrinth, which
offers a hundred entrances, opening out into corridors,
all of which, after various long and intricate windings,
finally lead out again, with the exception of a single one,
whose windings really take us to the centre, where the
idol stands. If one has hit upon this entrance one will
not fail to find the way, but one can never attain to the
goal by any other way. I do not conceal my opinion
that only the Will in us is the right end of the thread-
tangle, the true entrance to the labyrinth.

Now Descartes proceeded on the example of the metaphysics of Aristotle and the conception of substance, and
therewith we see also all his successors accommodate
themselves. He assumed, however, two kinds of substance, the thinking and the extended. These were supposed to act on one another through the *influxus physicus*,
which soon proved itself to be his remainder. It took
place, namely, not merely from without inward, in the
presentment of the corporeal world, but also from within
outward, between the Will (which was unhesitatingly assigned to thought) and the actions of the body. The
closer relations between these two kinds of substance
were the main problem on account of which such great
difficulties arose, and in consequence of which men were
driven to the system of *causes occasionelles* and of the

harmonia præstabilita, after the *spiritus animales* which had sufficed for the matter with Descartes, would no longer serve. Malebranche, for instance, holds the *influxus physicus* for unthinkable; but in this he does not take into consideration that the same thing is assumed without question in the creation and direction of the corporeal world by a God who is also a spirit. He replaces it therefore by the *cause causionelle* and *nous voyons tout en Dieu* — here lies his remainder. Spinoza, also, treading in the footsteps of his teacher, proceeded from the above conception of substance just as though it were a given thing. He nevertheless declared both kinds of substance, the thinking and extended, for one and the same, whereby the old difficulty was avoided. For this reason, however, his philosophy was chiefly negative, hinging on a mere negation of the two great Cartesian antitheses, for he also extended his identification to the other antithesis erected by Descartes, God and the World. The latter was nevertheless, properly speaking, a mere mode of teaching or form of presentation. It would have been too offensive to have said straight out: "It is not true that God has made this world, but it exists by its own perfection of power;" hence he chose an indirect phrase, and said: "The world itself is God;" to maintain which would never have occurred to him, if instead of proceeding from Judaism, he had started straightforwardly from nature itself. This phrase served at the same time to give his doctrines the appearance of positivity, though they are at bottom merely negative; and he therefore leaves the world unexplained, in that his doctrines issue in: "The world is because it is; and is as it is because it so is." (With this phrase Fichte was accustomed to mystify his students.) The deification of the world, arisen in the above manner, did not admit of any true ethics, and was, besides, in flagrant contradiction with the physical evils and the moral recklessness of this world. Here, then, is Spinoza's remainder.

The conception of substance from which Spinoza starts, he regards, as already said, as something given. He, indeed, defines it according to its ends, but he does not trouble himself as to its origin. For it was Locke, who, shortly after him, propounded the great doctrine that a philosopher, who wishes to deduce or demonstrate anything from conceptions, has in the first place to investigate the origin of such conception; for its content and what follows therefrom is determined entirely by its origin, as the source of all knowledge attainable by means of the same. But had Spinoza investigated the origin of this conception of substance, he must have found at last that it is simply MATTER, and therefore that the true content of the conception is nothing other than its essential and *a priori* assignable qualities. Indeed, everything attributed by Spinoza to his substance finds its confirmation in matter, and only there; it is uncaused, that is, causeless, eternal, singular, and unique, and its modifications are extension and consciousness, the latter, of course, as the exclusive quality of the brain. Spinoza is, therefore, an unconscious materialist, yet the matter, which, when carried out, realizes and empirically confirms his conceptions, is not the falsely-assumed and atomistic matter of Demokritos and of the later French materialists, which has none but mechanical qualities, but a correctly conceived matter, with all its inexplicable qualities attached to it; for this distinction I refer the reader to my chief work, vol. ii., chap. xxiv., p. 315 *seq.* (3d ed., p. 357 *seq.*). This method of assuming the conception of SUBSTANCE unnoticed, in order to make it the starting point, we find already with the Eleatics, as may especially be seen from the Aristotelean book "De Xenophane," etc. For Xenophanes also proceeds from the $\delta\nu$, that is, from substance, and its qualities are demonstrated without its previously being questioned or its being asked whence he has his knowledge of such a thing. If this had been done it would clearly have appeared what he was really speaking about, that is, what perception ultimately lies at the foundation of his conception and imparts to it reality, and in the end it would have been seen to be matter only, of which all that he says is true. In the following chapters on Zeno the coincidence with Spinoza extends itself even to the style and the expression. One can therefore scarcely refrain from assuming that Spinoza had known and used this work, since at his time, Aristotle, even though attacked by Bacon, still stood in high reputation, and good editions with Latin version were to be had. In this case Spinoza would be a mere resuscitator of the Eleatics as Gassendi was of Epicurus. We see once more, then, how extremely rare in any department of thought or knowledge is the really new and wholly original.

The above procedure of Spinoza on the conception of substance, moreover, rests, especially in its formal aspect, on the false assumption which he had taken over from his teacher Descartes, and he in his turn from Anselm of Canterbury, to wit, that *existentia* could proceed from *essentia*, *i.e.*, that from mere conception an existence could be deduced which would accordingly be a necessary one; or, in other words, that by virtue of the nature or definition of something merely THOUGHT, it should be necessary that it should be no longer something merely thought, but something really existent. Descartes had applied this false assumption to the conception of the *ens perfectissimum;* but Spinoza took that of *substantia* or *causa sui* (which latter expresses a *contradictio in adjecto*); see his first definition, which is his πρῶτον ψεῦδος in the introduction of the « Ethics, » and then proposition 7 of the first book. The difference between the basal conceptions of both philosophers consists almost entirely in expression, but their employment as starting points, that is as given, is with the one as with the other founded on the mistake of making a perceptual arise out of an abstract presentment; while in truth all abstract presentment arises from the perceptual, and is therefore based on the latter. We have here, therefore, a fundamental ὕστερον πρότερον.

Spinoza encumbered himself with a special difficulty by calling his one and only substance *Deus*, for since this word was already in use for the designation of quite another conception, he had continually to fight against misunderstandings which arose from it; the reader, instead of the conception assigned to it by Spinoza's first explanations, always attaching to it that which it otherwise signifies. If he had not employed the **word he**

would have been relieved of long and tedious expositions
in the first book. But he did so in order that his doctrines might find less opposition, an object in which he
nevertheless failed. In consequence, a certain double
sense pervades his whole exposition, which one might in
a manner term allegorical, especially as he adopts the
same plan with one or two other notions, as already observed (in the first essay). How much clearer, and consequently better, would his so-called "Ethics" have
turned out if he had spoken straightforwardly what was
in his mind, and called things by their name; and if he
had presented his thoughts, together with their grounds,
in an upright and natural manner, instead of making
them appear laced-up in the Spanish boots of propositions, demonstrations, scholia, and corollaries, in a garb
borrowed from geometry, which, instead of giving to
philosophy the certainty of the former, loses all significance as soon as geometry, with its construction of conceptions, ceases to stand inside it, whence the motto here
applies, *cucullus non facit monicum.*

In the second book he expounds the two modes of his
one substance as extension and presentment (*extensio et
cogitatio*), which is obviously a false division, since extension exists only for and in presentment, and ought
therefore to have been, not opposed, but subordinated,
to the latter.

Spinoza everywhere expressly and emphatically sounds
the praises of *lætitia*, and sets it up as condition and
sign of every praiseworthy action, while he rejects unconditionally all *tristitia* — although his Old Testament
might have told him, "Sorrow is better than laughter,
for by the sadness of the countenance the heart is made
glad" ("Ecclesiastes" vii. 3) — he does all this merely
for love of logicality, for if this world is a God, it is an
end to itself, and must glorify and rejoice at its own existence — *saute marquis! Semper* merry, *nunquam* sad!
Pantheism is essentially and necessarily optimism. This
compulsory optimism forces Spinoza to many other false
consequences, among which the absurd and very often
monstrous results of his moral philosophy take the first
rank, rising indeed in the sixteenth chapter of his "Trac-

tatus Theologico Politicus" to true infamy. On the other hand, at times he leaves the consequences out of sight,
where they would have led to correct views, as for instance in his as unworthy as false deliverances about
animals. (" Eth.," pars IV., appendices, cap. 26, ete jusdem
partis, prop. 37, " Scholion.") He speaks here, as a Jew
knows how, according to the first and ninth chapters of
Genesis, so that we, who are accustomed to purer and
worthier doctrines, are overpowered by the *fœtor judai-
cus.* Dogs he seems not to have known at all. To the
monstrous proposition with which the twenty-sixth chapter referred to opens, *præter homines nihil singulare in natura novimus, cujus mente gaudere et quod nobis amicitia,
aut aliquo consuetudinis genere jungere possumus,* the best
answer is given by a Spanish literateur of our day (" Lar-
ra," pseudonym " Figaro" in " Doncel," c. 33), *el que no
hà tenido un perro, no sabe lo que es querer y ser querido* (He
who has never kept a dog does not know what it is to
love and beloved).   The cruelties which, according to Cole-
rus, Spinoza for his amusement and amid hearty laughter was accustomed to practice on spiders and flies, coincide only too well with the propositions here attacked,
as also with the chapters of Genesis referred to.   Notwithstanding all this, Spinoza's " Ethica" is without doubt
a mixture of false and true, of the admirable and the
bad.   Toward the end, in the second half of the last
part, we see him in vain endeavoring to make himself
clear to himself.   He cannot do it, and therefore nothing remains for him but to become MYSTICAL, as happens
here.   But in order not to be unjust to this certainly
great mind we must consider that he had too little before him, hardly more than Descartes, Malebranche,
Hobbes, and Giordano Bruno.   The basal philosophical
conceptions were as yet insufficiently worked out, the
problems inadequately ventilated.

Leibnitz started similarly from the conception of substance as a given thing, but kept chiefly before him the
fact that it must be INDESTRUCTIBLE.   For this purpose it
must be simple since everything extended is divisible,
and hence destructible; it was, consequently, without extension, and therefore immaterial.   There remains then

no other predicates for his substance than the spiritual
ones of perception, thought, and desire. He assumed a
number of such simple, spiritual substances, which, although they are themselves unextended, lie at the foundation of the phenomenon of extension; hence he defines
them as formal atoms and simple substances, and bestows
upon them the name MONADS. These, therefore, lie at
the foundation of the phenomenon of the corporeal world,
which is, accordingly, a mere APPEARANCE without proper
and immediate reality, such merely accruing to the
monads, that remain within and behind it. The phenomenon of the corporeal world is, notwithstanding, on the
other side, in the perception of the monads (*i.e.*, those
that really perceive, which are very few, most of them
continuously sleeping) brought about by virtue of the
pre-established harmony, which the central monad produces entirely alone and at its own cost. We here get
somewhat into the dark. But, however this may be, the
connection between the mere thoughts of these substances
and the really and in itself extended, is regulated by a
pre-established harmony of the central monad. Here one
might say all is remainder. Meanwhile, in order to deal
justly with Leibnitz, we must remind the reader of the
way of regarding matter, which Locke and Newton had
made current, whereby, namely, matter exists as absolutely
dead, purely passive, and will-less, merely endowed with
mechanical forces, and only subordinated to mathematical
laws. Now Leibnitz rejects the ATOMS and the purely
MECHANICAL physics in order to put in its place a DYNAMI-
CAL, in all of which he prepared the way for Kant. (See
"Opera," edit. Erdmann, p. 694.) He recalls in the first
place the *formas substantialis* of the schoolmen, and attains
accordingly to the insight, that even the merely mechanical forces of matter, besides which, at that time scarcely
any others were known or admitted, must have something spiritual at their foundation. But he did not know
how to make this clear to himself otherwise than by the
extremely unhappy fiction that matter consisted of simple
souls, which were at the same time formal atoms, and
which, although existing for the most part in a state of
unconsciousness, nevertheless possessed an *analogon* of the

perceptio and the *appetitus.* This consequently misled him, so that he, like all the rest, made Knowledge the foundation and *conditio sine qua non* of everything spiritual rather than Will, the priority due to which I have been the first to vindicate, everything in philosophy being thereby turned round. In the meantime Leibnitz's endeavor to base spirit and matter on one and the same principle deserves recognition. One might even find therein a presentiment as well of the Kantian as of my own doctrines, but *quas velut trans nebulam vidit.* For his "Monadology" is based on the idea that matter is nothing in itself, but merely phenomenon, and that therefore the ultimate ground of even its mechanical action must not be sought in the purely geometrical, that is in what belongs to the phenomenon, such as extension, motion, figure, etc., and hence that impenetrability is not a mere negative quality, but the manifestation of a positive force. The opinion of Leibnitz we have praised is expressed most clearly in some of his smaller French writings, as the *Système nouveau de la nature*, etc., which are collected from the "Journal des Savans" in the edition of Dütens, in the edition of Erdmann, and in the letters, etc., (Erdmann, pp. 681–95.) There is also to be found a well-chosen collection of cognate passages of Leibnitz on pp. 335–40 of his "Smaller philosophical writings, translated by Köhler and revised by Huth," Jena, 1740.

But we see throughout this whole chain of strange dogmatic theories one fiction continually being brought to the support of another, just as in practical life one lie makes many others necessary. At the bottom of it lies Descartes' division of all existence into God and world, and of man into spirit and matter, to the last of which everything else is counted. To this must be added the error, common to him and to all philosophers who have ever yet been, of placing the final ground of our being in knowledge rather than in will, in other words, in making the latter the secondary, and the former the primary. These, then, were the original errors against which nature and the reality of things protested at every step, and to save which, the *spiritus animales*, the materiality of animals, the occasional causes, the seeing all things in God, the

pre-established harmony, the monads, optimism, and all
the rest of it, had to be invented. With me, on the
contrary, where things are seized by the right end, everything fits in of itself, everything appears in its proper
light, no fictions are required, and *simplex sigillum veri*.

Kant was not directly touched by the substance problem — he had got beyond it. With him the conception
of substance is a category, that is, a mere form of thought
a priori. By this, in its necessary application to sensible
perception, nothing is known as it is in itself; hence the
being which is at the foundation of bodies no less than
of souls is in itself one and the same. This is his doctrine. It paved the way for me to the insight that each
one's body is only the perception of his will arising in
his brain, a relation which, extended afterward to all
bodies, resulted in the resolution of the world into Will
and Presentment.

The conception of substance, however, which Descartes,
true to Aristotle, had constituted the leading conception
of his philosophy, and with whose definition, accordingly
(although in the fashion of the Eleatics), Spinoza also
starts, proclaims itself, when subjected to more rigorous
and honest investigation, as a higher but unjustified
abstractum of the conception of MATTER, which, by the
way, also includes the supposititious child, IMMATERIAL
SUBSTANCE, as I have already explained in my "Criticisms
of the Kantian Philosophy," pp. 550 *seq.* of the 2d ed.
(3d ed. 528–31 *seq.*). But apart from this the conception
of SUBSTANCE is invalid as the starting point of philosophy,
because it is in all cases an OBJECTIVE one. Nothing
objective is, for us, more than MEDIATE; the subjective
alone is the IMMEDIATE. This must not be passed over,
therefore, but must be made the absolute starting point.
Descartes has certainly done this; indeed, he was the
first who recognized it, and hence with him a new epoch
in philosophy opens. But he does it merely preliminarily
at the first starting off, after which he at once assumes
the absolute objective reality of the world on the credit
of the veracity of God, and from this time forward philos-
ophizes in an entirely objective manner. In this he is
guilty, in addition, of a noteworthy *circulus vitiosus*. He

demonstrates the objective reality of the objects of all our perpetual presentments from the existence of God as their author, whose veracity does not admit of his deceiving us. But the existence of God himself he demonstrates from the innate presentment which we are supposed to have of him as the all-perfect being. "*Il commence par douter de tout, et finit par tout croire,*" says one of his countrymen of him.

It was Berkeley who first showed himself in true earnest with the subjective starting point, and who irrefutably explained the indispensable necessity of it. He is the father of Idealism, which is the foundation of all true philosophy, and which has since then at least been universally retained as a starting point, although every successive philosopher has made his own modifications and variations of it. Thus even Locke started from the subjective, in that he ascribed a great part of the qualities of bodies to our sense impression. It is to be observed, however, that his reduction of all QUALITATIVE difference, as secondary qualities, to merely QUANTITATIVE, to wit, to size, figure, position, etc., as the sole primary or objective qualities, is at bottom the doctrine of Demokritos, who similarly reduced all qualities to the figure, composition, and position of atoms; as may be clearly seen from Aristotle's "Metaphysics," book i., chap. 4, and from Theophrastus's "De Sensu," chap. 61–65. Locke was, in so far, a resuscitator of the Demokritean philosophy, as Spinoza was that of the Eleatics. He also really paved the way for the succeeding French materialism. By his preliminary distinction between subjective and objective elements in perception, he led directly up to Kant, who, following his direction and track in a much higher sense, was enabled to sunder the subjective purely from the objective, by which process indeed so much accrued to the subjective, that the objective only remained as a kind of dark point, a something not farther recognizable — the thing in itself. I have now reduced this to the being which we discover in our self-consciousness as Will, and I have therefore again returned to the subjective source of knowledge. It could not happen otherwise, for, as already said, the objective is never more than the secondary, namely, a presentment. Hence, therefore, we must not seek the innermost kernel of our being, the thing in itself, without us, but within us, in other words, in the subjective side, as the only immediate. To this must be added that with the objective we can never attain to a point of rest, to an ultimate and original point, because we are there in the domain of PRESENTMENTS, and these are altogether and essentially subordinated to, and have for their form, the LAW OF CAUSATION in its four aspects, for which reason every object falls under and presupposes the requirements of the former. For instance, an assumed objective absolute carries with it the destructive questions, Whence? and Why? before which it must give way and fall. It is otherwise when we sink ourselves in the still, albeit obscure, depths of the subject. Here we are certainly threatened with the danger of falling into mysticism, and we must therefore only draw from this source what is actually true, compassable by each and all, and consequently undeniable.

The "Dianoialogy," which, as the result of investigations since Descartes, was current until Kant, may be found *en résumé* and expounded with *näive* clearness in Muratori, "Della Fantasia," chaps. 1–4 and 13; Locke there appears as a heretic. The whole is a nest of errors, by which it may be seen how very differently I have conceived and presented it, after having had Kant and Cabanis for predecessors. The above entire Dianoialogy and Psychology is based on the false Cartesian dualism. Everything must now in the whole work, *per fas et nefas*, be reduced to it, including many correct and interesting facts which are introduced. The whole procedure is interesting as a type.

SECTION 13.

SOME FURTHER OBSERVATIONS ON THE KANTIAN PHILOSOPHY.

There is a passage in Pope which would be very suitable as a motto for a critique of pure reason. It was written about eighty years earlier, and says: "Since it is **reasonable** to doubt most things, we should most of all doubt that reason of ours which would demonstrate all things. »

The true spirit of the Kantian philosophy, its leading idea and true sense, may be conceived and presented in many ways. Such various modes of expressing the matter are adapted, according to the variety of mind, to open out to this one or that the true understanding of these deep and therefore difficult doctrines. The following is one more attempt of this nature, in which I seek to infuse my clearness into Kant's depth.

Mathematics is based on perceptions, on which its demonstrations support themselves; but because these perceptions are not empirical, but are *a priori*, its doctrines are apodeictic. Philosophy, on the contrary, has, as the given element from which it proceeds, and which imparts to its demonstrations necessity (apodeicticity), mere CONCEPTS. For it cannot at once stand on the footing of simple empirical perception, inasmuch as it undertakes to explain the universal, not the particular, of things, its object being to lead beyond the empirically given. There remains nothing for it, then, but universal concepts, in so far as these are not perceptual or purely empirical. Such concepts must then furnish the foundation of its doctrines and demonstrations, and it must start from them as from something present and given. Philosophy is accordingly A SCIENCE FROM MERE CONCEPTS, while mathematics is a science from the CONSTRUCTION (perceptual presentment) of its concepts. Strictly speaking, however, it is only the demonstrations of philosophy which proceed from mere concepts. This cannot, like the mathematical, proceed from a perception, because such would have to be either purely *a priori* or empirical; but the latter gives no apodeicticity, and the former furnishes only mathematics. If it intends, therefore, to support its doctrines by any sort of demonstration, this must consist in the correct logical consequence from concepts at its foundation. Things had gone quite smoothly in this direction throughout the long period of Scholasticism, and even in the new epoch founded by Descartes, so tnat we see Spinoza and Leibnitz pursuing this method. At last it occured to Locke to investigate the origin of concepts, the result he arrived at being that all universal concepts, however abstract they may be, are derived from experience, that is, from the existent, sensuously perceivable, empirically real world, or else through inward experience such as the empirical self-observation of each offers, in short, that their whole content is derived from these two, and consequently can never furnish more than what outer or inner experience has placed there. From the foregoing it ought in strictness to have been inferred that they can never transcend experience, that is, can never lead to the goal; but Locke went, with the principles derived from experience, beyond experience.

In elaborate antithesis to his predecessors, and by way of correction of the Lockean doctrines, Kant showed that there are indeed some conceptions which make an exception to the above rule, that is, which do not spring from experience. But that these are at the same time partly derived from the pure, that is *a priori* given intuition of space and time, and partly constitute the special functions of our understanding itself, for the sake of their use in the experience which regulates itself according to them. Their validity only extends accordingly to possible experience of which sense is always the medium, inasmuch as they are only determined to generate this in us, together with its regular course; in other words they, themselves contentless, receive all material and content solely from SENSIBILITY, in order thereby to produce experience—but apart therefrom have neither content nor significance, inasmuch as they are only valid under the pre-supposition of perception resting on sense-feeling, and refer essentially to this. It follows from the above that they cannot supply us with clues to lead us beyond all possibility of experience, and from this again that metaphysics as the science of that which lies beyond nature, that is, beyond the possibility of experience, is impossible.

As now the one element of experience, namely, the universal, formal, and regulative, is knowable *a priori*, and therefore rests on the essential and regulative functions of our own intellect, while the other, namely, the particular, material, and accidental, arises from sense-feeling, it follows that both are of subjective origin. Hence it also follows that experience, in its totality, together with the world presented therein, is a mere PHENOMENON, that is, something which, directly and immediately, is only existent for the subject knowing it. But this phenomenon, nevertheless, points to a THING IN ITSELF lying at its foundation, but which, as such, is absolutely unknowable. These are the negative results of the Kantian philosophy.

I must here call attention to the fact, that Kant speaks as though we were only perceiving subjects, and had no datum outside the presentment, while we certainly possess another in the Will within us, which is *toto genere* distinct from the former. It is true he also took this into consideration, yet not in the theoretical, but only in the practical philosophy, from which with him it is quite separated, in other words, simply and solely in order to establish the fact of the pure and moral significance of our action, and thereupon to found a moral faith, to counterbalance our theoretical ignorance and the impossibility of all theology which follows therefrom.

Kant's philosophy in contradistinction, and indeed in antithesis to all others, is also designated as TRANSCENDENTAL PHILOSOPHY, or more accurately, TRANSCENDENTAL IDEALISM. The expression "transcendent" is not of mathematical, but of philosophical origin, since it was familiar to the scholastics. It was first introduced into mathematics by Leibnitz, in order to designate *quod algebrae vires transcendit*, that is, all operations, which common arithmetic and algebra do not suffice to complete, as, for instance, to find the logarithm of a number, or *vice versâ*, or to find the trigonometric functions of an arc, purely arithmetically, or *vice versâ*, and generally for all problems which are only to be solved by a calculus carried out to infinity. But the schoolmen designate as transcendent, such concepts as were more universal than the ten categories of Aristotle, and even Spinoza uses the word in this sense. Giordano Bruno ("De la Causa," etc., dial. iv.), calls those predicates transcendent which are more universal than the distinction of corporeal and incorporeal substance pertaining to substance generally. They concern, according to him, those common roots in which the corporeal is one with the incorporeal, and which is the true original substance; he even sees in this a proof that such must exist. Now Kant understands by TRANSCENDENTAL, in the first place, the recognition of the *a priori*, and therefore the merely formal in our knowledge AS SUCH, *i.e.*, the insight that such knowledge is independent of experience; indeed that this prescribes the unalterable rule, according to which it must proceed — such insight being at the same time bound up with the understanding why such knowledge is and accomplishes this, to wit, because it constitutes the form of our intellect, and is, in consequence, of subjective origin. Only Criticism of Pure Reason is, accordingly, transcendental. In opposition to this he calls transcendent the use, or rather the misuse, of the above purely formal element in our knowledge outside the possibility of experience; which he also terms hyperphysical. TRANSCENDENTAL, therefore, means in short, "before all experience," TRANSCENDENT, "beyond all experience." Kant it will be seen only admits Metaphysic as Transcendental Philosophy, that is, as the doctrine of the form contained in our knowing consciousness as such, and of the limitation thereby disclosed, by virtue of which the knowledge of things in themselves is impossible for us, since experience can furnish nothing but mere phenomena. The word "METAPHYSICAL," is however, not synonymous with "transcendental." Everything that is *a priori* certain, but which concerns experience, is termed by him metaphysical, whereas the doctrine that it is only on account of its subjective origin, and as purely formal, that it is *a priori* certain, is alone called transcendental. Transcendental is the philosophy which brings to one's consciousness that the primary and most essential laws of this world which is presented to us have their root in our brain, and for this reason can be known *a priori*. It is called transcendental, because it passes beyond the whole given phantasmagoria to its origin. Hence, as already said, the criticism of pure reason, and especially the Critical (*i.e.*, Kantian), philosophy, is alone transcendental; metaphysical, on the other hand.

are the "foundations of natural science," also those of
the "doctrine of Virtue," etc.

The conception of a transcendental philosophy, however,
may be taken in a deeper sense, if one undertakes to con-
centrate therein the innermost spirit of the Kantian philosophy, and somewhat in the following manner. That the
whole world is only given us, in a secondary manner, as
presentment or image in our head, as brain phenomenon,
while our own Will is given immediately in self-consciousness, and hence a separation, or indeed an opposition exists
between our own existence and that of the world — all thi
is a mere consequence of our individual and mere animal
existence, with the abolition of which it falls away. But
until then it is impossible for us to get rid in thought of
that fundamental and original form of our consciousness,
which is implied in the separation of subject and object,
since all thinking and presenting presupposes it. Hence
we count it for the all-essential and fundamental nature
of the world, while it is in reality only the form of our
animal consciousness and the phenomena occasioned by
the same. But from this arise all those questions, as to
beginning, end, boundary, and origin of the world, our
own continuance after death, etc. They rest accordingly
on a false assumption, which attributes to the thing-in-
itself what are only presentments occasioned by an animal,
cerebral consciousness, and assumes this to be the original and ultimate nature of the world. Such is the sense
of the Kantian expression — "all such questions are transcendent." They are, indeed, not merely subjectively, but
in and for themselves, that is objectively, susceptible of
no answer. For they are problems which wholly disappear
with the abolition of our cerebral consciousness and the
opposition based upon it, and are, nevertheless, stated as
though they were independent of it. For example, he
who asks whether he continues after his death, sets aside,
in hypothesi, his animal brain-consciousness, and asks, notwithstanding, as to the existence of something which presupposes this, inasmuch as it rests on its form, namely,
subject and object, space and time — to wit, as to his
individual continuance. Now philosophy, which brings all
these conditions and limitations, AS SUCH, to distinct con-

sciousness, is TRANSCENDENTAL, and, IN SO FAR AS IT
VINDICATES FOR THE SUBJECT, THE UNIVERSAL GROUND DE-
TERMINATIONS OF THE OBJECTIVE WORLD, IT IS TRANSCEN-
DENTAL IDEALISM. It will gradually be seen that the
problems of Metaphysics are only in so far insoluble, as
a contradiction is contained in the questions themselves.

Transcendental Idealism, in the meantime, does not
dispute the EMPIRICAL REALITY of the existing world, but
says only that it is not unconditioned, since it has our
brain-function, from which the forms of perception, time,
space, and causality arise, for its condition, and that
therefore this empirical reality itself is only the reality
of an appearance. If a multitude of existences manifest
themselves therein, of which one is always passing away
and another is arising, and we know, that only by means
of the percept-form of space, plurality, and only by
means of that of time, destruction and origination, is possible, we recognize that such a process has no absolute
reality, *i. e.*, that it does not belong to the beings-
in-themselves, which manifest themselves in that appearance. If we could withdraw these forms of knowledge,
as glass from the kaleidoscope, we should have, to our
astonishment, a single and enduring world before us, un-
transitory, unalterable, and amid all apparent change,
perhaps even right down to its individual determination,
identical. In accordance with this opinion, the following
three propositions may be stated: —

(1.) The sole form of reality is the actual; in it alone
the real is immediately met with and contained in its
completeness and fullness.

(2.) The true Real is independent of time and therefore, in every point of time, one and the same.

(3.) Time is the percept-form of our intellect, and hence
foreign to the things-in-themselves.

These three propositions are at bottom identical. He
who clearly sees their identity, no less than their truth,
has made great progress in philosophy, inasmuch as he
has grasped the spirit of transcendental Idealism.

How rich indeed in consequences is Kant's doctrine of
the ideality of space and time, dryly and tastelessly as
he has expounded it. On the contrary, nothing results

from the pompous, pretentious and purposely incomprehensible jargon of the three notorious sophists, who have drawn off from Kant the attention of a public that was unworthy of him. Before Kant, it may be said, we were in time, now time is in us. In the first case time is REAL, and we, like everything else that falls within it, are consumed by it. In the second case, time is IDEAL, but lies in us. The question respecting the future after death thus at once collapses. FOR IF I AM NOT, TIME IS NO MORE. It is only a deceptive illusion which shows me a time proceeding without me, after my death. All three divisions of time, past, present and future, are similarly my product, belong to me and not I to one any more than to another of them. Again, another consequence which may be drawn from the proposition that time does not belong to the essence of the things-in-themselves, would be this, that in one sense the past is NOT past, but that everything which has ever really, ever truly been, must still be, since time only resembles a stage-waterfall, which seems to stream down, but, being simply a wheel, never moves from its place. I have already in my chief work long ago compared, in a manner analogous to this, space to a glass cut into facets, which shows us that which exists singly in countless reproduction. If undeterred by the danger of becoming visionary, we plunge still deeper into the matter, it might appear to us as though, by a very vivid presentation of our own remote past, we received an immediate confirmation of the fact, that time does not touch the true being of things, but is only interpolated between their being and us as a mere medium of perception, after the removal of which all would again be there; as also, on the other hand, our true and living faculty of memory, in which this long past maintains an unwithered existence, bears witness to something within us that does not alter, and consequently, which is not within the domain of time.

The main tendency of the Kantian philsophy is to place before us the complete DIVERSITY OF THE IDEAL AND REAL after Locke had already broken ground. In the first place one can say, the Ideal is the perceptual figure dis-

playing itself spacially, with all the qualities perceivable
in it, while the Real is the thing by, in, and for itself,
independent of its being presented in the head of another
or its own. But the boundary between them is difficult
to be drawn, and yet it is precisely this upon which the
question turns. Locke had shown that everything in the
former which is figure, color, sound, smoothness, roughness, hardness, softness, cold, heat, etc. (secondary qualities), are merely IDEAL, and therefore do not belong to
the thing in itself, inasmuch as the being and nature of
the thing is not given therein, but only its ACTION, and
indeed a very one-sided definite action, an action, namely
on the quite specifically determined receptivity of our
five sense-organs, by virtue of which, for instance, sound
does not act on the eye, nor light on the ear. The action of bodies on the organs of sense consists in that it
sets the latter in a state of activity peculiar to them, almost in the same way as when I pull a thread which sets
a mechanism in play. As the Real, which belong to the
thing in itself, Locke left standing, extension, form, impenetrability, motion, or rest, and number, which he
therefore termed primary qualities. Now Kant demonstrated, subsequently, with infinitely superior insight,
that even these qualities do not belong to the objective
nature of the things or to the things in themselves, and
therefore cannot be absolutely REAL, since they are conditioned by space, time and causality, and that these in
their turn, according to their whole order and construction, are given us before all experience, and are exactly
known; and hence that they most reside in us preformed,
as much as the specific kind of the receptivity and activity of each of our senses. In accordance with this I
have said that these forms are the part taken by the
brain in perception as the specific sense-feelings are of
the respective sense-organs.* Even according to Kant
the purely objective, the nature of things which is independent of our presentment and its apparatus, which he

---

* As it is our eye which produces green, red, and blue, so it is our
brain which produces time, space, and causality (whose objectivized abstractum is matter). My perception of a body in space is the product
of my sense and brain function with χ.

calls the thing-in-itself, that is, the properly Real in contradistinction to the Ideal, is something totally distinct
from the figure which presents itself to us in perception
and to which, inasmuch as it is independent of space and
time, properly speaking, neither extension nor duration is
to be attributed, although it imparts the power of existence to all that possesses extension and duration. Spinoza has comprehended the subject in its general aspect,
as may be seen from "Eth.," p. ii., prop. 16, with the
2d coroll. also prop. 18, Schol.

The Lockean Real, in opposition to the Ideal, is at
bottom matter, stripped indeed of all its qualities, which
he casts on one side as secondary, that is as conditioned
by our sense-organs, for it is, *per se*, an extended, etc.,
existent, of which the presentment in us is the mere re-
flex or copy. As to this, I may recall that I (in the
"Fourfold Root," 2d ed., p. 77; 3d ed., p. 82, and at
less length in "The World as Will," etc., Presentment, 2d
ed., vol. i., p. 9, and vol. ii, p. 48; 3d ed., vol. i., p. 10; vol. ii.,
p. 52) have explained that the nature of matter consists simply in its action, that matter is nothing but causality, and
that conceived as such every special quality, that is, every
specific kind of action, is abstracted from it, so that it remains action or pure causality, deprived of all the other defi-
nitions, causality *in abstracto;* to which place, for a more
thorough understanding of the matter, I ask the reader to refer. But Kant had already taught, although it was I who
gave the first correct demonstration of it, that all causality is only a form of our understanding, and therefore,
only exists for the understanding and in the understanding. We see then the supposed Real of Locke, matter,
in this way retreats entirely into the Ideal, and therewith
into the subject, that is, exists only in the presentment
and for the presentment. Kant, by his presentment, certainly deprived the Real, or thing-in-itself, of its materiality, but with him it remained a completely unknown χ.
I have at last demonstrated the true REAL, or the
thing-in-itself, which alone has a real existence independent of the presentment and its forms, to be the WILL in
us, which had been hitherto inconsiderately reckoned to
the IDEAL. It will be seen, therefore, that Locke, Kant,

and I stand in close connection, inasmuch as we represent in the space of nearly two hundred years, the gradual development of a coherent, unified, process of thought. David Hume may be considered as a connecting link in this chain, although properly speaking, only so far as the law of causality is concerned. In respect of his influence I have to complete the above exposition with the following.

Locke, no less than Condillac, and the disciples who trod in his footsteps, have elaborated the fact that the feeling which enters into an organ of sense requires a cause of the same outside of our body, and that the differences of such action (sense-impression) also presuppose differences in the cause, whatever these may be; whence the above indicated distinction between primary and secondary qualities proceeds. With this they end, and an objective world in space stands ready made for them, composed of things in themselves, but which are colorless, odorless, soundless, neither warm nor cold, etc., and nevertheless, extended, figured, impenetrable, movable and numerical. But the axiom itself, by virtue of which the transition from the inner to the outer, and accordingly the whole derivation and installation of the things-in-themselves has taken place, namely, the law of causality, they, like all earlier philosophers, have assumed to be self-evident, and requiring no proof of its validity. Upon this point Hume directed his sceptical attack, inasmuch as he placed the validity of this law in doubt. For experience, from which, according to this philosophy, all our cognitions are derived, can never supply us with the causal connection itself, but only with the mere succession of states in time, in other words, never with a consequence, but only with a mere sequence, which, as such, must always be accidental, and never necessary. This argument, so antagonistic to common sense, yet not easily to be refuted, occasioned Kant to investigate the true origin of causality, which he found to lie in the essential and innate form of our understanding itself, that is, in the subject and not in the object, since it was not first brought to us from without. But by this the whole objective world of Locke and Condillac was drawn back into the subject, since Kant had shown the clue to it to be of subjective origin. For the rule is now found to be just as subjective as the sense-impression, according to which it is to be conceived as the effect of a cause, which cause it alone is, that is, perceived as the objective world. For the subject merely assumes an object without itself in consequence of the peculiar characteristic of its intellect, which to every change presupposes a cause, and therefore only projects it, as it were, out of itself in a space prepared for this purpose, this in its turn being a product of its own original construction, as well as of the specific impression on the sense-organs, at the instance of which the whole procedure takes place. The above Lockean objective world of things-of-themselves, had therefore been changed by Kant into a world of mere phenomena in our knowledge-apparatus, and this the more completely, since the space in which they present themselves, as also the time in which they pass, was proved by him to be undeniably of subjective origin.

But with all this, Kant, no less than Locke, allowed the thing-in-itself to exist, *i. e.*, admits something to exist independent of our presentments, which only furnish us with phenomena, and which lies at the foundation of these phenomena. Here, then, lay the Achilles's heel of his philosophy, which had, by the demonstration of its inconsequence, to forfeit the recognition it had already obtained as being of unconditioned validity and truth; but in the last resort it was, nevertheless, unjustly treated in this respect. For certainly the assumption of a thing in itself behind the phenomena, of a real kernel under so many shells, is in no wise untrue. The denial of it would be indeed absurd. It is only the way in which Kant introduced this thing-in-itself, and sought to unite it with his principles, which was faulty; at bottom it was only his exposition (this word taken in its most comprehensive sense) of the matter, and not the matter itself, which succumbed to his adversaries. In this sense it might be maintained that the argumentation made valid against him was, strictly speaking, addressed only *ad hominem*, not *ad rem*. Assuredly the Indian proverb finds an application here: " No lotus without a thorn." Kant was guided by the deeply-felt truth that behind every phenomenon a being in itself lies, from which it receives its subsistence; in other words, that behind the presentment something presented lies. But he undertook to deduce this from a given presentment itself by the addition of certain laws known to us *a priori*, and which, because they are *a priori*, cannot be deduced from something independent and distinct from the phenomenon or presentment; and hence for this purpose one must strike out another way. The inconsistencies in which Kant involved himself by the fallacious path he had taken in this respect, were demonstrated to him by G. E. Schultze, who, in a clumsy and diffuse manner, expounded the matter, at first anonymously in "Aenesidemus" (especially pp. 374–81), and subsequently in his "Critique of Theoretical Philosophy" (vol. ii., p. 205), against which Reinhold took up Kant's vindication, although without any special result; so that *haec potuisse dici, et non potuisse refelli* has its application.

I will here clearly set forth once for all in my way the truly essential of the matter, that which lies at the root of the whole controversy independently of Schultze's way of conceiving it. A strict deduction of the thing-in-itself Kant has never given, but he has inherited it from his predecessors, especially Locke, and has retained it as something, the existence of which was not to be doubted, since it was strictly self-evident; indeed, he was bound to do this to a certain extent. According to Kant's discoveries our empirical knowledge contains an element which is demonstrably of subjective origin, and another element of which this is not the case; the latter remains therefore objective, there being no ground for holding it to be subjective. Kant's transcendental Idealism denies, accordingly, the objective nature of things or their reality as independent of our perception, in so far as the *a priori* in our knowledge extends, but not farther, because the ground for the denial does not reach farther. What lies outside he allows to remain, that is, all such qualities of things as cannot be constructed *a priori*. For the whole nature of the given phenomena, namely, of the corporeal world is in no wise determinable by us *a priori*, but is merely the universal form of its phenomenon, and this may be reduced to space, time, and causality, together with the totality of the laws of these three forms. On the other hand, the indeterminate residuum present throughout all these *a priori* existent forms, in other words, that which pertains to chance, is precisely the manifestation of the thing-in-itself. Now the EMPIRICAL content of the phenomena, *i. e.*, every closer determination of the same, every physical quality appearing in them, cannot be known otherwise than as *a posteriori*. These empirical qualities (or rather their common source) remain therefore the thing-in-itself, as the manifestation of its special nature through the medium of the above *a priori* forms. This *a posteriori*, which in every phenomenon appears, as it were, clothed in the *a priori*, but yet imparting to every being its special and individual character, is accordingly the MATTER of the phenomenal world in contradistinction to its FORM. Now, since this matter is in no way deducible from the forms of the phenomenon inherent in the subject, so carefully sought out by Kant and so certainly demonstrated by the sign of *a priority* but rather remains after the abstraction of everything flowing from these, thereby proving itself a second perfectly distinct element of the empirical phenomenon, and a foreign addition to these forms; and at the same time, since it proceeds in no wise from the caprice of the knowing subject, but rather stands in opposition thereto — for these reasons, Kant did not hesitate to leave the MATTER of the phenomenon to the thing itself, and therefore to regard it as coming wholly from without, on the assumption that it must come from somewhere, or as Kant expressed it, have some ground. But as we cannot isolate such qualities as are known only *a posteriori*, nor conceive them as separated and purified from those which are certain *a priori*, but on the other hand, as they always appear enveloped in these latter, Kant teaches that we can know the existence of things in themselves, but nothing else about them; we can know THAT they are, but not WHAT they are. The nature of things in themselves remains therefore, for him, an unknown quantity, an χ. For the form of the phenomenon clothes and hides the nature of the thing-in-itself in all cases. We can say this at most—since the above *a priori* forms accrue to all things as phenomena, without distinction, proceeding as they do from our intellect, but the things at the same time show considerable diversity —that which determines this difference, that is, the specific variety of things, is the thing-in-itself.

Looked at in this way, Kant's assumption and presupposition of the things in themselves, notwithstanding the subjectivity of all our forms of knowledge, seems to be perfectly justified and well grounded. It is, nevertheless, shown to be untenable when its only argument, namely, the empirical content in all phenomena, is narrowly tested and traced back to its origin. It is certain that in empirical knowledge and its source, perceptual presentment, there is a MATTER which is independent of its form, which is known to us *a priori*. The next question is, as to whether this matter is of objective or subjective origin, since only in the first case can it insure for us the thing-in-itself. If we pursue it, therefore, to its origin, we find this nowhere else but in our SENSE-IMPRESSION. For it is a change occurring in the retina of the eye, in the nerves of the ear, or at the ends of the fingers, which induces the perceptual presentment, and thus first sets in play the whole apparatus of our forms of knowledge, which lie ready *a priori*, the result being the perception of an external object. On the change being felt in the sense-organ, THE LAW OF CAUSALITY is at once applied by means of a necessary and indispensable function of the understanding *a priori*. The above, with its *a priori* certainty and necessity, points to a CAUSE of this change which, since it does not stand in the arbitrary power of the subject, appears to it as something external. This quality receives its significance primarily by means of a form of space, which is added by the intellect itself for the purpose, the necessarily presupposed cause thereby appearing perceptually as an object in space bearing the alterations effected by it in our sense-organs, as though they were properties of the thing-in-itself. This whole process may be found adequately and thoroughly expounded in my treatise on the "Law of Cause," § 21. But the sense-impression, which constitutes the starting point of the process and furnishes undeniably the whole matter of empirical perception, is something altogether subjective, and as the entire knowledge-forms, by means of which the objective perceptual presentment arises out of this matter and is projected externally in accordance with Kant's correct demonstration, are no less of subjective origin, it is clear that the matter, as well as the form of perceptual presentment, arises from the subject. Our whole empirical knowledge is accordingly resolved into two elements, both of which have their origin IN OURSELVES, namely, in the sense-impression and in the forms given *a priori*, that is, in the forms embedded in the functions of our intellect or brain, time, space, and causality, to which Kant had added eleven other categories of the understanding, demonstrated by me, however, as superfluous and inadmissible. If the above be correct, perceptual presentment and our empirical knowledge resting on it, in truth furnish no data for conclusions as to things in themselves, and Kant was not justified on his principles in assuming such. The Lockean philosophy, like all earlier philosophies, had taken the law of causality as absolute, and was thereby justified in concluding from the sense-impression to the existence of real things external to and independent of us. This passage from the effect to the cause is, however, the only way to attain from the internal and subjectively given to the external and objectively existent. Kant therefore, after he had vindicated the law of causality for the knowledge-form of the subject, found this way no longer open to him. He had himself, moreover, often enough warned us against making a transcendent use of the category of causality, that is, a use extending beyond experience and its possibility.

In point of fact the thing-in-itself is never to be arrived at in this way, nor otherwise by that of pure OBJECTIVE knowledge, which always remains presentment, and as such has its root in the subject, and can never furnish anything really distinct from the presentment. But the thing-in-itself can only be arrived at by shifting the standpoint. that is, by instead of, as previously, starting from that which PRESENTS, once for all starting from that which is PRESENTED. But this is only possible in one single thing which is attainable by us all from within as well as from without, and is thereby given in a double manner: it is our own body which, in the objective world, exists as presentment in space, and at the same time proclaims itself as Will in our own self-consciousness. Thereby is furnished the key at once to the understanding of all its actions and motions produced by external causes (here motives), which without this internal and immediate insight into its essence, would remain just as incomprehensible and inexplicable as the changes occurring according to natural laws and as manifestations of natural forces, in those other bodies which are only given to us in objective perception; and hence to that of the permanent substratum of these actions, that wherein these forces have root, to wit the body itself. This immediate knowledge which each one has of the nature of his own phenomenon, given him like all others only in objective perception, must thereupon be transferred analogically to the remaining phenomena, which are really the only ones that can properly be said to be given, and becomes then the key to the knowledge of the inner nature of things, or, in other words, of the things-in-themselves. One could only attain to this by a way quite different from pure objective knowledge, which remains mere presentment, by taking the SELF-CONSCIOUSNESS of the subject, which always appears as animal individual, to aid, and by making it the exponent of the CONCIOUSNESS OF OTHER THINGS, *i.e.*, of the perceptive intellect. This is the way which I have followed, and it is the only right one, the narrow gate to truth.

But instead of men striking out this way, Kant's exposition was confounded with the essence of the subject, and it was believed that with the former the latter was refuted; what in reality were mere *argumenta ad hominem*, were believed accordingly to be *argumenta ad rem*, and in consequence of these Schultzian attacks Kant's philosophy was declared untenable. The field was now open for the sophists and wind bags. The first to set up in this line was Fichte, who, because the thing-in-itself had come into discredit, straightway proceeded to construct a system without any thing-in-itself, and therefore rejected the assumption of anything but what was our presentment pure and simple, making the knowing subject all in all, or at least making it produce everything from its own resources. For this purpose he did away at once with the essential and valuable in Kant's doctrines,—the distinction between *a priori* and *a posteriori*,—and thereby that between the phenomenon and the thing-in-itself, inasmuch as he declared everything to be *a priori*, while being naturally without any proof of such a monstrous assumption, he offered us partly sophistical and partly absurd sham demonstrations, whose futility hid itself under the garb of depth and of the assumed incomprehensibility arising therefrom. He laid claim, moreover, openly and audaciously, to intellectual intuition,—in other words, to inspiration. For a public destitute of all power of judgment, and unworthy of Kant, this certainly sufficed. Such a public held self-assumption for excellence, and immediately declared Fichte to be a much greater philosopher than Kant. At the present day, indeed, there are not wanting philosophical writers who are anxious to foist the false fame of Fichte, now become traditional, on to the new generation, and quite seriously assure us that what Kant merely attempted Fichte had accomplished, and that he was properly the right man. These gentlemen, by their Midas-judgment, expose their entire incapacity to understand Kant, and, indeed, lay bare so palpably their deplorable ignorance, that it is to be hoped the rising and finally disillusionized generation will guard themselves from destroying their time and brains with the countless histories of philosophy and other writings produced by them. I take this opportunity of recalling a little work, from which it may be seen what impression Fichte's personal appearance and ways made on an unprejudiced contemporary. It is called the "Cabinet of Berlin Characters," and appeared in 1808 without indication of place of printing; it is said to be by Buchholz, but as to this I am not certain. With it may be compared what the jurist Anselm Von

Feuerbach, in the letters issued in 1852 by his son, says about Fichte; as also "Schiller's and Fichte's Correspondence," 1847; from all of which a correct idea may be formed of this sham philosopher.

It was not long before Schelling, worthy of his predecessor, trod in Fichte's footsteps, which he nevertheless forsook in order to proclaim his own invention, the absolute identity of the objective and subjective, or the Ideal and Real, which would imply that all which great minds like Locke and Kant, had, with incredible expenditure of acuteness and consideration, separated, should be again dissolved in the broth of his said absolute identity.   For the doctrines of the two former thinkers may be very suitably designated as those of the ABSOLUTE DIVERSITY OF THE IDEAL AND REAL, OR OF THE SUBJECTIVE AND OBJECTIVE.   But now things went further from confusion to confusion, by Fichte having introduced incomprehensibility of speech, and having put the appearance of depth in the place of thought, the seeds being scattered which were to result in one corruption after another, and finally in that total demoralization of philosophy, and, through philosophy, of all literature which has appeared in our day.

After Schelling followed a philosophical creature of ministers, the great philosopher Hegel, manufactured from above with a political but miscalculated purpose, a flat, commonplace, repulsive, ignorant charlatan, who, with unparalleled presumption, conceit, and absurdity, pasted together a system which was trumpeted by his venal adherents as immortal wisdom; and by blockheads really taken for it, whereby such a perfect chorus of admiration arose as had never before been known.   The extended intellectual influence thus violently acquired by such a man had as its consequence the ruination of the learning of a whole generation.   The admirer of this pseudo-philosophy has the mockery of posterity in store for him, a mockery which is already preluded by the delightfully audible laughter of neighbors.   For should it not sound delightful to my ears when the nation, whose learned caste has for thirty years spurned my labors as worth nothing and less than nothing, not even a passing

glance, should have the reputation among its neighbors
of having revered and even deified throughout these thirty
years, as the highest and most unheard-of wisdom, what
is wholly bad, absurd, nonsensical, and subservient merely
to material ends ? I ought, I suppose, as a good patriot,
to go my way in the praise of the Germans and of Ger-
manism, and rejoice to have belonged to them and to
no other nation ? But it is as the Spanish proverb says:
"*Cada uno cuenta de la feria, como le va en ella*" (Everyone reports respecting the fair, according as it has fared
with him there). Go to the Democolacs and get yourself
praised. Well-developed, unwieldy, minister-bepuffed,
nonsense-mongering charlatans, without intellect and
without merit, such as these belong to the Germans, not
men like myself! Such is the testimony which I have to
give them in parting. Wieland (" Letters to Merck," p.
239) calls it a misfortune to be born a German; Bürger,
Mozart, Beethoven, and others would have agreed with
him; I also. It rests upon the fact that σοφὸν εἶναί δει τὸν
ἐπιγνωσόμενον τὸν σοφόν or *il n'y a que l'esprit qui sent l'esprit.*

To the most brilliant and meritorious sides of the Kantian philosophy, belongs incontestably the "Transcendental Dialectic," by which he has so far raised speculative
theology and psychology from their foundations, that since
then no one has been able, even with the best intentions,
to set them up again. What a blessing for the human
mind! For do we not see, throughout the whole period
from the revival of the sciences to Kant, that the
thoughts of even the greatest men receive a twist, indeed are often completely distorted, in consequence of
these two absolutely sacred presuppositions, which cripple
all intellect, which are removed from all investigation,
and therefore dead to it ? Are not the first and most
essential convictions respecting ourselves and all things
twisted and falsified, if we start with the presupposition
that everything is produced and ordered from without,
according to the notions and preconceived purposes of a
personal and therefore individual being ? In the same
way the fundamental essence of man is assumed to be a
thinking essence, and to consist of two wholly hetero-

geneous parts, which have come together and been soldered together without knowing how, and had to accommodate themselves to each other as well as they could, in order to be again forever severed, *nolentes volentes ?* How powerfully Kant's critique of these fancies and of their grounds has acted upon all the sciences, is obvious from the fact that since then, at least in the higher German literature, these presuppositions appear only in a figurative sense, and are no longer seriously made, being left for popular literature and for the professors of philosophy, who earn their bread by them. Our works on natural science keep themselves especially free from them, while, on the contrary, the English, by aiming at them in their modes of expression and diatribes, or else by apologies, lower themselves in our eyes. Immediately before Kant, indeed, things were quite different in this respect; we see, for instance, even the eminent Lichtenberg, whose early education was pre-Kantian, in his treatise on physiognomy, earnestly and with evident conviction adhering to this antithesis of soul and body, and thereby injuring his cause.

He who has estimated the high value of the "Transcendental Dialectic," will not find it superfluous if I here deal with it somewhat more in detail. In the first place, therefore, I lay before those who know and interest themselves in the critique of reason, the following essay on the critique of rational psychology, as it is presented in its entirety in the first edition—for in the following editions it appears castrated. The argument which is there criticised, p. 361, *seq.*, under the title "Paralogism of the Personality," ought to be quite otherwise conceived and therefore criticised. For Kant's certainly profound exposition is not only too subtle and difficult to be understood, but it may also be objected to it, that it assumes the object of self-consciousness, or in Kant's language, of the internal sense, suddenly and without further justification, as the object of an alien consciousness, or indeed of an external perception, in order thereupon to judge it according to the laws and analogies of the corporeal world. Two distinct times are even allowed to be assumed (p. 363), the one in the consciousness of the judged, the other in that of the judging subject, which do not coincide. I would give the argument in question, from the personality, quite another turn, and present it accordingly in the two following propositions:—

1. One can establish *a priori* respecting all motion in general, no matter of whatever kind it may be, that it is primarily perceptible by the comparison with something resting; whence it follows that the course of time, with all that is in it, could not be perceived were it not for something that has no part in it, and with whose rest we compare its motion. It is quite true that we here judge according to the analogy of motion in space; but space and time must always serve mutually to explain each other. For this reason also we have to imagine time under the figure of a straight line in order to apprehend it perceptually, to construct it *a priori*. In accordance therewith, we cannot imagine that if everything in our consciousness at once and together moved forward in the flux of time, that this forward movement would nevertheless be perceptible, but in order to this we must assume something fixed, past which time with its content flows. For the perception of the external sense, this is accomplished by matter as the enduring substance under the change of accidents, as Kant also explains in the demonstration to the "First Analogy of Experience," p. 183 of the 1st edition. In this very place, however, he commits the insupportable blunder, already criticised by me elsewhere, and which contradicts, moreover, his own doctrine, of saying that it is not time that flows, but only the phenomena in time. That this is fundamentally false is proved by the fixed certainty implanted in us all, that if all things in heaven and on earth suddenly stood still time would continue its course undisturbed thereby; so that if nature were later on again to get under way the question as to the length of the previous pause would be capable in itself of a perfectly exact answer. Were it otherwise, time would have to stand still with the watch or when the latter got too fast, go along with it. But precisely this relation, together with our certainty *a priori* respecting it, proves incontrovertibly that time has its course, and therefore its essence, in our

head and not outside of us. In the realm of external intuition, as I have said, the enduring is matter; with our argument from the personality the argument is on the other hand respecting the perception of the internal sense, in which that of the external is again taken up. I said, therefore, that if our consciousness with its entire content moved forward uniformly in the stream of time, we could not be aware of this motion. For this, then, there must be something in the consciousness that is itself immovable. But this cannot be anything other than the knowing subject itself which contemplates, unmoved and unaltered, the course of time and the change of its content. Before its gaze life pursues its course like a drama. We shall be sensible how little part it has itself in this course if in old age we recall vividly to ourselves the scenes of youth and childhood.

2. Internally in self-consciousness, or to speak with Kant, through the internal sense, I only know in time. But objectively considered, nothing permanent can exist in mere time, since such implies a duration, but this a simultaneity and this again space. (The justification of this proposition will be found in my treatise on "The Law of Cause," § 18, besides in "The World as Will and Presentment," 2d ed., vol. i., § 4, pp. 10 and 11, and p. 531; 3d ed., pp. 10 and 11, and 560.) Notwithstanding all this, I find myself as a matter of fact as the substratum of the same, which endures, that is, which ever remains, in spite of all change in my presentments, which is related to the presentments as matter is to its changing accidents, and consequently no less than the latter deserves the name of SUBSTANCE, and since it is not spacial and therefore unextended, that of SIMPLE SUBSTANCE. Since now, as already said, no permanency can take place in mere time by itself alone, but the substance in question is perceived on the other hand, not by the external sense and consequently not in space, we must, in order as against the flux of time to think it as permanent, assume it as something lying outside time and say accordingly, all object lies in time, but the specially knowing subject, not. As now outside time there is no cessation or end we should have in the knowing subject a

permanent, albeit neither spacial nor temporal, and therefore indestructible, substance.

In order then to demonstrate the argument from the
personality, as thus stated, to be a paralogism, one should
have to say that the second proposition of the same takes
an empirical act to aid — to which this other may be opposed — that the knowing subject is bound up with life,
and indeed with waking, that its continuance during both
in nowise proves that it can exist apart from them. For
this actual permanence, during the period of the conscious state, is far removed, even *toto genere* distinct,
from the permanence of matter (the origin and sole real-
ization of the conception substance), which we know in
perception, and in which we discern *a priori* not merely
its actual duration, but its necessary indestructibility, and
the impossibility of its annihilation. Yet it is according
to the analogy of this truly indestructible substance that
we would wish to assume a thinking substance in ourselves, which would then be certain of an endless continuance. But apart from the fact that this latter would be
an analogy with a mere phenomenon (matter), the error
which the dialectical reason, in the above demonstration,
commits, consists in that it treats the permanence of the
subject, throughout the change of all its presentments
in time, like the permanence of the matter given to us
in perception, and accordingly includes both under the
conception of substance. Everything which it, although
under the condition of perception, can predicate of matter *a priori*, especially continuance through all time, can
be attributed to the pretended immaterial substance, and
this although the permanence of the latter only rests
upon the fact that it is assumed as existing in no time
at all, let alone in all times, and as a result the conditions of perception, in consequence of which indestructibility is predicated of matter *a priori*, are here expressly
abolished, especially the SPACIAL. But on this precisely
rests (as has been shown in the above quoted passages
of my writings), the permanence of the same.

As to the demonstrations of the immortality of the soul,
from its assumed simplicity and consequent indissolubil-
ity, by which the only possible kind of decay, the disso-

lution of the parts, is excluded; it may be said generally
that all laws respecting origination, dissolution, change,
continuance, etc., which we know either *a priori* or *a posteriori*, are only valid of the corporeal world given us
objectively, and also conditioned by our intellect. As
soon, therefore, as we depart from this, and talk of immaterial essences, we have no longer any justification
for applying those laws and rules in order to maintain
whether the origination and dissolution of such essences
is possible or not, for here every clue fails us. In this
connection, all such proofs of immortality from the simplicity of the thinking substance are invalid. For the
amphiboly lies in that an immaterial substance is spoken
of, and then the laws of material substance are interpolated in order to be applied to it.

In the meantime the paralogism of the personality, as
I have apprehended it, gives in its first argument the
demonstration *a priori* that something permanent must
lie in our consciousness; and in the second argument it
proves the same thing *a posteriori*. Taken altogether, it
will seem that the truth which, according to the rule,
lies at the foundation of every error, rational psychology
included, has its root in the above. This truth is, that
even in our empirical consciousness an eternal point can
assuredly be shown, but only a point, and only shown TO
BE, without the material for any further demonstration
being derived from it. I refer here to my own doctrines, according to which that is the knowing subject
which knows all, but is not itself known. We therefore
conceive it as the fixed point past which time, with its
presentments, flows, the very course of time being only
known in opposition to something permanent. I have
called this the point of contact of the object with the
subject. The subject of knowledge is with me, like the
body whose brain-function it objectively presents, a phenomenon of the will, which, as the only thing-in-itself,
is here the substratum of a correlate of all phenomena,
that is, of the subject of knowledge.

If we now turn to RATIONAL COSMOLOGY we find pregnant expressions, in its antinomies, of the perplexity arising from the law of cause, perplexities which have from

time immemorial forced men to philosophize.   To emphasize this in another, clearer, and less complex manner than has been done by Kant, is the object of the
following exposition, which, unlike the Kantian, is not
merely dialectical, operating with abstract concepts, but
which applies itself immediately to the perceptive consciousness.

Time can have no beginning, and no cause can be
primal.   Both are *a priori* certain, and therefore undeniable, for all beginning is in time, and therefore presupposes time, and every cause must have a previous one
behind it, whose effect it is.   How, then, could a first
beginning of the world and the things therein have ever
taken place? (The first verse of the Pentateuch would
seem a *petitio principii*, and this in the most literal sense
of the term).   On the contrary, if a first beginning had
not been, the real present would not be now, but would
be long past, for between it and the first beginning we
must assume some time, however limited, but which —
if we deny the beginning, in other words, if we push
it back to infinity — is also pushed back to infinity.
But even if we assume a first beginning, this does
not assist us in the last resort, for we have thereby
arbitrarily cut off the causal chain, after which we
shall immediately find mere time itself a difficulty.
The ever-renewed question, namely, " why this first beginning did not take place earlier? " will follow it up
further and further through time, whereby the chain
of causes lying between it and us is carried up higher and
higher, so that it can never be long enough to reach down to
the actual present, and accordingly it will have always NOT YET reached the present.   But this is con-
tradicted by the fact that the present is really there,
and constitutes indeed our only datum for the reckoning. The justification of the foregoing inconvenient
question arises from the fact that the first beginning
as such, implies no preceding cause, and therefore
might just as well have occurred trillions of years
earlier.   For if it required no cause for its occurrence,
it did not have to wait for any, and must accordingly
have taken place infinitely sooner, since there existed

nothing to prevent it. For as nothing need precede the first beginning as its cause, so nothing need precede it as its hindrance; it has, therefore, to wait for nothing, and never comes soon enough. It matters not in what point of time we fix it, we can never see why it should not have existed much sooner. This, therefore, pushes it ever further back, for since time itself can have no beginning, there is always an infinite time elapsed up to the present moment, so that the throwing backward of the beginning of the world is always endless, every causal chain from it to us proving too short, the consequence being that we never reach from it to the present time. Hence it comes that a given fixed point of connection (*point d'attache*), fails us, and therefore we have to assume such a one arbitrarily, but it always vanishes before our hands backward into infinity. And so it also happens that when we posit a first beginning and proceed therefrom we never attain from it to the present time.

If, on the other hand, we start from the really given present we never attain, as already indicated, to the first beginning. For every cause to which we proceed must always be the effect of a previous one, which finds itself in the same case and can reach no end. The world is therefore now beginningless, like infinite time itself, in the contemplation of which our imaginative faculty is wearied, and our understanding receives no satisfaction.

These two opposite views may be compared to a stick of which one end, it matters not which, may be easily grasped, while the other extends itself forever into infinity. The essential of the matter may be resumed in the proposition that time, which is absolutely infinite, must always be too great for a world conceived as finite. But at bottom the truth of the "antithesis" of the Kantian antinomy is confirmed thereby, for if we proceed from that which is alone certain and really given, the beginninglessness of time results. On the other hand, the first beginning is merely an arbitrary assumption, which cannot be united as such, with what we have said is the only certain and real, the present. For the rest we must regard these considerations as disclosing the absurdities ensuing from the assumption of the absolute reality of time, and consequently as confirmations of the main thesis of Kant.

The question as to whether the world is bounded in space or is unbounded, is not *per se* transcendent, but rather empirical, since the question always lies within the realm of possible experience, the reduction of it to reality being only forbidden us by our own physical conformation. *A priori* there is here no demonstrably certain argument, either for the one or the other alternative, so that the question really resembles an antinomy, inasmuch as with the one as with the other assumption considerable difficulties present themselves. A bounded world in infinite space vanishes, let it be ever so large, to an infinitely small quantity, and one asks what is the remaining space there for? On the other hand, one cannot conceive that no fixed star should be the farthest in space. It may be observed, by the way, that the planets of such a star would only have a starry heaven at night during a half of their year, during the other half a starless heaven, which would certainly make a very uncanny impression on the inhabitants. The foregoing question, therefore, may be thus expressed, "Is there a fixed star whose planets stand in this predicament or not?" Here it evinces itself as obviously empirical.

In my critique of the Kantian philosophy, I have shown the whole assumption of the antinomies to be false and illusory. With due consideration, however, everyone will at once recognize it as impossible that conceptions, correctly drawn from phenomena and their *a priori* certain laws, should, when combined according to the laws of logic into judgments and conclusions, lead to contradictions. For if this were the case, contradictions would have to lie in the perceptually-given phenomenon itself, or in the regulative connection of its members, which is an impossible assumption. For the perceptual, as such, knows no contradiction at all; the latter term has in respect of it no meaning or significance, since it exists merely in abstract knowledge or reflection. One can perfectly well, either openly or covertly, assume something and at the

same time not assume it, in other words, contradict oneself, but something real cannot at the same time both be
and not be. The opposite of the foregoing, Zeno the
eleatic certainly sought to prove with his well-known
sophisms, as also Kant with his antinomies. I therefore
refer the reader to my critique of the latter.

Kant's service to SPECULATIVE THEOLOGY has already
been generally touched upon. In order to emphasize it
still more I will now as shortly as may be, endeavor to
make the essential of the matter as comprehensible as
possible in my way.

In the Christian religion the existence of God is a thing
presupposed and raised above all discussion. This is only
natural, for it is essential thereto, and is in this case based
upon revelation. I regard it therefore as a blunder of
the Rationalists when they attempt in their dogmas to
demonstrate the existence of God otherwise than from
the Scriptures. They in their innocence do not know how
dangerous is this amusement. Philosophy, on the other
hand, is a science, and as such has no articles of faith.
In philosophy, therefore, nothing may be assumed as existent, except either what is directly given in experience,
or what is demonstrated by indubitable arguments. The
latter people certainly long believed themselves to be in
the possession of when Kant disillusionized the world on
this point, and so decisively demonstrated the impossibility
of such proofs, that since then no philosopher in Germany
has again attempted to resuscitate them. Herein Kant
was perfectly justified, and what he did was of the highest service, for a theoretical dogma which presumes to
stamp everyone who refuses to admit its validity as a
rogue, deserves once for all to be seriously put to the
test.

The case of the assumed demonstration is as follows.
Inasmuch as the REALITY of the existence of God cannot
be shown by empirical reasoning, the next step should
properly be to establish its POSSIBILITY, in the course of
doing which one would encounter enough difficulties.
But, instead of this, its NECESSITY was undertaken to be
proved, *i. e.*, it was undertaken to demonstrate God as
NECESSARY ESSENCE.

Now NECESSITY, as I have often shown, is never anything more than the dependence of a consequence on its cause, in other words, the appearance or positing of the effect because the cause is given. To this end accordingly the choice lay between the four forms of the principle of cause demonstrated by me, and of these the two first only were found to be admissible. There arose therefore two theological demonstrations, the cosmological and the ontological, the first derived from the principle of the ground of Becoming (cause), the other from that of the ground of Knowing. The first seeks to establish the necessity referred to as PHYSICAL according to the law of CAUSALITY, inasmuch as the world is conceived as an effect which must have a CAUSE. To this cosmological demonstration the assistance and support of the physico-theological is added. The cosmological argument is most powerfully expressed in the Wolffian version of it, which is as follows: "If any thing at all exists, there exists an absolutely necessary Being." By this is to be understood either that which is itself given, or the first of the causes through which it attains to existence. The latter is then assumed. This demonstration has obviously the weakness of being a conclusion from the consequence to the cause, to which form of conclusion logic refuses all claim to certainty. It ignores the fact which I have often pointed out, that we can only think any thing as necessary in so far as it is effect, not in so far as it is cause of another given thing. Besides, the law of causality when applied in this way proves too much. For if it would carry us from the world back to its cause, it does not allow us to remain by this, but leads us further back still to the cause of the cause, and so onward and remorselessly onward *in infinitum*. This is involved in its very nature. We are in the position of Goethe's magician's apprentice, whose imp began indeed at command, but refused to leave off again. Add to this that the force and validity of the law of causality only extends to the form of things and not to their matter. It is the clue to the change of forms and nothing more; the matter remains untouched by all their coming and going, a fact which we discern before all experience, and therefore know with certainty.

Finally, the cosmological demonstration is upset by the transcendental argument that the law of causality is demonstrably of subjective origin, and therefore merely applicable by our intellect to PHENOMENA, and not to THINGS IN THEMSELVES.*

As already said, the physico-theological demonstration is given as a subsidiary aid to the cosmological, in order that it should afford confirmation, substantiation, plausibility, color, and form to the assumption introduced by the former. But it can only come in with the presupposition of the first demonstration, the explanation and amplification of which it is. Its procedure consists in that it raises the already presupposed cause of the world to a knowing and willing being, inasmuch as by induction from the many effects which may be explained by such a cause, it seeks to establish this cause. But induction can, at most, afford strong probability, certainty never. Besides, as already said, this whole demonstration is conditioned by the previous one. But if one goes more closely and seriously into this favorite physico-theology, and tests it in the light of my philosophy, it is seen to be the carrying-out of a fundamentally false view of nature, which degrades the immediate phenomenon or objectivation of the will to a mere mediate one, and thus, instead of recognizing in natural existences the original,

* Looking at things realistically and objectively, it is as clear as the noonday that the world maintains itself. Organic beings subsist and propagate themselves by virtue of their own inward and original vital force. Inorganic bodies bear in themselves the forces of which physics and chemistry are the mere description, and the planets proceed in their course from inward powers by virtue of their inertia and gravitation. The world, therefore, requires no one outside itself for its subsistence, for it is *Vishnu;* but to say that this world in time with all its indwelling forces has not always been, but has been produced from nothing by a foreign power existing outside it, is a wholly superfluous supposition which nothing can confirm, more particularly as all its forces are bound up with matter, the origination and destruction of which we cannot even so much as think. This conception of the world reaches back to Spinozism. That men in their uttermost need have everywhere conceived beings which control the forces of nature and their course, in order to appeal to such, is perfectly natural. Greeks and Romans, however, were content to leave the matter with the control of its own sphere by each divinity; it never occurred to them to assert that any one of them had made the world and the forces of nature.

primarily powerful, knowingless, and, therefore, infallibly
certain action of the will, it explains it as something
merely secondary, only produced by the light of knowledge and the clue of motives; and, accordingly, it conceives that which has been produced from within
outward as something becarpentered, bemodeled, and
molded from the outside.   For if the Will, as thing-in-
itself, which is NOT in any sense Presentment, emerges
in the act of its objectivation from its originality into
Presentment, and we assume that what displays itself
in this presentment is something brought about in the
world of presentment itself; in other words, in consequence of KNOWLEDGE, then, certainly, it appears only possible by means of an immeasurably perfect knowledge, a
knowledge which comprehends at once all objects and
their connection,— in short, as a work of the highest wisdom.   As to this point I refer the reader to my treatise
on " Will in Nature," especially pp. 43–62 of the 1st ed.
(pp. 35–54 2d ed., pp. 37–58 3d ed.), under the heading
" Comparative Anatomy," and to my chief work, vol. ii.,
beginning of cap. 26.

The second theological demonstration, the ontological,
as stated, does not take the law of causality, but the
principle of the ground of knowledge as its clue, whereby
the necessity of the existence of God becomes here a
LOGICAL one.   It is sought here, namely, to deduce the
existence from the conception of God by a mere analytical judgment, in such wise that it is not possible to
make this conception the subject of a proposition in
which this existence is denied, by making such denial
contradict the subject of the proposition.   This is logically
correct, but is also a very obvious and only too transparent conjuror's trick.   After having, by using the concept " perfection " or " reality " as a handle to be employed
as *terminus medius*, the predicate of existence is introduced into the subject, it cannot fail that it is afterward
found there again, and is exposed by means of an
analytical judgment.   But the justification for establishing the whole concept is in nowise proved thereby; on
the contrary, it is either excogitated in a purely arbitrary
manner, or introduced through the cosmological demon-

14

stration according to which everything turns on purely
physical necessity. Christian Wolff seems, indeed, to have
seen this, for in his metaphysics he has only made use
of the cosmological argument, and expressly takes note of
the fact. The ontological demonstration will be found
carefully investigated and estimated in the second and
third edition of my treatise on the "Fourfold Root of
the Principle of Adequate Cause," § 7, and to this I
refer the reader.

The two theological demonstrations mutually support
each other, but cannot stand any the more on that
account. The cosmological has the advantage that it
takes account how it has come by the conception of a
God, and by its adjunct the physico-theological demonstration seeks to make this demonstration probable.
The ontological, on the other hand, is quite unable to
prove how it has come by its conception of the most
real of all essences, and, in consequence, either alleges
it to be innate or borrows it from the cosmological
demonstration, and seeks to uphold it by imposing-
sounding talk of the Being which cannot be thought of
except as existing, whose existence lies already in its conception, etc.

In the meantime, we shall not deny the merit of acuteness and subtlety to the invention of the ontological
demonstration if we consider the following. In order to
explain a given existence, we point to its cause, in respect
of which it then appears as something necessary, and
this serves as its explanation. But this way leads, as
already sufficiently shown, to a "*regressus in infinitum*,"
and can never, therefore, attain the something final
which would furnish a fundamental ground of explanation. The case would be otherwise if the EXISTENCE of
any being could be really deduced from its ESSENCE, that
is, from its mere concept or definition. For then, indeed,
it would be known as something NECESSARY (by which
here, as elsewhere, is only meant that "which follows
from its cause") without thereby being bound to anything other than its own concept,— in other words, without its necessity being merely transitory and momentary,
itself being again conditioned, and so on, leading to an

infinite series as is always the case with CAUSAL necessity. The mere ground of knowledge would then have
transformed itself into a ground of reality, that is, into
a cause, thereby excellently qualifying itself to serve as
the final, and hence certain, point of attachment for all
causal series, in which case we should have what we
sought.

But we have seen above that all this is illusory, and
it looks as if Aristotle himself had been desirous of
avoiding such a sophistication when he said, τὸ δὲ εἶναι
οὐκ οὐσία οὐσία οὐδένι, *ad nullius rei essentiam pertinet existentia* (Analyt. post. ii. 7).

Without troubling himself about this, Descartes, following Anselm of Canterbury, who had already led the way
to a similar line of thought, posited the conception of
God as one which fulfilled the requirement,— Spinoza,
however, that of the world as the only existing substance
which could be *causa sui*, i. e., *quæ per se est et per se concipitur quamobrem nulla alia re eget ad existendum*, conferring
on the world so established the title God, *honoris causa*,
in order to satisfy everyone. But it is always the same
tour de passe-passe, which endeavors to palm off the
LOGICALLY necessary as a REAL necessary, and which, together with other similar deceptions, at last gave occasion
to Locke's great investigation into the origin of concepts,
with which the foundation of the critical philosophy was
laid. A more detailed exposition of the procedure of
both dogmatists is contained in my treatise on the " Principle of Cause, " 2nd and 3rd ed., §§ 7 and 8.

After Kant by his critique of speculative theology had
given the latter its death blow, * he had to seek to modify the impression produced by this, and to apply, as it
were, a soothing medicine or anodyne; the procedure of
Hume was analagous, who in the last of his, as readable
as irrefutable, "Dialogues on Natural Religion, " explains to us that the whole thing has merely been a
joke, an *exercitium logicum*. In the same way Kant gave
as substitute for the demonstration for the existence of
God, his postulate of the practical reason, and the moral

* Kant discovered, namely, the alarming truth that philosophy
must be something other than Jewish mythology.

theology arising therefrom which without any claim to objective validity, so far as knowledge or the theoretical reason was concerned, should have complete validity in respect of conduct, or for the practical reason, whereby a belief without knowledge might be founded — so that at all events people should have something in hand. His exposition properly understood, says nothing else than that the assumption of a just God rewarding and punishing after death is a useful and sufficient regulative scheme for the explanation of the serious ethical significance felt to belong to our conduct, as also for the regulation of this conduct itself. He set up, as it were, an allegory of the truth, so that in this respect, which alone has any significance in the last resort, his assumption might take the place of the truth, even though theoretically or objectively it was not to be justified. An analogous scheme of similar tendency, but of much greater validity, stronger plausibility, and consequently more immediate worth, is the dogma of Brahminism of a rewarding or punishing Metempsychosis, according to which we must at some time be reborn in the form of every being that has been injured by us, in order to suffer the same injury. Kant's moral theology must be taken in the sense indicated, remembering at the same time that he himself dare not express himself so plainly as is here done on the real state of affairs, but in setting up the monstrosity of a THEORETICAL doctrine of merely PRACTICAL validity reckoned on the *granum salis* of the wiser sort. The theological and theosophical writers of a later time far removed from the Kantian philosophy, have endeavored for the most part to give the matter the appearance as though Kant's moral theology were a real dogmatic Theism, a new proof of the existence of God. Yet it is not so by any means, but is only valid inside the moral sphere, merely for the assistance of morality, and not a straw's breadth further.

Not even the professors of philosophy allowed themselves to be satisfied with this for long, although they were placed in conspicuous embarrassment by Kant's critique of speculative theology, for they had from of old recognized it as their special calling to demonstrate the existence and attributes of God, and to make Him the chief subject of their philosophizing. When, therefore, Scripture teaches that God nourishes the ravens in the field, I must also add, and the professors of philosophy in their chairs. Even nowadays, they assert with perfect coolness that the Absolute (well-known as the new-fangled title for God) and its relation to the world is the proper subject of philosophy, and to define this more closely, and to paint it with their imagination, exercises them now as before, for assuredly the governments which provide money for such philosophizing desire to see good Christians and zealous Church-goers come out of the philosophical class-rooms. How must it then have suited these gentlemen of the lucrative philosophy when Kant upset the concept by the proof that all demonstrations of speculative theology are untenable, and that all cognitions concerning their chosen theme were simply impossible for our intellect? At first they tried to help themselves by their well-known method of ignoring, and afterward by contesting, but this did not answer in the long run. They next threw themselves upon the assertion that the existence of God was indeed incapable of any demonstration, but that it did not require any; for it was obvious, indeed the most established fact of the world, which we could not doubt since we had a "divine consciousness" within us, our reason being the organ for the immediate knowledge of supernatural things, and our instruction on this point being derived immediately from it, whence it was therefore called REASON! (I earnestly beg the reader to consult respecting this my treatise on the "Principle of Cause," 2d and 3d ed., § 34, as also my "Fundamental Problems of Ethics," pp. 148–154, finally also my "Criticism of the Kantian Philosophy," 2d ed., pp. 584–584, 3d. ed., pp. 617–618.)

As regards the genesis of this divine consciousness we have recently received a remarkable pictorial illustration, to wit, an engraving displaying a mother placing her three-year-old child with folded hands and in a kneeling position against the bed, for the purpose of praying, certainly a frequent occurrence constituting the genesis of the divine consciousness. For it is not doubtful that when the brain

in the earliest stages of its growth, and at the tenderest
age is so molded, the "divine consciousness" will grow as
firmly imbedded in it as though it were really inborn.
According to others the reason merely furnishes sugges-
tions, while others again possess intellectual intuitions.
There were, still further, those who invented Absolute
Thought, *i. e.*, a Thought by which man did not require
to look around him at the things, but which determined
in Divine Omniscience how they were to be once for all.
This is undoubtedly the most convenient of all the foregoing inventions. They one and all seized upon the word
"absolute" which is nothing but the cosmological demonstration *in nuce*, or rather so strongly compressed that it
has become microscopic and invisible, and thus is allowed
to pass unnoticed, and as such is proclaimed as something
requiring no explanation. For in its true form it dare no
longer show itself after the Kantian *examen rigorosum* —
as I have already shown at greater length in the 2d
edition of my treatise on "The Principle of Cause," p.
36 (3d ed., p. 37), and also in my criticism of the Kantian
philosophy, 2d. ed., p. 544 (3d ed., p. 574). I do not
know who was the first who fifty years ago made use of
the trick of smuggling in under this comprehensive word
Absolute the exploded and proscribed cosmological demonstration, *incognito*, but the dodge was well suited to
the capacities of the public, for up to this day the word
"absolute" passes current as true coin.

In short, in spite of the critique of the reason and its
demonstrations, the professors of philosophy have never
failed in authentic accounts of the existence of God and
his relation to the world in the detailed exposition of
which in their eyes philosophy properly consists. But in
the words of the proverb, "copper money, copper wares;"
this God requiring no explanation of theirs has neither hand
nor foot; and for this reason they keep him hidden behind a mountain, or rather behind a noisy edifice of words,
so that scarcely a sign of him is visible. If one could
only compel them to explain themselves clearly as to what
is to be understood by the word God we should be able
to see whether it required no explanation. Not even a
natura naturans (into which their God often appears to

pass) requires no explanation since we find Leukippus, Demokritos, Epikurus, and Lukretius constructed a world without any such; and these men, with all their errors, were worth a great deal more than a legion of weather-cocks whose trade-philosophy turns round with the wind. But a *natura naturans* is a long way from being God. In the conception of such the truth is merely contained that behind the ever-fleeting and restlessly changing phenomena of the *natura naturata* an imperishable and untiring force must lie hidden by virtue of which the former is continually renewing itself, since it remains un-touched by the dissolution of things. As the *natura naturata* is the subject of physics, so is the *natura natu-rans* that of metaphysics. This shows us that we ourselves ultimately belong to nature, and consequently, know less of *natura naturata* than of *natura naturans* — that we are the nearest and the clearest, and indeed that we possess in ourselves the only specimen of it to which access can be obtained from within. Now inasmuch as a serious and exact reflection upon ourselves discloses the Will as the core of our being, we have in this an immediate revela-tion of the *natura naturans*, which we are accordingly justified in transferring to all other beings which are only one-sidedly known to us. We attain thereby to the great truth that the *natura naturans*, or the thing-in-itself is the Will in our own heart, while the *natura naturata*, or the phenomenon, is the presentment in our head. But even apart from this result it is sufficiently obvious that the mere distinguishing of a *natura naturans* and a *natura naturata* is not only not Theism, but is not even Pan-theism; for even to the latter, if it is not to be a mere manner of speaking, the addition of certain moral quali-ties is necessary, which clearly do not accrue to the world, *e.g.*, goodness, wisdom, blessedness, etc.

For the rest, Pantheism is a conception which destroys itself, for the conception of a God presupposes as its es-sential correlate that of a world distinct from him. If, on the other hand, the world takes over his rôle, there remains an absolute world without God, and hence Pan-theism is only a euphemism for Atheism. But this last expression in its turn also contains a subreption, since it

assumes at the outset that Theism requires no explanation, whereby it dexterously evades the *affirmanti incumbit
probatio*, while it is rather the so-called Atheism that has
the just *primi occupantis*, and has therefore to be first
driven out of the field by Theism.   I allow myself here
the observation that men came into the world uncircum-
cised, and therefore not as Jews.   But even the assumption of some cause of the world distinct therefrom is not
Theism.   Theism requires not only a cause distinct from
the world, but an intelligent, a knowing and willing, that
is a personal, in short, an individual cause; such a cause
alone does the word God connote.

An impersonal God is no God at all, but merely a
misapplied word, a misconception, a contradicfion *in adjecto*, a shibboleth for professors of philosophy who, after
having given up the thing, are anxious to smuggle in the
word.   The personality, on the contrary, that is, the self-
conscious individuality which first knows, and then in
accordance with the knowledge wills, is a phenomenon
known to us solely from the animal nature which is
present on our small planet, and is so intimately connected with this that we are not only not justified in
thinking it as separate and independent, but are not even
capable of doing so.   But to assume a being of such a
kind, as the origin of nature herself and of all existence
is a colossal and daring conception which would startle
us if we heard it for the first time, and if it had not by
dint of earliest teaching and continuous repetition become familiar to us as a second nature, I might also say
a fixed idea.   Hence I may observe, by the way, that
nothing has so well accredited to me the genuineness of
Casper Hauser as the statement that the so-called natural
theology which was expounded to him did not seem to
enlighten him as much as was expected.   To which may
be added that he (according to the " Letters of Count
Stanhope to the Schoolmaster Meyer ") exhibited an extraordinary reverence for the sun.   But to teach in philosophy that this theological notion requires no explanation,
and that the reason is only the capacity immediately to
comprehend the same and recognize it as true, is a shameless proceeding.   Not only has philosophy no right to

assume such a conception without the fullest demonstration, but it is by no means essential even to religion. This is attested by the religion which counts the largest number of adherents on earth, the ancient, highly moral, indeed ascetic Buddhism,—whose adherents now number three hundred and seventy millions,—a religion which also maintains the most numerous body of clergy of any— inasmuch as it does not admit such a conception, but rather expressly stigmatizes it, and is thus *ex professo*, according to our notions, atheistic.*

According to the foregoing, Anthropomorphism is an essential characteristic of Theism, and it is expressed not merely in the human form nor even in human affections and passions, but in the fundamental phenomenon itself, to wit, in the one will furnished with an intellect for its guidance, which phenomenon, as already said, is known to us only in animal nature and most perfectly in human nature, which is only thinkable as Individuality, and which when it is endowed with reason is called

---

* The Zaradobura, the high priest of the Buddhists in Ara, in a treatise on his religion which he gave to a Catholic Bishop, reckons among the six damnable heresies the doctrine that a Being exists who has created the world and all things in the world, and who is alone worthy of worship. ("Francis Buchanan on the Religion of the Burmas," in "Asiatic Researches," vol. vi., p. 268.) It is mentioned in the same series, vol. xv., p. 148, viz, that the Buddhists bow their heads before no idol, giving as their reason that the Primal Being interpenetrates all nature and consequently is also in their heads. Similarly the learned Orientalist and member of the St. Petersburg Academy, J. J. Schmidt, in his "Researches in the Domain of the Ancient History of Central Asiatic Culture" (Petersburg, 1848), p. 180, says: "The system of Buddhism knows no eternal uncreated single divine being existent before all time, and who created all things visible and invisible. This idea is quite foreign to it, and there is not the slightest trace of it to be found in the Buddhist books. Just as little is there a creation." Where, then, is the "divine consciousness" of Kant and those professors of philosophy who pervert the truth? How is it to be explained that the language of the Chinese, who constitute about two-fifths of the whole human race, has no expressions for God and creation? For this reason the first verse of the Pentateuch could not be translated into Chinese to the great perplexity of the missionaries whom Sir George Staunton tried to assist by means of a book which he entitled, "An inquiry into the proper mode of rendering the word 'God' in translating the Sacred Scriptures into the Chinese language." London, 1848.

Personality.   This is confirmed by the expression, "as truly as God lives"; He is indeed a living being, that is, one willing with knowledge.   Hence a God requires a heaven in which he is enthroned and whence he governs. Much more on this account than because of the expression in the Book of Joshua was the Kopernican system at once received with distrust by the Church, and we find accordingly a hundred years later Giordano Bruno as the champion at once of this system and of Pantheism. The attempts to purify Theism from Anthropomorphism, notwithstanding that they are only meant to touch the shell, really strike at the innermost core.   In their endeavor to conceive its object abstractly they sublimate it to a dim cloud-shape whose outline gradually disappears entirely in the effort to avoid the human figure; so that at last the whole childish idea becomes attenuated to nothing.   But besides all this the rationalistic theologians, who are especially fond of these attempts, may be reproached with contradicting the Holy Scriptures, which say, "God created man in his own image; in the image of God created he him."   Let us then away with the jargon of the professors of philosophy!   There is no other God than God, and the Old Testament is his revelation — especially the Book of Joshua.   From the God who was originally Jehovah, philosophers and theologians have stripped off one coating after the other, until at last nothing but the word is left.

One might certainly, with Kant, call Theism a practical postulate, although in quite another sense to that which he meant it.   Theism is indeed no product of the Understanding but of the Will.   If it were originally theoretical, how could all its proofs be so untenable?   But it arises from the Will in the following manner: the continual need with which the heart (Will) of man is now heavily oppressed, now violently moved, and which keeps him perpetually in a state of fear and hope, while the things of which he hopes and fears are not in his power — the very connection of the chain of causes which produce them only being traceable for a short distance by his intelligence — this need, this constant fear and hope, causes him to frame the hypothesis of personal beings on whom everything depends. It is assumed of such that they, like other persons, are susceptible to request and flattery, service and gift — in other words, that they are more tractable than the iron Necessity, the unbending, the unfeeling forces of nature, and the mysterious powers of the world-order. At first, as is natural, and as was very logically carried out by the ancients, these Gods were many, according to diversity of circumstances. Later on, owing to the necessity of bringing sequence, order, and unity into knowledge, these Gods were subordinated to one, which, as Goethe once remarked to me, is very undramatic, since with a solitary person one can do nothing. The essential, however, is the impulse of anxious humanity to throw itself down and pray for help in its frequent, bitter, and great distress and also in its concern for its eternal happiness. Man relies rather on external grace than on his own merit. This is one of the chief supports of Theism. In order therefore that his heart (Will) may have the relief of prayer and the consolation of hope, his intellect must create a God; and not conversely, because his intellect has deduced a God, does he pray. Let him be left without needs, wishes, and requirements, a mere intellectual will-less being, and he requires no God and makes none. The heart, that is the Will, has in its bitter distress the need to call for almighty and consequently supernatural assistance. Hence, because a God is wanted to be prayed to he is hypostatized, and not conversely. For this reason the theoretical side of the theology of all nations is very different as to the number and character of their gods; but that they can and do help when they are served and prayed to, thus much is common to them all, since it is the point upon which everything depends. It is at the same time the birthmark by which the descent of all theology is recognizable, to wit, that it proceeds from the Will, from the heart, and not from the head or the intelligence, as is pretended. This is implied also in that the true reason why Constantine the Great, as also Chlodowig, the king of the Franks, changed their religion, was that they hoped from their new god better support in war. There are some few races which, preferring the minor to the major, instead of gods possess mere spirits, who are prevented from doing harm by sacrifice and prayer. But the final result shows no great difference. The original inhabitants of the Indian peninsula and Ceylon, before the introduction of Brahminism and Buddhism, appear to have been such races, and their descendants would seem to have in part even now a similar cacodæmonological religion, like many other savage peoples. From this source springs the Kappuism which is mixed with the Cinghalese religion, Buddhism. In the same way the devil worshippers of Mesopotamia, visited by Layard, seem to belong to this category. Intimately connected with the true origin of all Theism, as here expounded, and equally proceeding from the nature of man, is the impulse to bring sacrifices to his gods in order to purchase their favor, or if they have already shown such, to ensure its continuance or to buy off evils from them. ("Sanchoniathonis Fragmenta," ed. Orelli, Lips., 1826, p. 42.) This is the meaning of every sacrifice, and hence the origin and support of every god; so that it may be said with truth the gods live upon sacrifice. For precisely because the impulse to appeal to and to purchase the assistance of supernatural beings as the child of need and intellectual limitation, is natural to man, for its satisfaction and requirement he creates God for himself. Hence the universality of sacrifice in all ages and with the most diverse races, and its identity amid the greatest difference of circumstance and of intellectual development. Thus, for example, Herodotus relates that a ship from Samos, through the exceptionally advantageous sale of its cargo in Tartessus, had acquired an unprecedented fortune, whereupon the Samians expended the tenth part of it to the amount of six talents on a large brazen and artistically worked vase, which they presented in the Temple of Here. And as a counterpart to these Greeks, we see in our days the miserable nomad reindeer Lapp, with figure shrunk to the dimensions of a dwarf, hiding his spare money in various secret recesses of the rocks and glens, which he makes known to no one except it be in his dying hour to his heir, and even to him there is one such hiding place which he never reveals — that namely wherein he has secreted a

treasure brought as a sacrifice to the *genius loci*, the pro-
tecting God of his territory (S. Albrecht Pancritius
Hägringar, " Reise durch Schweden, Lappland, Norwegen,
und Dänemark im Jahre 1850," Königsberg, 1852, p. 162).
The belief in gods thus has its root in egoism.   In Christianity alone has the sacrifice proper disappeared, although
in the form of masses for souls, of cloister, church, and
chapel building, it is still there.   For the rest, and especially with Protestants, praise and thanksgiving have to
serve as the surrogate of sacrifice, and hence they are
carried to the extremest superlative even on occasions
which to the outsider seem little suited thereto — a proceeding analogous to that of the State which also does
not always reward merit with gifts, but sometimes with
mere testimonials of honor, thereby maintaining its continuance.   In this respect what the great David Hume
says deserves to be recalled: " Whether this god, therefore, be considered as their peculiar patron, or as the
general sovereign of heaven, his votaries will endeavor
by every art to insinuate themselves into his favor; and
supposing him to be pleased, like themselves, with praise
and flattery, there is no eulogy or exaggeration which
will be spared in their addresses to him.   In proportion
as men's fears or distresses become more urgent, they
will invent   new   strains of   adulation; and   even he
who outdoes his predecessors in swelling up the titles of
his divinity, is sure to be outdone by his successors in
newer and more pompous epithets of praise.   Thus they
proceed, till at last they arrive at infinity itself, beyond
which there is no farther progress." (" Essays and
Treatises on Several Subjects," London, 1777, vol. ii.,
p. 429.) And again: " It appears certain that, though
the original notions of the vulgar represent the divinity
as a limited being, and consider him only as the particular cause of health or sickness, plenty or want, prosperity or adversity, yet when more magnificent ideas
are urged upon them, they esteem it DANGEROUS TO
REFUSE THEIR ASSENT. Will you say that your deity is
finite and bounded in his perfection; may be overcome
by a greater force; is subject to human passions, pains,
and infirmities; has a beginning, and may have an end?

This they dare not affirm, but thinking it SAFEST TO COMPLY WITH THE HIGHER ENCONIUMS, THEY ENDEAVOR, BY AN AFFECTED RAVISHMENT AND DEVOTION, TO INGRATIATE THEMSELVES WITH HIM. As a confirmation of this we may observe that the assent of the vulgar is, in this case, merely verbal, and that they are incapable of conceiving those sublime qualities which they seemingly attribute to the Deity. Their real idea of him, notwithstanding their pompous language, is still as poor and frivolous as ever." (*Ibid.*, p. 432.)

In order to mitigate the heterodoxy of his "Critique of all Speculative Theology," Kant added thereto not only moral theology, but also the assurance that even though the existence of God had to remain unproven, it would be just as impossible to prove the opposite, an assurance with which many have consoled themselves, without observing that he, with pretended simplicity, ignored the *affirmanti incumbit probatio*, as also that the number of things whose existence cannot be proved is infinite. He has naturally taken still more care not to bring forward the arguments which might be employed for an apagogic counter-demonstration when once one ceased to adopt a merely defensive attitude, and began to act on the aggressive. The proceeding would be somewhat as follows:—

1. In the first place the unhappy constitution of a world in which living beings subsist by mutually devouring each other, the consequent distress and dread of all that has life, the multitude and colossal magnitude of evil, the variety and inevitability of grief often attaining to horror, the burden of life itself hurrying forward to the bitterness of death cannot honestly be reconciled with its being the work of a united All-Goodness, All-Wisdom, and All-Power. To raise an outcry against what is here said is just as easy as it is difficult to meet the case with solid reasons.

2. There are two points which not only occupy every thinking man, but also which the adherents of every religion have most at heart, and on which the strength and persistence of religion is based; firstly, the transcendent moral significance of our conduct; and secondly, our continuance after death. When once a religion has taken

care of these two points everything else is secondary. I
will therefore test Theism here in respect of the first,
and later on in that of the second point.

With the morality of our conduct Theism has a double
connection, *viz*, one *a parte ante*, and one *a parte post*,
that is, with respect to the causes and consequences of
our action. To take the last point first; Theism indeed
gives morality a support, albeit one of the roughest kind,
one indeed by which the true and pure morality of conduct is fundamentally abolished, inasmuch as every disinterested action is at once transformed into an interested
one by means of a very long dated but assured bill of
exchange which is received as payment for it. The God,
viz, who was in the beginning the Creator, appears in
the end as an avenger aad paymaster. Regard for such
an one can certainly call forth virtuous actions, but these
are not purely moral since fear of punishment, or hope
of reward are their motive, the significance of such
virtue being reducible rather to a wise and well-con-
sidered egoism. In the last resort it turns solely on the
strength of belief in undemonstrable things; if this is
present no one will certainly stick at accepting a short
period of sorrow for an eternity of joy, and the really
guiding principle of morality will be "we can wait."
But every one who seeks a reward for his deeds, either
in this or in a future world, is an egoist. If the hoped-
for reward escape him, it is the same thing, whether
this happens by the chance which dominates this world,
or by the emptiness of the illusion which builds for him
the future one. For these reasons Kant's Moral Theology, properly speaking, undermines morality.

Again, *a parte ante*, Theism is equally in contradiction with morality, since it abolishes freedom and responsibility. For with a being which in its *existentia*
and *essentia* alike, is the work of another, neither fault
nor merit can be conceived. Vauvenargues says very
rightly: "*Un être, qui a tout reçu, ne peut, agir que par
ce qui lui a été donné; et tout la puissance divine qui est
infinie, ne saurait le rendre indépendant*" ("Discours sur la
Liberté," see "Œuvres complètes," Paris, 1823, tom. ii.,
p. 331). Like every other thinkable being it cannot

operate otherwise than according to its nature, and make
known this nature in its operations; it is created as we
here find it. If it acts badly this comes from the fact
that it is bad, in which case the fault is not its own, but
his who made it. The originator of its existence and
its nature, to which we may add the circumstances in
which it has been placed, is inevitably the originator of
its conduct and its deeds, which are as certainly determined by the former as the triangle is by two angles
and a line. The correctness of this argumentation has
been very well recognized and admitted by St. Augustine, by Hume, and by Kant, while others have glossed
over and timidly ignored it, a point I have fully dealt
with in my prize essay on the "Freedom of the Will,"
p. 67, sq. (2d ed., p. 66, sq.). In order to elude this
fearful and exterminating difficulty the freedom of the
Will, the *liberum arbitrium indifferentiæ*, was invented, a
theory which contains an utterly monstrous fiction, and
was therefore long ago discarded by all thinking minds,
but has perhaps never been so systematically and thoroughly refuted as in the work just quoted. If, notwithstanding, the common herd content themselves with
freedom of the Will — even the literary, the philosophical, common herd — what matters that to us? The assertion that a given being is FREE, that is, under given
circumstances can act thus and also otherwise, implies
that it has an *existentia* without any *essentia*, *i.e.*, that it
can BE without being SOMETHING, in short, that it at the
same time IS and is NOT. This, of course, is the acme of
absurdity, but none the less, good enough for people
who seek not the truth but their fodder, and hence will
never allow anything to obtain which does not suit the
stuff, the *fable convenu*, on which they live; ignoring
suits their obtuseness better than refuting. And ought
we to attach any weight to the opinions of such βοσκήματα,
in terram prona et ventri obedientia? All that IS is
also something, has an essence, a nature, a character,
in accordance with which it must operate. It must conduct itself (that is, act according to motive), when the
external occasions arise which call out its particular
manifestations. Whence it gets its actuality, its *exist-*

entia, there also it gets its construction, its *essentia*, since the two, although distinguishable in conception, are not separable in reality. But that which has an *essentia*, that is, a nature, a character, a construction, can only act in accordance therewith, and never otherwise. It is merely the precise moment, and special form and manner of the individual actions which are determined by the incoming motive. That the creator made man FREE, that he gave him an *existentia* without an *essentia*, in other words, an existence merely *in abstracto*, inasmuch as he left it to him to be what he would, is an impossible proposition. On this point I beg the reader to refer to section 20 of my treatise on the "Foundations of Morality." Moral freedom and responsibility, or accountability, necessarily presupposes *Aseity*. Actions are always based on character, that is, they proceed with necessity from the peculiar, and therefore unchangeable structure of a being under the influence and according to the measure of motive. Hence, if it is to be responsible, it must exist originally by virtue of its own power. It must, as regards its *existentia* and *essentia*, be its own work, and the creator of itself, if it is to be the true creator of its acts. Or, as I have expressed it in my two Prize Essays, its freedom cannot consist in its *Operari*, but must reside in its *esse*, for there it certainly is.

Since all this is not merely demonstrable *a priori*, but is clearly taught us by daily experience, to wit, that every one brings his moral character already complete into the world with him, and remains unchangeably true to it to the end, and since this truth is presupposed tacitly but certainly in our practical life, inasmuch as everyone bases his confidence or his misconfidence in another, once for all on the traits of character that other has manifested —this being so, one might wonder how, for about sixteen hundred years, the opposite has been theoretically asserted and taught, namely, that all men are in respect of morality originally the same, and that the great diversity of their conduct arises not from innate disposition and character, and just as little from accidental circumstances and causes, but, properly speaking, from nothing

15

at all, which nothing at all receives the name of free-will. But this absurd doctrine is made necessary by an-other, in the same way, purely theoretical assumption with which it exactly hangs together, namely, that the birth of man is the absolute beginning of his existence, since he is created out of nothing (*a terminus ad hoc*). If now, under this presupposition, life is to retain a moral significance and tendency, these must have their origin in the course of it, and must indeed originate from noth-ing, just as the supposed man himself is from nothing; for every connection with a preceding condition, a previous existence or a timeless act to which, neverthe-less, the immeasurable original and innate variety of moral characters clearly points, remains once for all ex-cluded. Hence the absurd fiction of a free will. Truths, it is well known, all stand in mutual connection; but er-rors also are necessary to each other just as one lie requires a second, or as two cards stood up against one another reciprocally support each other so long as noth-ing overturns them both.

3. On the assumption of Theism it does not fare much better with our continuance after death than with the freedom of the will. That which has been created by another has had a beginning of existence. Now that that which for an infinite time has not been, should from all eternity continue to be, is an outrageously bold assumption. If at my birth I have come from nothing and been created out of nothing, then it is the highest probability that at death I shall again become nothing. Endless continuance *a parte post*, and nothing, *a parte ante*, do not go together. Only that which is itself orig-inal, eternal, uncreated, can be indestructible. ("Aris-toteles de Cœlo," i. 12, 282, a, 25 fg., and Priestley, on "Matter and Spirit," Birmingham, 1782, vol. i., p. 234.) Those, therefore, may certainly be anxious in death who believe that before thirty or sixty years they were a pure nothing, and out of this nothing have proceeded as the work of another, for they have the difficult task of assuming that an existence so arisen, notwithstanding its late beginning, which has come about after the lapse of an infinite time, will, nevertheless, be of infinite dur-

ation. On the other hand, why should he fear death who recognizes himself as the original and eternal being, the very source of all existence, who knows that outside him nothing, properly speaking, exists at all—he who closes his individual existence with the saying of the Holy Upanishads, "*hæ omnes creaturæ in totum ego sum, et præter me ens aliud non est,*" on his lips or even in his heart. He alone, can with logical consistency, die peacefully. For, as already said, *aseity* is the condition of immortality as of accountability. In accordance with the foregoing, contempt of death and the most complete indifference to, or even joy in dying, is thoroughly at home in India. Judaism, on the contrary, originally the sole and only pure monotheistic religion, teaching a real God-creator of heaven and the earth, has with perfect logicality no doctrine of immortality, and hence no recompense after death, but only temporal punishments and rewards, whereby it distinguishes itself from all other religions, though possibly not to its advantage. The two religions sprung from Judaism, in so far as they took up the doctrine of immortality, which had become known to them from other and better religious teaching, and at the same time retained the God-creator, acted illogically in doing so.

That, as already said, Judaism is the only pure monotheistic religion, *i. e.*, one teaching that a God-creator is the origin of all things; is a service which for unknown reasons it has been sought to conceal by continually maintaining and teaching that all nations reverence the true God, although under other names. There is not merely much wanting in this procedure, but everything. That Buddhism, that is, the religion which, by possessing the greatest number of adherents, is the most important on earth, is throughout expressly atheistic, is placed beyond a doubt by the agreement of all unfalsified testimonies and original documents. The Vedas also teach no God-creator, but a world-soul called Brahm (neuter), of which the Brahma sprung from the navel of Vishnu, with the four faces, and forming part of the *trimurti*, is merely a popular personification; in the very lucid manner of Hindoo mythology. It represents obvi

ously the generation, the arising of beings, as Vishnu
does their acme, and as Shiva does their destruction.
The generation of the world is moreover a sinful act, like
the world-incarnation of Brahm. The Ormuzd of the
Zendavesta has, as we know, Ahriman as his counterpart, and both have proceeded from the immeasurable
time *Zervane Akerene* (if the ordinary view of this be correct). Similarly, in the very beautiful COSMOGONY OF THE
PHŒNICIANS, written by Sanchoniathon, and preserved for
us by Philo Byblius, which is perhaps the original of the
Mosaic Cosmogony, we find no trace of Theism or world-
creation by a personal being. We see here, also, as in
the Mosaic Genesis, the original chaos sunk in night, but
no God appears commanding, "Let there be light! let
there be this, and let there be that!" Oh, no! but ἠράσθη
τὸ πνεῦμα τῶν ἰδίων ἀρχῶν. The spirit fermenting in the
mass embodies itself in its own being, whereby a mixture of those original elements of the world arises (and
arises indeed, very effectively and significantly), from
which, in consequence of the longing, πόθος, which, as
the commentator correctly observes, is the Eros of the
Greeks, it develops itself from the primeval slime, and
out of this proceed, finally, plants, and last of all intelligent beings, that is, animals. For up to this time, as it
is expressly stated, everything went on without intelligence; αυτὸ δὲ οὐκ ἐγίγνωσκε τὴν ἑαυτοῦ κτίσιν. Thus does it
stand, adds Sanchoniathon, in the Cosmogony written
by Taaut, the Egyptian. A more detailed Zoogony then
follows upon his Cosmogony. Certain atmospheric and
terrestrial occurrences are described which really suggest
the correct assumptions of our modern geology. At
last, after heavy floods of rain, comes thunder and
lightning, startled by the crashing of which intelligent
animals awake into existence. "And there moves now
on the earth and in the sea, male and female."
Eusebius, whom we have to thank for this fragment
of Philo Byblius ("Præparat. Evangel.," 1. ii., c. 10),
justly accuses this cosmogony of atheism, which it is,
incontestably, like all and every theory of the origin of
the world, with the single exception of the Jewish. In
the mythology of the Greeks and Romans we find, indeed,

God as father of Gods, and sometimes also of men (although these were rather the potter's work of Prometheus), but no God-creator. For that later a few philosophers to whom Judaism had become known, wanted to transform father Zeus into such, does not affect the matter; just as little as that Dante, without having sought his permission, identifies him without scruple in his hell with Domeneddio, whose unparalleled vengeance and cruelty is stigmatized and pictured (*e. g.*, c. 14, 70; c. 31, 92). Finally (for everything has been brought into requisition), the endlessly repeated statement that the North American Indians worshiped God, the Creator of heaven and earth, under the name of the Great Spirit, and hence were pure Theists, is entirely incorrect. This error has recently been refuted in a treatise on the North American Indians, which John Scouler read before a sitting of the London Ethnographical Society in 1846, and of which "l'Institut, Journal des Sociétés Savantes," sect. 2, Juillet, 1847, gives an extract. It says: "When we are told in reports on the superstitions of the Indians, about the GREAT SPIRIT, we are apt to assume that it designates a conception agreeing with that which we associate with it, and that their belief is a simple natural Theism. But this interpretation is very far from correct. The religion of these Indians is rather a pure Fetichism, which consists in magical practices and Incantations In the report of Tanner, who lived among them from childhood, the facts are trustworthy and remarkable, albeit very different from the inventions of certain writers. One sees from it namely, that the religion of the Indians is only a Fetichism similar to that which was formerly met with among the Finns, and is still among the Siberian tribes. With the Indians dwelling eastward of the Mountains the Fetich consists simply of any object, it matters not what, to which mysterious qualities are attributed," etc.

In accordance with all this, the opinion here in question has to make way for its opposite, to wit, that only one very small and unimportant nation, despised by all contemporary nations, and living alone among them all without the belief in a continued existence after death, but nevertheless selected for the purpose, has possessed a pure monotheism, or the knowledge of the true God; and this, moreover, not through philosophy, but only through revelation, as was indeed suitable; for what value would a revelation have which only taught one what one knew without it? That no other nation has ever conceived such an idea must accordingly contribute to our estimate of the revelation.

SECTION 14.

SOME OBSERVATIONS ON MY OWN PHILOSOPHY.

There is scarcely any philosophical system so simple and constructed out of such few elements as my own; a fact rendering it readily comprehensible at a glance. This results from the complete unity and consistency of its fundamental positions, and is certainly a favorable augury for its truth, truth being allied to simplicity ἁπλοῦς ὁ τῆς ἀληθείας λόγος ἔφυ. *Simplex sigillum veri.* My system might be signalized as IMMANENT DOGMATISM, since its doctrines, although dogmatic, do not transcend the given world of experience, but merely explain WHAT THE LATTER IS, by analyzing it into its ultimate elements. The old dogmatism overturned by Kant (and not less the air-bubbles of the three modern University-Sophists), is TRANSCENDENT in that it passes beyond the world, to explain it by something foreign thereto: it makes the world the consequence of a cause which is inferred from itself. My philosophy, on the other hand, began with the doctrine that cause and effect possess meaning solely within the world, and that only under the presupposition of it are there causes and effects; inasmuch as the principle of cause in its four modes is merely the most universal form of the intellect, and that in this alone, as its true *locus mundi*, the objective world exists.

In other philosophical systems, the consequence is reached through a chain of propositions. But this necessarily demands that the special content of the system be present in the very earliest of these propositions; whereby the rest, as derived from them, can scarcely appear otherwise than monotonous, poor, empty, and tedious, being simply a development and repetition of what was contained in the original premises. This unhappy consequence of demonstrative deduction is most felt in Christian Wolff; but even Spinoza, who strictly followed this method, was unable entirely to escape its drawbacks, although his genius knew how to compensate for them. My doctrines, on the other hand, do not, for the most part, rest on a chain of syllogisms, but immediately on the sensible world itself, and the strict consequence, as visible in my own, as in any other system, is, as a rule, not simply arrived at by a logical process, but is rather the natural agreement of doctrines, necessarily resulting from their being based, in their entirety, on intuitive cognition, *i.e.*, on the sensible perception of the one OBJECT, successively contemplated from different sides, or in other words, on the REAL WORLD, which in all its phenomena is subject to the consciousness wherein it presents itself.

For this reason I have never had a care as to the mutual consistency of my doctrines; not even when some of these appeared to me inconsistent, as was the case for some time; for the agreement came afterward of itself in proportion to the numerical completeness of the doctrines; consistency in my case being nothing more than the consistency of reality with itself, which, of course, can never fail. This is analogous to when, on looking at a building for the first time on one side only, we fail to understand the symmetry of its parts, yet feel perfectly sure that it is not wanting, but will be visible to us on the completion of our view. But the above consistency is a perfectly certain one, because of its origination, and because it stands under the continual control of experience; while that which is deduced, and whose validity is derived from syllogisms, may easily be found false in some particular; should, for instance, a member of the long chain be ungenuine, loosely fitted, or otherwise faulty in its construction. My philosophy, accordingly, has a wide basis, on which everything stands immediately and, therefore, firmly; while other systems resemble lofty towers, where if one support breaks, the whole edifice falls to the ground. The foregoing may be summed up in the statement that my philosophy has arisen, and is presented, in an analytic rather than a synthetic manner.

I may adduce as a special characteristic of my philosophizing, that I seek everywhere to arrive at the foundation of things, and that I am not satisfied till I have found the ultimate given reality. This is in accordance with the natural bent of my mind, which renders it well-nigh impossible for me to rest in any more general and abstract and, therefore, undetermined knowledge, in mere conceptions, least of all in mere words; but drives me forward till I have the final basis of all conceptions and propositions which is always an intuitive one, exposed before me, and which I then must either leave as an ultimate phenomenon, or, if possible, resolve it into its elements, but either way, follow out the essential nature of the thing to its uttermost. On this account, it will be recognized one day (though certainly not during my lifetime) that the handling of the same subject by any earlier philosopher is tame as compared with mine. Mankind has learned much from me that will never be forgotten, and my writings will not pass into oblivion.

Theism also assumes the world to be the production of a Will — a Will that guides the planets in their orbits, and calls forth nature upon their surface. But theism, in childish fashion, places this Will outside the Universe, and only allows it to operate indirectly on the things, namely, through the medium of cognition and matter, in a Human manner; while with me the Will works not so much ON things, as IN them; they themselves being indeed naught else but its visible manifestation.

This agreement proves, however, that we cannot regard the original of things in any other light than as Will. Pantheism calls this ever-active Will that is in things by the name of God; an absurdity frequently and strongly enough exposed by me. I have designated it the WILL TO LIVE; because this expresses the finality of our knowledge on the subject. The above relation of the Mediate to the Immediate presents itself also in the sphere of Morals. The Theists would have a reconciliation between

what one does and what one suffers, and so would I.
But they make this take place through the medium of
time, and the interposition of a Judge and Avenger. I,
on the other hand, immediately, since I demonstrate the
same being in the actor and the sufferer. The moral
consequences of Christianity to the most extreme Asceticism are present with me, but based on the reason
and the connection of things; while in Christianity they are
supported by mere fables. The belief in these is daily
waning; people will, therefore, be forced to turn to my
philosophy. The Pantheists can have no seriously-meant
morality, since they regard everything as equally divine and excellent. It has often been made a reproach
to me that in philosophy, namely theoretically, I have
represented life as miserable and no way to be desired;
it should be remembered, however, that practically, he
who lays little store by his life is praised, nay admired,
and he who is careful and troubled as to its preservation is despised. My writings had scarcely begun to
awaken the curiosity of some persons before the question
of priority arose with reference to my fundamental
thought, it being represented that Schelling had once
said, "Will is Being"; and anything else of this kind
which could be adduced. With regard to this matter, it
may be observed that the root of my philosophy is
already present in the Kantian, especially in Kant's doctrine of empirical and intelligible character, but above
all, in that whenever Kant brings the thing-in-itself
nearer the light, it always appears through its veil as
Will; a point to which I have expressly called attention
in my "Critique of the Kantian Philosophy," and have
said accordingly that my philosophy is no more than
its complete thinking-out. It is not to be wondered at
then, if the philosophizings of Fichte and Schelling, who
equally started from Kant, also show traces of the same
fundamental idea; although they there appear without
consequence, connection, or development, and therefore
may be regarded as a mere foretaste of my doctrines.
But, in general, as regards this point, it may be remarked that every great truth before its discovery is
announced by a previous feeling, a presentiment, a faint

outline as in fog, and an unavailing attempt to grasp it; simply because the progress of the time has prepared it. It is, therefore, preluded by disjointed utterances. But he alone, who has recognized a truth from its causes, and thought it out to its consequences, developed its whole content, cast his eyes over the extent of its domain, and after this, with a full consciousness of its value and importance, clearly and connectedly expounded it, he alone is its originator. When, on the other hand, it happens on some occasion or other, to have been expressed either in ancient or modern times, with a half consciousness, almost as an utterance in sleep, and is hence to be found only if expressly looked for, it has little further significance, even though it stand there *totidem verbis,* than if it were there merely *totidem litteris.* Just as the finder of a thing is he, who knowing its value, picks it up and keeps it; and not he who chances to take it into his hand, and let it fall again; or, once more, Columbus is the discoverer of America, and not the first shipwrecked sailor the waves cast up there. This is precisely the meaning of the Donatian *pereant qui ante nos nostra dixerunt.* Had my critics desired to establish an effective priority against me on the strength of such chance sayings, they should have sought farther back when, for instance, they might have adduced Clemens Alexandrinus (Strom. II., c. 17): προηγεῖται τοίνυν πάντων τὸ βούλεσθαι· αἱ γὰρ λογικαὶ δυνάμεις τοῦ βούλεσθαι διάκονοι πεφύκασι (*Velle ergo omnia antecedit: rationales enim facultates sunt voluntatis ministræ* ("Sanctorum Patrum Opera Polemica," vol. v. Weissburghi, 1779; "Clementis Alex. Opera," tom. ii., p. 304); as also Spinoza: *Cupiditas est ipsa unius cujusque natura, seu essentia,* ("Eth.," p. iii., prop. 57) and before: *Hic conatus, cum ad mentem solam refertur, Voluntas appellatur; sed cum ad mentem et corpus simul refertur, vocatur Appetitus, qui proinde nihil aliud est, quam ipsa hominis essentia* (p. iii., prop. 9, schol., and finally, p. iii. Defin. I., explic.). Helvetius remarks with great justice: *Il n'est point de moyens que l'envieux, sous l'apparence de la justice, n'emploie pour dégrader le mérite. . . . C'est l'envie seule qui nous fait trouver dans les anciens toutes les découvertes modernes. Une phrase vide de sens, ou du moins inintelligible avant ces découvertes, suffit pour faire crier au plagiat* ("De l'Esprit," iv. 7). There is one more passage in Helvetius I shall take the liberty of recalling, having reference to the matter in question, the quotation of which I must beg the reader not to lay down to vanity and arrogance, but simply to bear in mind the justice of the thought expressed and consider whether or not something in it will be found capable of application to myself. *Quiconque se plaît à considérer l'esprit humain voit, dans chaque siècle, cinq ou six hommes d'esprit tourner autour de la découverte que fait l'homme de génie. Si l'honneur eu reste à ce dernier, c'est que cette découverte est, entre ses mains, plus féconde que dans les mains de tout autre ; c'est qu'il rend ses idées avec plus de force et de netteté ; et qu'enfin on voit toujours à la manière différente, dont les hommes tirent parti d'un principe ou d'une découverte à qui ce principe au cette découverte appartient* ("De l'Esprit," iv. 1).

As a consequence of the old, irreconcilable war, that has everywhere and always been waged by incapacity and stupidity against intellect and understanding — by legions on the one side against individuals on the other — he who brings to light anything valuable and genuine has to fight a hard battle with incompetence, dullness, depraved taste, private interests and envy, all in that worthy alliance, respecting which Chamfort says: *en examinant la ligne des sots contre les gens d'esprit on croirait voir une conjuration de valets pour écarter les maîtres.* In my case there was, in addition, an unusual enemy engaged; the greater part of those, whose business it was to guide public opinion in my department, were appointed and paid to propagate and to laud to the very skies that worst of all systems — the Hegelian. But this cannot succeed if one is determined that the good shall produce its effect, even though it be only in a measure. The above may explain to my future readers the, to them, otherwise unaccountable fact, that I have remained as unknown to my own contemporaries as the man in the moon. It must be acknowledged, notwithstanding, that a system of thought which, in the absence of any participation on the part of others, has been able to engage its originator throughout a long life unceasingly and cheerfully, and to spur him on to unremitting and unrewarded labor possesses in itself a testimony to its value and its truth. Destitute of any encouragement from outside, the love of my work alone has through the many days of my life upheld my endeavors, and not allowed me to tire. I have, therefore, looked with contempt on the noisy celebrity of the worthless. For upon my entry upon life my genius laid before me this choice, either to acknowledge the truth, but therewith to please no one; or, like others, to teach falsehood with support and applause; and the choice was not difficult for me. Accordingly, the fortune of my philosophy was the opposite of that of the Hegelian, so entirely so, indeed, that one may regard them both as the opposite sides of the same sheet, according to the construction of both philosophies. Hegelianism, devoid alike of truth, clearness, and intelligence, nay, of human understanding, and in addition appearing in the shape of the most sickening Gallimathias that had ever been heard of, was a subsidized and privileged academ-ical philosophy, consequently a species of nonsense which supported its author. My philosophy appearing simultane-ously with it had, indeed, all the qualities which it lacked; but it was not cut out for any ulterior purposes, was not at all suited at that time for the chair, and, therefore, as the expression is, there was nothing to be made out of it. It followed then, as day follows night, that Hegelianism was the flag to which all ran, while my philosophy found neither applause nor adherents; but was rather with a uniform purpose completely ignored, treated with silence, and where possible smothered, because through its pres-ence the above miserable game would have been spoiled, as shadows on the wall are by the incoming daylight. Hence I became the Iron Mask, or as the excellent Dorguth says, the Kaspar-Hauser of the professors of philosophy: shut out from air and light that no one might see me, and that my natural claims might not be recognized. Now, however, the Man who should have been killed by the silence of the professors of philosophy is again risen from the dead, to the great consternation of the pro-fessors of philosophy, who do not know at all what face they shall assume.

ON PHILOSOPHY AND ITS METHOD.*

THE ultimate basis on which all our cognitions and sciences rest, is the inexplicable. Every explanation leads back to this by means of more or less intermediate stages; as in the sea the plummet finds the bottom, now in greater, now in lesser depths, but must nevertheless everywhere reach it at last. This inexplicable falls to the share of Metaphysics.

Almost all men unceasingly think they are this and this man (τις ἄνθρωπος), together with the corollaries which result therefrom. On the other hand, that they are **Man** in general (ὁ ἄνθρωπος), and the corollaries which follow from this, scarcely ever occurs to them, but is nevertheless the main point. The few who pay more attention to the latter than to the former proposition are philosophers. But the tendency of the others is reducible to the fact that they never see anything in the things except the particular and individual, and not their universality. Only the more highly gifted see more or less, according to the degree of their intelligence, the universal in particular things. This important distinction interpenetrates the whole faculty of knowledge so far indeed that it extends itself down to the intuition of the most everyday objects; hence in the highly gifted head these are other than in the ordinary head. This grasp of the universal in the particular, which always presents itself, is coincident with that which I have called the pure will-less Subject of Knowledge, and have postulated as the subjective correlate of the Platonic Idea. This is proved because, when directed on the universal, the intelligence may remain will-less, while, on the contrary, the objects of the Will lie in particular things; for which reason the intelligence of animals is strictly limited to these particulars, and accordingly their intellect remains

* The following essays are from the second volume of the "Parerga and Paralipomena," and are headed "Detached yet systematically arranged thoughts on many different subjects."

exclusively in the service of their will.   The above direction of the mind to the universal is the indispensable condition of genuine achievements in philosophy, poetry, and in the arts and sciences generally.

For the intellect in the SERVICE OF THE WILL, that is, in practical use, there are only particular things.   For the intellect which pursues art and science, in other words, which is active for its own sake, there are only UNIVERSALITIES, whole kinds, species, classes, IDEAS, of things, for even the creative artist wishes to present the Idea, that is, the kind in the individual.   This comes about because the Will is turned directly merely to individual things; these are, properly speaking, its objects, for these alone have empirical reality.   Concepts, classes, species, can, on the contrary, become objects only very indirectly. Hence the common man has no sense for universal truths. But genius overlooks and misses the individual element. The compulsory occupation with the particular, as such, in so far as it constitutes the matter of practical life, is an irksome bondage.

The two first conditions of philosophizing are these: firstly, to have the courage to set one's heart upon no question; and, secondly, to bring all that which is obvious in itself to clear consciousness in order to comprehend it as problem.   Finally, in order, properly speaking, to philosophize, the mind must be truly at leisure.   It must pursue no purposes, and thus not be led by the Will, but give itself over undividedly to the teaching which the perceptive world and its own consciousness impart to it. Now professors of philosophy are concerned as to their personal use and advantage, and what leads thereto; there the serious point for them lies.   For this reason they fail altogether to see so many obvious things, indeed do not so much as once come to reflection on the problems of philosophy.

The poet brings pictures of life, human character, and situations before the imagination, sets everything in motion, and leaves it to everyone to think into these pictures, as much as his intellectual power will find for him therein.   On this account he can satisfy men of the most diverse capacities, even fools and wise men at the same time.   Now the philosopher does not bring in the same way life itself, but the completed thoughts which he has abstracted from it, and demands that his reader should think just in the same way, and just as far as he himself, and his public is, in consequence, very small.   The poet may therefore be compared to him who brings the flowers, the philosopher to him who brings the quintessence.

Another great advantage which poetical achievements have over philosophical is this, that all poetical works can stand without hindrance to each other side by side; while a philosophical system has hardly come into the world, but it contemplates the destruction of all its brothers, like an Asiatic sultan on ascending the throne.   For as there can only be one queen in a beehive, so there can only be one philosophy on the order of the day.   Systems are of as unsociable a nature as spiders, of which each sits alone in its web, and sees how many flies will let themselves be caught in it, but only approaches another spider in order to fight it.   Thus, while the works of poets pasture peacefully next each other like lambs, those of philosophers are born ravening beasts, and their destructive impulses are even directed primarily against their own species, like those of scorpions, spiders, and the *larvæ* of certain insects.   They come into the world like the armed men from the seed of Jason's dragons' teeth, and have till now like these mutually exterminated each other.   This battle has already lasted more than 2,000 years.   Will a final victory and lasting peace ever result from it ?

In consequence of its essentially polemical nature, this *bellum omnium contra omnes* of the philosophical systems, it is infinitely more difficult to obtain recognition as philosopher than as poet.   The work of the poet demands nothing further from the reader than to enter into the series of the writings which amuse or elevate him, and the devotion of some few hours to them.   The work of the philosopher, on the contrary, is intended to revolutionize his whole mode of thought; it requires of him that he shall acknowledge all he has learned and believed

in this department to be error, his time and trouble to
be lost, and shall begin again from the beginning. It,
at most, leaves some rudiments of its predecessor standing in order to build its foundation upon them. To this
is added that, in every teacher of an already existing
system, it has a professional opponent, and that sometimes even the state takes a philosophical system that
pleases it under its protection, and by the help of its
powerful material resources prevents the success of any
other. Again, one must consider that the size of the
philosophical public is proportioned to that of the poetical, as the number of people who want to be taught to
those who want to be amused, and one will be able to
judge, *quibus auspiciis* a philosopher makes his entry.
It is indeed true, on the other hand, that it is the applause of thinkers of the elect of all periods and all
countries without difference of nation which rewards the
philosopher; the multitude gradually learns to reverence
his name on the strength of authority. In accordance
with the foregoing, and on account of the slow but deep
effect of the progress of philosophy on which the whole
human race proceeds, since thousands of years the history of philosophers goes with that of kings, and counts
a hundred times fewer names than the latter. Hence it
is a great thing to procure for one's own name an enduring place therein.

The philosophical writer is the guide, and his reader
is the wanderer. If they are to arrive together they
must, above all things, start together; that is, the author
must take his reader to a standpoint which they have in
common; but this can be no other than that of the empirical consciousness which is common to all of us. Let
him, then, grasp him firmly by the hand, and see how
high above the clouds he can attain, step by step, along
the mountain path. This is how Kant proceeds. He
starts from common experience, as well of one's own self
as of other things. How mistaken it is, on the other
hand, to seek to start from the standpoint of an assumed
intellectual intuition of hyperphysical relations, or processes, or even of a reason which perceives the supersensi-

ble, or of an absolute, self-thinking Reason. For all this means starting from the standpoint of not directly communicable cognitions, when therefore even at starting the reader does not know whether he is near his author, or miles distant from him.

Conversation with another, and serious meditation and inward contemplation of the things, is as a machine to a living organism. For only in the latter case is everything cut from one piece, or as it were played in one key, whereby alone it can acquire clearness, intelligibility, and true coherence — in fact, unity. Otherwise, heterogeneous pieces of very different origin are stuck together, and a certain unity of movement is forced, which often unexpectedly stops. It is only oneself that one understands perfectly; others only half, for one can at most attain to community of concepts, but never to the perceptual point of view lying at their foundation. Hence deep philosophical truths are never brought to light by way of common thinking in dialogue. Such, however, is very serviceable as practice to the hunting up of problems, to their ventilation, and afterward to the testing, controlling, and criticising of the proposed solution. Plato's dialogues are composed in this sense, and accordingly the second and third academies which issued from his school took on a more and more sceptical direction. As form for the communication of philosophical ideas the written dialogue is only serviceable where the subject admits of two or more wholly different or even opposite views respecting which the judgment of the reader shall either remain suspended, or which, taken together, shall lead to a complete and accurate understanding of the matter. To the first case belongs the refutation of objections raised. The dialogue form chosen for this purpose must, however, be genuinely dramatic; in that the differences of opinion are laid bare to their foundations and thoroughly worked out. There must really be two speaking. Without this, it is, as is mostly the case, mere idle play.

Neither our knowledge nor our insight will be ever specially increased by the comparison and discussion of what

16

has been said by others; for that is always like pouring
water from one vessel into another. Only by the contemplation of things oneself, can insight and knowledge
be really increased; for it alone is the living source, always ready, and always at hand. It is curious to see
how would-be philosophers are forever occupied with
the first method, and seem not to know the other at all,
being always concerned with what this one has said and
with what that one may have meant. So that they are,
as it were, perpetually turning old casks upside down in
order to see whether some drop may not have remained
behind, while the living wellspring lies neglected at their
feet. Nothing so much as this betrays their incapacity,
or gives the lie more to their assumed mien of importance, depth, and originality.

Those who hope to become philosophers by the study
of the history of philosophy ought to conclude from it that
philosophers, like poets, are only born, and that, indeed,
much more rarely.

A curious and unworthy definition of philosophy which
even Kant gives, is that it is a science of mere concepts.
For the whole property of concepts is only what has been
placed in them after it has been begged and borrowed
from perceptual knowledge, the real and inexhaustible
source of insight. Hence a true philosophy cannot be
spun out of mere abstract concepts, but must be founded
on observation and experience, inner no less than outer.
It is not by attempts at the combination of concepts such
as has been so often practiced, but especially by the
sophists of our time, by Fichte and Schelling, and in its
worst form by Hegel (in "Morals" also by Schleiermacher)
that any good will be achieved in philosophy. Like art
and poetry, it must have its source in our perceptual
view of the world. Moreover, however much the head
ought to have the upper hand, it must not be treated so
cold-bloodedly, but that at last the whole man with head
and heart should come into action, and be stirred throughout. Philosophy is no algebraic formula. Vauvenargues
is right when he says: "*Les grandes pensées viennent du cœur.*

Considered as a whole, the philosophy of all times may be conceived as a pendulum which swings from side to side between Rationalism and Illuminism, that is, between the employment of the objective and subjective sources of knowledge.

Rationalism, which has for its organ the intellect, originally determined for the service of the WILL, and therefore directed OUTWARD, appears first as Dogmatism, as which it maintains a completely objective attitude. Then it changes to Scepticism, and becomes in consequence finally Criticism, which undertakes to settle the dispute by a consideration of the subject; in other words, it becomes transcendental philosophy. I understand by this, every philosophy which starts from the proposition that its nearest and most immediate object is not the world of things, but only the human CONSCIOUSNESS of the things, and that this, therefore, can never be left out of consideration. The French call this rather inexactly the *méthode psychologique*, in opposition to the *méthode purement logique*, by which they understand, without more ado, the philosophy proceeding from objects, or objectively thought concepts, in short, Dogmatism. Having reached this point, Rationalism attains to the knowledge that its *organon* apprehends only the phenomenon, and does not reach the ultimate inner and original essence of things.

At all its stages, but most of all here, Illuminism asserts itself as its antithesis. ILLUMINISM, which essentially turned inward has as its *organon* internal illumination, intellectual intuition, higher consciousness, immediately-cognizing Reason, divine consciousness, etc., and which contemns Rationalism as the "light of nature." If a religion, it is MYSTICISM, its root-failing being that its knowledge is not mediate; partly because for the internal perception there is no criterion of the identity of the objects of different subjects; partly because such a knowledge would have to be communicated by language, but the latter, which has arisen for the sake of the knowing faculty of the Intellect, as directed outward by means of its own abstraction, is quite unsuited to express those internal states which are different from it, and which

form the material of Illuminism. The latter must, therefore, construct a language of its own, which again, for
the reason above given, does not work. Not being mediate a knowledge of this kind is undemonstrable, the
consequence being that Rationalism again enters the field
hand in hand with Scepticism. Illuminism is already
discoverable in certain places in Plato; but it appears
more distinctly in the philosophy of the Neo-Platonists,
the Gnostics, in that of Dionysius Areopagita, as also in
Scotus Erigena; among the Mohammedans in the doctrines of the SUFI; in India it is dominant in the Vedanta
and Mimansa; but most distinctly of all in Jacob Bœhme,
and all the Christian Mystics. It always appears when
Rationalism has run its course without attaining its goal.
Thus it came toward the end of the scholastic philosophy and in opposition thereto, especially among the
Germans, as the Mysticism of Tauler, and the author of
the "German Theology" among others. And, similarly,
in modern times as opposition to the Kantian philosophy
in Jacobi and Schelling, also in Fichte's last period.
Philosophy, however, must be MEDIATE knowledge, hence,
Rationalism. I have accordingly, at the close of my own
philosophy, indicated the sphere of Illuminism as present,
but have taken special care not to place so much as a
foot upon it. On the contrary, I have not even attempted
to give the final clues to the existence of the world, but
only went as far as was possible on the objective Rationalistic path. I have left the ground free for Illuminism
to solve all problems in its own fashion, without its coming in my way or having to polemicize against me.

Meanwhile a hidden Illuminism may often enough lie
at the basis of Rationalism, to which the philosopher
looks as to a hidden compass, while he only admits that
he steers his course by the stars, that is, the external
objects which lie clearly before him, and that he takes
them alone into his reckoning. This is admissible, since
he does not undertake to communicate the immediate
knowledge, his communications remaining purely objective and rational. Such may have been the case with
Plato, Spinoza, Malebranche, and some others; it does

not concern any one, for it is the secret of their own breast. But the noisy invocation of intellectual intuition, and the barren narration of its content, with the claim for its objective validity, as in the case of Fichte and Schelling, is shameless and abominable.

For the rest, Illuminism is a natural, and in so far a legitimate, attempt to fathom the truth. For the intellect directed outward, as mere *organon* for the purposes of the Will, and consequently merely secondary, is nevertheless only a part of our entire human nature. It belongs to the phenomenon, and its knowledge merely assumes the phenomenon, which is there only for its own sake. What can be more natural than that when we have failed to succeed with the objectivity-knowing intellect we bring into play our whole remaining being — which is also Thing-in-itself, and as such pertains to the true nature of the world, and consequently must bear within it the solution of all problems — in order to seek help from it, just as the ancient Germans, when they had played away everything else, finally staked their own persons. But the only correct and objectively-valid way of carrying this out is that we apprehend the empirical fact of a Will proclaiming itself in our inmost being, and constituting our only nature, and apply it to the explanation of our objective, external knowledge, as I have accordingly done. The way of Illuminism, on the other hand, for the reasons above explained, does not lead to this goal.

Mere cleverness suffices for the sceptic but not for the philosopher. Meanwhile scepticism is in philosophy what opposition is in Parliament; it is as beneficial as it is necessary. Is is always based on the fact that philosophy is not capable of evidence of such a kind as Mathematics; just as little as the man is capable of the tricks of animal instinct which are also certain *a priori*. Hence scepticism will ever be able, as against every system, to lay itself in the other scale. But its weight will at last become so little against the other that it will no more hurt it than the arithmetical quadrature of the circle, which is also only approximative.

THAT WHICH ONE KNOWS has a double value, if at the same time one admits oneself not to know THAT WHICH ONE DOES NOT KNOW. For thereby the former is free from the suspicion to which one exposes it, if, like for instance the Schellingites, one proposes also to know what one does not know.

Every one forms certain propositions which he holds for true without investigation, declarations of reason. Such propositions he could not bring himself seriously to test, since this would involve his calling them in question for the nonce. They have come into this unshakeable credit with him because ever since he began to speak and to think he has heard them perpetually spoken of, and they have thereby become indoctrinated into him. Hence his habit of thinking them is as old as his habit of thinking at all; they have grown up into his brain. What is here said is so true that it would, on the one hand, be superfluous, and on the other, of doubtful desirability, to substantiate it with examples.

No conception of the world which has arisen from an objective perceptual apprehension of things, and which has been logically carried out, can be entirely false; it is in the worst case only one-sided, as for instance complete Materialism, absolute Idealism, etc. They are all true, but they are equally so — consequently their truth is only relative. Every such conception is true, namely, only from a particular standpoint; just as a picture only displays a landscape from one point of view. But if one lifts oneself above the standpoint of such a system one recognizes the relativity of its truth, that is, its one-sidedness. Only the highest standpoint which overlooks and takes into account all, can furnish absolute truth. It is true, accordingly, when I, for example, conceive myself as a mere natural product arisen in time, and destined to complete destruction — after the manner of the Koheleth.

But it is equally true that everything that was or will be, I am, and that nothing exists outside me. It is just as true, when I, after the manner of Anakreon, place the highest happiness in the enjoyment of the present time, but it is equally true when I recognize the wholesomeness of suffering, and the nothingness, nay, the injuriousness, of all pleasure, and conceive death as the object of my existence.

All this has its reason in that each view logically carried out is only a perceptual and objective apprehension of nature translated into concepts, and thereby fixated; but nature, *i. e*, the perceptual, never lies nor contradicts itself since its essence excludes any such thing. Where, therefore, contradiction and lie are, there are thoughts which have not sprung from objective apprehension—*e. g.*, optimism. But an objective apprehension may be incomplete and one-sided; it then requires completion, not refutation.

People are never tired of reproaching Metaphysics with its small progress in view of the great progress of the Physical sciences. Even Voltaire exclaims: "O méta-physique! nous sommes aussi avancés que du tems des premiers Druides" ("Mel. d. phil.," ch. 9). But what other science has like it always had as a hindrance an antagonist, *ex officio*, a paid fiscal prosecutor, a king's champion in full armor, to attack it defenseless and weaponless? It will never show its true powers, never be able to make its giant-strides, so long as it is required of it with threats, that it shall suit itself to dogmas cut out with a view to the small capacity of the great mass. They first bind our arms, and then mock us because we cannot accomplish anything.

Religions have seized upon the metaphysical faculties of men, which they first of all lame by the early instilling of their dogmas, respecting which they taboo all free and unprejudiced expressions of opinion, so that free research respecting the most important and interesting of problems, respecting man's existence itself, is in part directly forbidden, in part indirectly hindered, being rendered subjectively well-nigh impossible by mutilation, and thus the most noble of man's faculties lies in fetters.

In order to make us patient under contradiction, and

tolerant of views opposed to our own, nothing is, perhaps, more powerful than the remembrance how often we have successively held quite opposite views on the same subject, and have changed them repeatedly, sometimes, indeed, within a very short period, how we have rejected and again taken up, now this opinion, now its opposite, according as the subject presented itself to us, now in one, now in another light.

In the same way there is nothing more calculated to procure acceptance with another for our contradiction of his own opinion than the phrase, "I used to think the same myself, but," etc.

A fallacious doctrine, whether founded on a false opinion or sprung from a bad intention, is only designed for special circumstances, and consequently for a certain time; but the truth is for all time, even though it may be misunderstood or smothered for a while. For as soon as a little light comes from within, or a little air from without, some one will be found to proclaim or to defend it. For since it has not originated in the interests of any party, every superior mind will be its champion at any time. It resembles the magnet which always and everywhere points to an absolutely definite part of the compass; the false doctrine, on the contrary, resembles a statue which points with the hand toward another statue, but once removed from it loses all significance.

What stands most in the way of the discovery of truth is not the false appearance proceeding from the things and leading to error, nor even directly the weakness of the understanding; but it is the preconceived opinion, the prejudice which as a bastard *a priori*, opposes itself to the truth, and then resembles a contrary wind which drives the ship back from the direction in which the land lies, so that rudder and sail work in vain.

I comment as follows on Goethe's verse in "Faust";

«What thou hast inherited from thy fathers
Inherit it in order to possess it.»

That which thinkers have discovered before us, it is of great service and value to ourselves to discover by our own means, independently of them, and before we know them, for one understands what one has thought out for oneself much more thoroughly than what one has learned, and when one afterward finds it with these predecessors, one receives an unhoped-for confirmation, speaking strongly for its truth from an independent and recognized authority. In this way one gains confidence and assurance to champion it against every opponent.

When, on the other hand, one has found something first of all in books, and then attained the same result by one's own reflection, one never knows for certain that one has thought and reasoned this out oneself, and not merely been the echo in one's feelings, or one's speech, of these predecessors. But this makes a very great difference in respect to the certainty of the matter. For in the latter case it may happen that one has erred with one's predecessors owing to one's preoccupation with them, just as water readily takes to a ready-made course. If two persons, each for themselves, make a calculation and reach the same result, the result is certain, but not when the calculation has merely been looked through by the other.

It is a consequence of the construction of our Intellect, sprung as it is from the Will, that we cannot help conceiving the world either as END or as MEANS. The first would assert that its existence was justified by its essence, and was definitely preferable to its nonexistence. But the knowledge that it is only a place of struggle for suffering and dying beings renders this idea untenable. Again, the infinity of Time already passed does not admit of its being conceived as means, for every end to be obtained would long ago have been accomplished. From this it follows that the foregoing application of the natural presupposition of our intellect to the whole of things, or to the world, is TRANSCENDENT, that is, it is valid IN the world, but not OF the world. This is explicable from the fact that it arises from the nature of an

Intellect, which as I have shown has itself arisen for the service of an individual WILL, *i.e.*, for the attainment of its objects, and hence being exclusively concerned with ends and means, neither knows nor conceives of anything else.

When we look outward, where the immeasurableness of the world and the countlessness of its beings display themselves to us, oneself as mere individual shrinks up to nothing and seems to vanish. Carried away by the immensity of mass and number, one thinks further that only the philosophy directed OUTWARD, that is, the OBJECTIVE philosophy, can be the right way, and to doubt as to this never occurred to the oldest Greek philosopher.

Let us now look inward. We find, in the first place, that every individual takes an immediate interest only in himself, indeed that his SELF he takes more to heart than all else put together; which comes from the fact that he knows himself immediately but everything else only mediately. If one adds to this that conscious and knowing beings are thinkable solely as individuals, and that beings without consciousness have only a half, a mere mediate existence, it follows that all proper and true existence obtains only in the individual. If, finally, one considers that the object is conditioned by the subject, and that, therefore, this immeasurable outer world has its existence only in the CONSCIOUSNESS of knowing beings and, consequently, is bound up with the existence of individuals which are its bearers, so much so that in a sense it may be looked upon as a mere equipment, an accident of the always individual consciousness; if one I say, keeps all this in view one is driven to the opinion that only the philosophy which is directed INWARD proceeding from the subject as immediately given — in other words, that of the modern, since Descartes — is on the right way, and that the Ancients have overlooked the main points. But one first receives the complete conviction of this, when turning within upon oneself, one brings to one's consciousness the feeling of origination which lies in every knowing being. More than this, everyone, even the most insignificant human being, finds in his simple self-consciousness himself as the most real of all beings, and recognizes necessarily in himself the true centre of the world, the ultimate source of all reality. And does this ultimate consciousness lie? Its most powerful expression is to be found in the words of the Upanishad: "hæ omnes creaturæ in totum ego sum, et præter me ens aliud non est, et omnia ego creata feci" ("Oupnekh," i., p. 122), which is certainly there the transition to Illuminism, or indeed, to Mysticism. This is, therefore, the result of contemplation directed inward; while that directed outward shows us as the goal of our existence —a heap of ashes.*

Respecting the division of philosophy, which is of special importance with regard to its exposition, it should, from my point of view, be treated as follows:

Philosophy, indeed, has experience for its subject, but not, like the other sciences, this or that definite experience, but experience itself generally and as such, according to its possibility, its range, its essential content, its inner and outer element, its form and matter. That philosophy must assuredly have empirical foundations, and not be spun out of purely abstract conceptions, I have adequately explained in the second volume of my chief work, chap. xvii., pp. 180–185 (3d ed., 199 *seq.*), and have given a short *résumé* of it above. Hence it follows further that the first thing which it has to contemplate must be the medium in which experience-in-general presents itself, together with its form and construction. This medium is presentment, knowledge, in short, intellect. For this reason every philosophy must begin with the investigation of the faculty of knowledge, its forms and

---

* FINITE and INFINITE are concepts, having significance merely in respect of time and space, inasmuch as both these are INFINITE, *i. e.*, endless, as also infinitely divisible. If we apply these two concepts to other things it must be to such things as fill space and time, and can participate in their qualities. From this it may be judged how great is the abuse which philosophasters have in this century carried on with these concepts.

its laws, as also its validity and limits. Such an investigation will, therefore, be a *Philosophia prima*. It falls asunder into the consideration of the primary, *i.e.*, perceptual presentments, which part may be called Dianoialogy, or doctrine of the Understanding; and into the consideration of the secondary, *i.e.*, abstract presentments, together with the order of their treatment as LOGIC, or doctrine of Reason This universal part conceives, or rather represents, that which was formerly termed Ontology, and which was put forward as the doctrine of the most universal and essential qualities of things in general, and as such; inasmuch as what only accrues to things in consequence of the form and nature of our faculty of presentment — since all essences to be apprehended by the latter must present themselves in accordance therewith, whereby they bear certain characteristics common to them all — were held to be the qualities of the things in themselves. This may be compared to attributing the color of a glass to the objects seen through it.

The philosophy following upon such investigation is in the narrower sense of the word METAPHYSICS, since it not only teaches us to know that which is actually present, nature conceived in its order and connection, but it apprehends it as a given, though in some way, conditioned phenomenon, in which a being distinct from itself, in other words, the thing-in-itself, displays itself. This it endeavors to learn more closely, the means thereto being partly the bringing together of outer and inner experience; partly the attainment of an understanding of the whole phenomenon by a discovery of its meaning and connection, to compare the reading of the hitherto indecipherable characters of an unknown writing. In this way it attains from the appearance to the thing appearing, to that which is hidden behind it, hence τὰ μετὰ τὰ φυσικά. It may be divided in consequence into three parts:

> «Metaphysic of Nature,
> Metaphysic of the Beautiful,
> Metaphysic of Morals.»

The deduction of this division, however, presupposes Metaphysics. For this points to the thing-in-itself, the inner and ultimate essence of the phenomenon, as our Will. Hence, after a consideration of it as presented in external nature, Metaphysic investigates its quite different and immediate manifestation in ourselves, whence proceed the Metaphysic of Morals. But, previously to this, the completest and purest apprehension of its external or objective phenomenon is taken into consideration which give us the Metaphysic of the Beautiful.

Rational Psychology, or doctrine of the soul, there is not; for, as Kant has proved, the soul is a transcendent, and as such, an undemonstrated and unjustified hypostasis, so that the antithesis of " spirit and nature " is left for the Philistines and Hegelians. The essence in itself of the human being can only be understood in conjunction with the essence in itself of all things, that is, of the world. Hence Plato, in the " Phædrus," makes Socrates put the question in a negative sense: Ψυχῆς οὖν φύσιν ἀξίως λόγου κατανοῆσαι οἴει δυνατὸν εἶναι ἄνευ τῆς τοῦ ὅλου φύσεως; (*Animæ vero naturam absque totius natura sufficienter cognosci posse existimas ?*) The Microcosm and the Macrocosm reciprocally explain each other, whereby they evince themselves as essentially the same. This consideration, connected with the inner side of man, interpenetrates and suffuses the whole of Metaphysic in all its parts and cannot, such being the case, again appear separately as Psychology. Anthropology, on the other hand, as an empirical science has its justification, but it is partly anatomy and physiology, partly mere empirical Psychology, that is, a knowledge of the moral and intellectual manifestations and peculiarities of the human race, as also of the variation of individuals in this respect, derived from observation. The most important part of it is, nevertheless, necessary as empirical material to be taken up and worked out by the three parts of Metaphysic. What remains over requires fine observation and intelligent apprehension, indeed, a contemplation from a somewhat higher standpoint, I mean from that of a cer-

tain superiority, and is, therefore, only to be enjoyed
in the writings of specially gifted minds, such as
Theophrastus, Montaigne, Larochefoucauld, Labruyère,
Helvetius, Chamfort, Addison, Shaftesbury, Shenstone,
Lichtenberg, etc., but is not to be sought nor to
be endured in the compendiums of unintelligent,
and therefore intelligence-hating, professors of philosophy.

SOME REFLECTIONS ON THE ANTITHESIS OF THING-IN-ITSELF AND PHENOMENON.

THING-IN-ITSELF signifies the existent independently of our perception, in short, that which properly is. This was, for Demokritus, formed matter. It was the same at bottom for Locke; for Kant it was = x; for me it is Will.

How entirely Demokritus took the matter in the above sense, and hence belongs at the head of this exposition, is confirmed by the following passage from "Sextus Empiricus" (Adv. Math. 1. vii., § 135), who had his works before him, and for the most part, cites verbally from them : Δημόκριτος δὲ ὅτι μὲν ἀναιρεῖ τὰ φαινόμενα ταῖς αἰσθήσεσιν, καὶ τούτων λέγει μηδὲν φαίνεσθαι κατ᾽ ἀλήθειαν, ἀλλὰ μόνον κατὰ δόξαν· ἀληθὲς δὲ ἐν τοῖς οὖσιν ὑπάρχειν τὸ ἀτόμους εἶναι καὶ κενόν, etc. (*Demokritus autem ea quidem tollit, quæ apparent sensibus, et ex iis dicit nihil ut vere est apparere, sed solum ex opinione ; verum autem esse in iis, quæ sunt, atomos et inane.*) I recommend the reader to look over the whole passage where also the following occurs: ἐτεῇ νυν οἷον ἕκαστον ἔστιν, ἢ οὐκ ἔστιν, οὐ συνίεμεν· (*vere quidem nos, quale sit vel not sit unumquodque, neutiquam intelligimus*), also: ἐτεῇ οἷον ἕκαστον (ἔστι) γιγνώσκειν ἐν ἀπόρῳ ἔστι· (*vere scire quale sit unum quodque, in dubio est*). All this is as much as to say: "We do not know the things as they may be in themselves, but only as they appear," and opens up the series starting from the most decided Materialism but leading to Idealism, which closes with me. A surprisingly clear and definite distinction between the thing-in-itself and the phenomenon, even in the Kantian sense, we find in a passage of Porphyry which Stobæos has preserved ("Eclog.," L. I., c. 43, Fragm. 3). It says, Τὰ κατηγορούμενα τοῦ αἰσθητοῦ καὶ ἐνύλου ἀληθῶς ἐστι ταῦτα, τὸ πάντη εἶναι διαπεφορημένον, τὸ μεταβλητὸν εἶναι, etc. Τοῦ δὲ ὄντως ὄντος καὶ καθ᾽ αὑτὸ ὑφεστηκότος αὑτοῦ, τὸ εἶναι ἀεὶ ἐν ἑαυτῷ ἱδρυμένον· ὡσαύτως τὸ κατὰ ταῦτὰ ἔχειν, etc.

As we only know the surface of the earth, and not the great solid mass of the interior, so we know nothing whatever empirically of things and the world, but only of their PHENOMENON, *i.e.*, their surface. The exact knowlege of this is Physics taken in its widest sense. But that this surface presupposes an interior which is not mere surface, but has a cubic content, is, together with the conclusions as to its nature, the subject of Metaphysics. To attempt to construct the nature of things in themselves, according to the laws of the mere phenomenon, is an undertaking which may be compared to the attempt to construct from mere surfaces and their laws the stereometric body. Every transcendent dogmatic philosophy is an attempt to construct the thing-in-itself according to the laws of the phenomenon which results similarly to that of attempting to cover two absolutely dissimilar figures with one another, which must always miscarry, since, turn them as one will, now this, now that, corner projects.

Inasmuch as every being in nature is at the same time a PHENOMENON and a THING-IN-ITSELF, that is, *natura naturata* and *natura naturans*, it is capable of a double explanation, a PHYSICAL and a METAPHYSICAL. The physical is always from the CAUSE; the metaphysical always from the WILL; for this it is which displays itself in consciousless nature as natural force, higher up, as vital force, but in animal and man receives the name Will. Taken strictly, in a given human being, the degree and the direction of his intelligence, and the moral construction of his character, might possibly be purely physically produced, the first, viz, from the structure of his brain and nervous system, together with the circulation of the blood which affects it, the latter from the structure and combined action of his heart, cellular system, blood, lungs, liver, spleen, kidneys, intestines, genital organs, etc., but for this would certainly be requisite a much closer acquaintance with the laws which regulate the *rapport du physique au moral* than even Bichât and Cabanis possessed. Both would then be reducible to more distant physical causes, to wit, the structure of his parents, since these could only furnish the germ of a being like themselves, but not of a higher and better one. METAPHYSICALLY, on the other hand, the same human being must be explained as the phenomenon of his own perfectly free and original Will, which has created in him the corresponding intellect. Hence all his deeds, however necessarily they proceed from his character, in conflict with the given motive (and this again appears as the result of his corporization), are nevertheless to be wholly attributed to him. Metaphysically, moreover, the distinction between him and his parents is not an absolute one.

All UNDERSTANDING is an act of PRESENTING, and remains, therefore, essentially within the domain of PRESENTMENT; but since this only furnishes phenomena it is limited to the phenomenon, where the thing-in-itself begins the phenomenon leaves off, consequently also the presentment, and with this the understanding. But its place is here taken by the EXISTENT itself, which is conscious of itself as WILL. Were this self-consciousness immediate we should have a completely adequate knowledge of the thing-in-itself. But because it is thereby rendered possible that the Will creates this organic body, and by means of part of the same an intellect, and finds and recognizes itself first through this, in self-consciousness as Will—it follows that this knowledge of the thing-in-itself is primarily conditioned by the separation of a knowing and a known, and then by the form of time, which is inseparable from the cerebral self-consciousness, and that it is hence not completely exhausted and adequate. (Compare chap. xviii. in 2d vol. of my chief work.)*

---

* The distinction between the thing-in-itself and the phenomenon may be expressed as that between the SUBJECTIVE and OBJECTIVE essence of a thing. Its pure SUBJECTIVE essence is the thing-in-itself, but this is no object of knowledge. For in order to be such it is essential that it should always be present in a knowing consciousness as its presentment, and what displays itself there is the objective essence of the thing. This is accordingly object of knowledge, but as such it is mere presentment, and as it can only become so by means of a presentment-apparatus which must have its own structure and the laws resulting therefrom, it is a mere phenomenon which must

17

With this is connected the truth presented by me in
my Essay on "Will in Nature," under the heading "Physical Astronomy," p. 86 (2d ed., p. 79; 3d ed., p. 86):
that in proportion to the clearness with which a process or relation may be comprehended, does it pertain
to the mere phenomenon and not to the thing-in-itself.

When we observe and contemplate any natural being,
as for instance an animal, in its existence, life, and
action, it stands before us, in spite of all that zoology
and zootomy teach respecting it, as an impenetrable
mystery. But does nature, then, from mere obstinacy
remain eternally dumb to our questioning? Is it not like
everything great, open, communicative, and even naïve?
Can its answer, therefore, fail from any other reason
than because the question was wrongly put, was one-sided,
proceeded from false assumptions, or perhaps, even contained a contradiction? For is it easy to think that a
connection of causes and consequences could obtain where
it must eternally and essentially remain undiscovered?
THAT assuredly not. But it is unfathomable, because we
search for causes and effects in a region to which this
form is foreign, and hence we pursue the chain of causes
and effects on an entirely wrong track. We seek to attain
the inner essence of nature, namely, which confronts us
in every phenomenon on the lines of the principle of
cause — whereas this is the mere form with which our
intellect apprehends the phenomenon, i.e., the surface of

connect itself with the thing-in-itself. This obtains also where there
exists a self-consciousness, that is, a self-cognizing I. For this also
knows itself only in its intellect, i. e., its apparatus of presentment,
and indeed through the external senses as organic form, by the internal as Will whose acts it sees as simultaneously repeated by that
form as the latter is by its shadow, whence it concludes as to the
identity of both and terms the result I. But on account of this double
knowledge, as well as on account of the great proximity in which the
intellect here stands to its source or root, the Will, the knowledge of
objective being, that is, of the phenomenon, differs here much less
from the subjective or thing-in-itself than in the case of knowledge by
means of the external sense or the consciousness of other things in
opposition to self-consciousness. For to this, in so far as the internal
sense alone cognizes it, the form of time alone cleaves, and no longer
that of space and time together, time therefore and the separation
of subject and object is all that divides it from the thing-in-itself.

things, and we expect by this means to get beyond the phenomenon. But within the range of the phenomenon it is useful and sufficient. For example, the actuality of a given animal may be explained from its generation. This in the last resort is no more mysterious than the sequence of any other, even the simplest effect, from its cause, since even in such a case the explanation abutts ultimately upon the incomprehensible. The fact that in generation a few middle links in the chain of connection fail us makes no difference essentially, for even if we had them we should still come back to the incomprehensible. All this is because the phenomenon remains phenomenon and does not become thing-in-itself.

The inner essence of things is foreign to the principle of cause. It is the thing-in-itself, and that is pure Will. It is because it wills and it WILLS because it is. It is the simple Real in every being.

The fundamental character of all things is perishability. We see everything in nature from the metal to the organism consuming and destroying itself, partly by its very existence, partly by conflict with something else. How could nature endure the maintaining of its form, and the renewing of its individuals, the countless repetition of its life process throughout an endless time without tiring, if its own innermost core were not timeless, and hence completely indestructible, a thing-in-itself of a kind quite other than its phenomena — a metaphysical thing quite distinct from the physical thing? This is the Will in ourselves and in all things.

We complain of the obscurity in which we live without understanding the connection of existence in the whole, and above all, not even of our own self with the whole; so that not only is our life short, but our knowledge is exclusively limited to it, since we can neither look backward beyond our birth, nor forward beyond our death, and hence our consciousness is but a flash of lightning that momentarily illumines the night. It would seem, indeed, as though a spiteful demon had closed up for us all further knowledge that he might enjoy our embarrassment. But this complaint is, properly speaking, unjustified, for it springs from an illusion which is brought about by the fallacious opinion that the totality of things has proceeded from an INTELLECT, consequently, existed as mere PRESENTMENT before it became real; and that accordingly having arisen from knowledge, it must be also accessible to knowledge, and penetrable and exhaustible by it. But, in truth, the matter stands rather thus, that all that which we complain that we do not know, is known to no one, is indeed in itself not knowable, *i. e.*, not presentable. For the PRESENTMENT in the domain of which all knowledge lies, and to which therefore all knowledge refers, is only the external side of existence, a secondary added thing, something that is, which was not necessary to the maintenance of things generally, in other words, of the world-whole, but merely to the maintenance of individual animal beings. Hence the existence of things in general and as a whole, appears only *per accidens* in knowledge and, therefore, in a very limited manner; it only forms the background of the picture in the animal consciousness where the objects of the Will are the essential, and occupy the first place. There arises now, by means of this accident, the whole world in space and time, that is, the world as presentment, which has no existence of this kind outside knowledge. Its internal essence, on the other hand, that which is existent in itself, is quite independent of this kind of existence. But since, as already said, knowledge is only there for the sake of the maintenance of each animal individual, so its whole structure all its forms, as time, space, etc., are merely there for the purposes of such an individual. But the latter merely requires the knowledge of relations between particular phenomena, and in no way those of the nature of the thing and of the world-whole.

Kant has proved that the problems of metaphysics which disturb everyone more or less, are capable of no direct, of no sufficient solution whatever, but are based in the last resort on the fact that they have their origin in the forms of our intellect, time, space and causality, while this intellect is merely designed to supply the motives to the individual will, *i. e.*, to show it the objects of its willing together with the ways and means to attain them. When, however, this intellect is abusively turned to the nature of things-in-themselves, to the totality and the complex of the world, the aforesaid forms pertaining to it of the coexistence succession and causation of all possible things give birth to the metaphysical problems as, for instance, of origin and purpose, beginning and end of the world, and of one's own self, of the destruction of the latter by death, or of its continued duration in spite of it, of the freedom of the Will, etc. Let us conceive these forms as once abolished, and a consciousness of the things as, nevertheless, present — these problems would then be not, indeed, solved, but would have entirely vanished, and their expression would have no more meaning. For they take their origin entirely from these forms, which are designed not for the understanding of the world and of existence, but merely for an understanding of our personal ends.

This whole consideration affords us an explanation and OBJECTIVE justification of the Kantian doctrines, which were only justified by their founder from the SUBJECTIVE side, viz, that the forms of the understanding are merely of imminent, not transcendent, application. One might, instead of the above, also say the intellect is physical, not metaphysical, i. e., as it has grown out of the Will as pertaining to its objectivation, it is there also only for its service; that this merely obtains IN nature, and not in anything lying outside of it. Every animal possesses (as I have explained and substantiated in "Will in Nature") its intellect obviously only for the purpose of finding and obtaining its food, and its degree is determined thereby. With Man it is not otherwise, only that the greater difficulty of his maintenance, and the infinitely greater number of his wants has here made a much higher degree of intellect necessary. It is only when this is exceeded, through an abnormity, that the perfectly free SURPLUS remains, over which, if considerable, is called GENIUS. In the first instance, such an intellect as this is truly objective only; but it can easily go so far that it may become to a certain extent even metaphysical, or at least endeavor to be so. For precisely in consequence of its objectivity, nature itself, the totality of things, becomes its object and its problem. For nature here first begins properly to perceive itself as something which is and yet might NOT be, or which might be OTHERWISE, while in the ordinary, merely normal, intellect it does not clearly perceive itself, just as the miller does not hear his mill, nor the perfumer smell his shop. It seems to require no explanation, the intellect is involved in it. Only in certain clearer moments is it aware of it, and becomes almost frightened at it, but this soon passes off. How much such normal heads are ever likely to achieve in philosophy, however numerously they congregate, is easy to see. If, on the contrary, the intellect were originally and by constitution metaphysical, it could further philosophy like every other science, especially with united forces.

SOME WORDS ON PANTHEISM.

ONE might illustrate allegorically and dramatically the controversy carried on at the present time among the professors of philosophy respecting Theism and Pantheism, by a dialogue which took place in the pit of a theatre at Milan during the performance. The one interlocutor, convinced that he is in the great and celebrated Marionette Theatre of Girolamo, admired the art with which the director has arranged the marionettes and guides their play. The other says, on the contrary, "Not at all! That they were in the Theatro della Scala, that the director and his associates were playing themselves, and were concealed really in the persons before them;—and that the poet was also playing."

It is delightful to see how the professors of philosophy coquet with Pantheism as with a forbidden thing which they have not the heart to seize. Their attitude in this respect I have already described in my essay on "The University-Philosophy," which reminds one of Bottom the weaver in "The Midsummer Night's Dream." It is, indeed, a sour piece of bread, the bread of the professors of philosophy! One has first to dance to the pipe of ministers, and when one has done that satisfactorily, one may still be fallen upon from outside by those wild men-eaters the real philosophers, who are capable of pocketing and running off with one, in order to produce one opportunely as a pocket-pulcinello to give zest to their expositions.

Against Pantheism I have chiefly this objection only, that it says nothing. To call the world God is not to explain it, but only to enrich language with a superfluous synonym of the word "world." Whether it says "the world is God," or "the world is the world," comes to the same thing. If indeed we start from God as the given thing to be explained, and say, "God is the world," there we have to a certain extent an explanation, in so far as we return from the unknown to the known; still it is only a verbal explanation. But if we start from the really given, viz, the world, and say "the world is God," it is as clear as daylight that we have said nothing thereby, or that at least *ignotum* is explained *per ignotius;* hence Pantheism presupposes Theism as having preceded it. For only in so far as one starts with a God, and therefore has him already in advance, and is intimate with him, can one finally bring oneself to identify him with the world, in order to put him on one side in a decent manner. We have not started impartially from the world as the thing to be explained, but from God as the given thing; after we did not know what to do with the former, the world had to take over his rôle. This is the origin of Pantheism. For on a first and impartial view it would never occur to anyone to regard the world as a God. It must obviously be a very ill-advised God who knew no better amusement than to transform himself into a world such as this: into a hungry world, in order there to endure misery, suffering, and death, without measure or end, in the shape of countless millions of living, but anxious and tormented beings, who only maintain themselves for a while by mutually devouring each other: *e. g.*, in the shape of six million negro slaves, who daily on an average receive sixty million blows of the whip on their bare bodies, and in the shape of three million European weavers who, amid hunger and misery, feebly vegetate in stuffy attics or wretched workshops, etc. That would indeed be a pastime for a God! who as such must be accustomed to things very different.

The supposed great progress from Theism to Pantheism, if taken seriously and not merely as a masked negation, as above suggested, is accordingly, a progress from the unproven, and hardly thinkable to the actually absurd. For however unclear, vacillating, and confused may be the conception which one associates with the word God, two predicates are at all events inseparable from it — the highest power and the highest wisdom. But that a being armed with this should have placed himself in the position above described, is an actually absurd idea; for our position in the world is obviously such as no intelligent, let alone an all-wise being, would place himself in. Theism, on the other hand, is merely unproven, and even if it is difficult to conceive that the infinite world should be the work of a personal, and therefore individual being, such as we only know from animal nature, it is nevertheless not exactly absurd. For that an almighty and, at the same time, an all-wise being should create a tormented world is always conceivable, although we may not know the wherefore of it. Hence, even if we attribute to him the quality of the highest goodness, the incomprehensibility of his judgment is always the refuge by which such a doctrine escapes the reproach of absurdity. On the assumption of Pantheism, however, the creating God is himself the endlessly tormented, and on this small earth alone dies once in every second, and this of his own free will, which is absurd. It would be much more correct to identify the world with the devil, as has been actually done by the venerable author of "The German Theology," inasmuch as on p. 93 of his immortal work (according to the restored text, Stuttgart, 1851), he says: "Therefore are the evil spirit and nature one, and when nature is not overcome there also is the evil one not overcome."

The Pantheists obviously give to the SANSARA the name God. The Mystics, on the other hand, give the same name to the NIRVANA. Of this, however, they relate more than they know, which the Buddhists do not do; and hence their NIRVANA is but a relative nothing. The Synagogue, the Church, and Islam use the word God in its proper and correct sense.

The expression one often hears nowadays, "the world is end to itself," leaves undecided whether it is to be explained by Pantheism or by mere Fatalism, but allows it at all events only a physical and no moral significance, since on the assumption of this latter the world always presents itself as means to a higher end. But this notion that the world has only a physical and no moral significance is the most hopeless error that has ever sprung from the perversity of the human mind.

ON ETHICS.

PHYSICAL truths may have much external significance, but they are wanting in internal significance. The latter is the privilege of intellectual and moral truths, which have as their theme the highest stages of the objectivation of the Will, while the former have only the lowest. For instance, if we attain to certainty as to what is now merely supposition, to wit, that the sun at the equator produces thermoelectricity, this the magnetism of the earth, and this again the polar light, these truths would be of much external significance, but internally poor. Examples of internal truths are not only furnished by high and truly spiritual philosophizings, but also by the catastrophe of every good tragedy; also indeed by the observation of human conduct in the extreme expressions of its morality and immorality, in other words, of its evil and goodness. For in all this the essence appears whose phenomenon the world is, and at the highest stage of its objectivation brings to light its innermost core.

That the world has merely a physical, and no moral significance, is the greatest, the most pernicious, the fundamental error, the true perversity of opinion, and is at bottom that which faith has personified as Anti-Christ. Nevertheless, and despite all religions, which one and all maintain the contrary, and seek to explain it in their mythical fashion, this root-error never quite dies out, but ever and again raises its head anew, till universal indignation compels it once more to hide it.

But certain as is the feeling of a moral significance of the world and of life, its explication and the unraveling of the contradiction between it and the course of the world is, nevertheless, so difficult, that it was reserved for me to expound the true only genuine and pure, and therefore everywhere and at all times operative foun-

(266)

dation of morality, together with the goal to which it leads. In this I have the reality of moral progress too much on my side, that I need fear ever again to be superseded and displaced by another.

As long, however, as my "Ethics" remain unnoticed by the professors, the Kantian moral principle obtains at the universities, and among its various forms that of the "Dignity of Man" is now the most accepted. I have already exposed its emptiness in my essay on the "Foundation of Morality," § 8, p. 169 (2d ed., 166). For this reason we say only thus much here on this point. If one were to ask on what this pretended dignity of man rested, the answer would come to saying that it rested on his morality. Thus the morality rests on the dignity, and the dignity on the morality. But apart from this, the conception of dignity seems to me to be only ironically applicable to a being so sinful in will, so limited in intellect, so easily injured, and so feeble in body as man:

"Quid superbit homo? cujus conceptio culpa,
   Nasci poena, labor vita, necesse mori!"

I would therefore postulate the following rule in opposition to the aforesaid form of the Kantian moral principle: Do not attempt in the case of any man with whom you come in contact an objective valuation of him as to worth and dignity; hence do not take into consideration the badness of his will, nor the limitation of his understanding, nor the perversity of his ideas, for the first can easily evoke hatred, the last contempt against him; but bear in mind only his sufferings, his need, his anxiety, his pains. In this way we shall continually feel ourselves related to him, sympathize with him, and instead of hatred or contempt, experience that sympathy with him which is the only ἀγάπη to which the Gospel admonishes us. The standpoint of sympathy is alone suited to prevent hatred or contempt arising toward him, and not certainly the opposite one of seeking after his pretended dignity.

The Buddhists, in consequence of their deeper ethical and metaphysical insights, do not start from cardinal

virtues, but from cardinal vices, as the antitheses or
negations of which the cardinal virtues first appear.
According to J. J. Schmidt's "History of the Eastern
Mongolians," p. 7, the cardinal vices of the Buddhists
are lust, idleness, anger, and greed. But probably pride
ought to stand in the place of idleness, as given in the
"Lettres Édifiantes et Curieuses," edit. de 1819, vol. vi., p.
372; envy or hatred being there added as a fifth. For
my correction of the statement of the highly deserving
J. J. Schmidt, its agreement with the doctrines of the
Sufis, who were certainly under the influence of Brahm-
ism and Buddhism, speaks strongly in favor. For these
also postulate the same cardinal vices, and indeed very
effectively, pairwise, so that lust appears related to greed,
and anger to pride. (See Tholuck's "Collection of Blos-
soms from Oriental Mysticism," p. 206.) We already find
lust, anger, and greed in the "Bhagavat Gita" (xvi. 21),
postulated .as cardinal vices, which attests the great age
of the doctrine. Similarly in the "Prabodha-Chandrodaya,"
a philosophico-allegorical drama, extremely important for
the Vedanta-philosophy, these three cardinal vices also
appear as the three generals of the King Passion in his
war against King Reason. As the cardinal virtues opposed to the above cardinal vices, modesty and generos-
ity, together with mildness and humility, would result.

If we compare with these deeply-conceived oriental
root-ideas of ethics the so-celebrated and so-many-thou-
sand-times-repeated cardinal virtues of Plato, justice, bravery, moderation, and wisdom, we shall find them to be
without a clear guiding root-conception, and therefore
superficially chosen, and in part even clearly false. Virtues
must be qualities of the Will, but wisdom belongs directly to the intellect. The σωφροσύνη, which is translated
by Cicero *Temperantia*, and in German *Mässigkeit* (moderation), is a very indeterminate and ambiguous expression,
under which many things may be brought, such as reflection, abstinence, holding one's head up; it comes probably
from σῶον ἔχειν τὸ φρνεῖν, or as Hierax says in "Stobæus"
(Flor. tit. J., § 60, vol. i., p. 134, Gaisf.) . . . Ταύτην
τὴν ἀρετὴν σωφροσύνην ἐκάλεσαν σωτηρίαν οὖσαν φρονησέως. Bravery
is no virtue at all, although it may sometimes be the

servant or tool of virtue; albeit it is equally ready to serve the cause of the greatest unworthiness, being, properly speaking, a mere characteristic of temperament. Geuliux ("Ethica, in Præfatione,") rejected the cardinal virtues of Plato and postulated these; *diligentia, obedientia, justitia, humilitas;* obviously a bad selection. The Chinese name five cardinal virtues: sympathy, justice, politeness, knowledge, and uprightness ("Journ. Asiatique," vol. ix., p. 62). "Sam. Kidd, China" (London, 1841, p. 197), calls them benevolence, righteousness, propriety, wisdom, and sincerity, and gives an exhaustive commentary on each. Christianity has no cardinal, but only theological virtues: faith, love, and hope.

The point at which the moral virtues and vices of men first part is the above antithesis of our fundamental attitude toward others, which either takes on the character of envy or of sympathy. For these two diametrically opposite characteristics every man bears within himself, since they spring from the unavoidable comparison of his own state with that of another; and accordingly, as the result affects his individual character, will the one or the other quality become his fundamental attitude of mind and the source of his conduct. Envy builds up the more firmly the wall between thou and I; for sympathy it becomes thin and transparent; sometimes, indeed, it is thrown down altogether, in which case the distinction between I and not-I vanishes.

Bravery, as discussed in the foregoing, or rather the courage which lies at its foundation (for courage is only bravery in war) deserves a closer investigation. The ancients reckoned courage among the virtues and cowardice among the vices; but the Christian moral sense, which is directed toward well-wishing and suffering, and whose doctrine forbids all enmity, properly indeed all resistance, does not involve this, and hence it has disappeared with the moderns. We must nevertheless admit that cowardice is not easily compatible with a noble character if only on account of the excessive concern for one's person which betrays itself therein. Courage is reducible to the fact that one willingly encounters evils threatened at the present moment, in order to avoid greater ones looming in the future, while cowardice does the opposite. Now patience is of the former character, since it consists in the clear consciousness that there are greater evils than the present ones which might be brought on by the violent flying from or warding off of these. Courage would therefore be a form of PATIENCE, and because it is this which enables us to endure privations and self-conquest of every kind, so, by means of it, courage is at least akin to virtue.

But perhaps it admits of a higher mode of contemplation One might reduce all fear of death to a want of that natural and therefore merely felt metaphysic by virtue of which man bears within himself the certainty that he exists just as much in all things, yes, in all things, as in his own person, the death of which need therefore little concern him. From this certainty, accordingly, arose the heroic courage and consequently (as the reader may remember from my " Ethics") from the same source as the virtues of justice and human love. This certainly means seizing the matter from above; nevertheless it is not easily to be explained otherwise why cowardice appears contemptible, and personal courage, on the contrary, noble and sublime. For one cannot see from any lower standpoint why a finite individual who is himself all — is himself indeed the fundamental condition of the existence of the rest of the world — should not put the maintenance of himself before all else. An exclusively immanent, that is purely empirical explanation, inasmuch as it could only be based on the utility of courage, would be insufficient. From this it may have arisen that Calderon pronounces a sceptical but significant view of courage, when he denies its reality, and does this indeed out of the mouth of an old wise minister as against his young King:—

> « Que aunque el natural temor,
> En todos obra igualmente,
> No mostrale es ser valiente,
> Y esto es lo que hace el valor. »
> « La Hija del Aire, » P. II. tom, 2.

" For although natural fear is active in the same way in all men, one is brave in so far as one does not let it be seen, and this indeed constitutes bravery." ("The Daughter of the Air," Part. II., A. 2.)

Respecting the above-mentioned differences between the estimation of courage among the ancients and among the moderns it must, however, be taken into consideration that the ancients understood by virtue, *virtus*, ἀρετή, every excellence, every quality praiseworthy in itself, whether moral or intellectual, or, indeed, merely corporeal. But after that Christianity had demonstrated the ground-tendency of life to be moral, moral excellencies alone were thought of under the conception of virtue. Meanwhile we find the earliest sense in the older Latinists and even in the Italian, as is proved by the well-known meaning of the word *virtuoso*. Learners ought to have their attention especially directed to this extended range of the conception Virtue among the ancients, as otherwise it may easily give rise to a secret perplexity in them. To this end I particularly recommend two passages preserved for us by Stobæus; the one apparently emanating from the Pythagorean Metopos in the first chap. of his "Florilegium," § 64 (Vol. i., p. 22, Gaisf.), where the capacity of each member of our body for ἀρετή is explained, and the other in his "Eclog. Eth." I. II., cap. 7 (p. 272, ed. Heeren). It there speaks as follows . . . σκυτοτόμου ἀρετὴν λέγεσθαι καθ᾽ ἥν ἀποτελεῖν ἄριστον ὑπόδημα δύναται. (*Sutoris virtus dicitur secundum quam probum calceum novit parare.*) This explains why virtues and vices are spoken of in the "Ethics" of the ancients and find no place in our own.

Just as the place of bravery among the Virtues is doubtful so is that of avarice among the Vices. Only one must not confound it with the greed which is directly expressed by the Latin word *avaritia*. We will therefore for the nonce allow the *pro* and *contra* to be brought forward and heard, so that the final judgment may be left to each reader.

A. Avarice is not a vice, but its opposite, EXTRAVAGANCE, which arises from an animal limitation to the present time against which the future, existing as it does merely in thought, can attain no power, and is based on the illusion of the positive and real value of sensuous pleasures. Future want and suffering are accordingly the price for which the spendthrift purchases these vacuous, fleeting, and often imaginary pleasures, or feeds his empty, brainless conceit in the posturings of the parasites who laugh at him behind his back, and in the astonishment of the common people and of those envious of his magnificence. For this reason one ought to fly from him as from one plague-stricken, and after we have discovered his vice to break with him as soon as possible; so that we may not have, later, when the consequences appear, either to help to bear them, or to play the rôle of the friends of Timon of Athens. In the same way it is not to be expected that he who has thoughtlessly run through his own fortune will leave untouched that of another when it comes into his hands; but as Sallust has very rightly put it, *sui profusus, alieni appetens* (Catil. c. 5). Hence extravagance leads not merely to poverty but through this to crime; the criminals from the well-to-do classes have almost all become so in consequence of extravagance. Truly does the Koran say (Sure 17, v. 29): "Spendthrifts are brothers of Satan." Avarice, on the contrary, has superfluity in its train, and when is this undesirable? But that must surely be a good vice that has good consequences. The avaricious man, namely, proceeds from the correct principle that all pleasures act merely negatively and that hence a happiness compounded of them is a chimera, and that on the contrary pains are positive and very real. Hence he denies for himself the former, in order the better to secure himself against the latter, so that *sustine abstine* are its maxims. And since he further knows how inexhaustible are the possibilities of misfortune, and how countless the paths of danger, he takes his measures against them, in order, if possible, to surround himself with a threefold wall of defense. Who could say then where precautions against accidents begin to be excessive? Only he who knew where the tricks of fortune attain their end. And even if precautions are excessive, this mistake at most brings harm to himself, not to others. Will he never have need of the treasures he hoards up? In this case they will accrue at some time to the benefit of others to whom nature has given less forethought. That until then money has been withdrawn from circulation is no harm, for money is not an article of consumption; it is a mere representative of real, useful goods, not such itself. Ducats are at bottom themselves mere reckoning counters; it is not they which have value, but that which they represent, and this cannot be withdrawn from circulation. Besides, through his retention of the money, the value of that which remains in circulation is by so much raised. If, as is sometimes maintained, many misers at last come to love money directly for its own sake, so, on the other hand, and just as certainly does many a spendthrift love the spending and wasting of money for its own sake. But friendship, or, indeed, relationship with the miser, is not only without danger but desirable, since it may bring him the greatest advantages. For at all events those nearest to him reap the fruits of his self-restraint after his death. But even during his life there is, in cases of great need, something to be hoped from him — more at least than from the penniless spendthrift who is helpless and in debt. "Mas dà el duro, que el desnudo" ("The hardhearted man gives more than the naked") says a Spanish proverb. In consequence of all this, avarice is no vice.

B. It is the quintessence of the vices! If physical pleasures seduce man from the right path, his sensuous nature, the animal within him, is to blame. Carried away by excitement, and overpowered by the impression of the moment, he acts without consideration. When, however, through bodily weakness or old age he has reached a stage at which the vices which he could never forsake, finally forsake him, in that his capacity for sensual enjoyments has died out, the intellectual appetite survives the fleshly, and he turns to avarice. Money, which is the representative of all the good things of the world — which is their *abstractum* — is now the withered stem to which his dead appetites cling, as egoism *in abstracto*. They regenerate themselves henceforth in the love of mammon. Out of the fleeting, sensuous appetite a well considered and calculating appetite for money has developed itself, which like its object is of symbolical nature, and like it also is indestructible. It is the stiff-necked love of the enjoyments of the world, as it were outliving itself, the perfected inconvertibility, the subli-mated and spiritualized lust of the flesh, the abstract fo-cus in which all lusts centre, to which it is, therefore related as the universal concept to particular things. Avarice, accordingly, is the vice of age, as extravagance is that of youth.

The *disputatio in utramque partem* just heard is assur-edly suited to force as to the *juste milieu* morality of Aristotle. The following consideration is also favorable thereto.

Every human perfection is akin to a fault into which it threatens to pass over; and conversely every fault is akin to a perfection. Hence the mistake respecting a man in which we are often landed, rests upon the fact that at the beginning of our acquaintance we confound his faults with their kindred perfections, or *vice versâ*. The prudent man thus seems to us cowardly, the econom-ical man avaricious; the spendthrift seems liberal, the discourteous man straightforward and upright, the block-head endowed with a noble self-confidence, etc.

He who lives among men feels himself ever anew tempted to the assumption that moral badness and intel-lectual incapacity are closely connected, since they spring directly from one root. But that this is not so, I have conclusively shown in the second volume of my chief work, chap. xix., No. 8. The foregoing illusion, which merely arises from the fact that both are often found together, is entirely to be explained from the very fre-quent appearance of both, in consequence of which it often happens to them that they have to dwell beneath the same roof. But it is not to be denied, however, that they play into one another's hands to reciprocal advan-tage, whence is brought about the so unedifying appear-ance which only too many men offer, and the world goes as it goes. Stupidity is especially favorable to the clear exposure of falseness, meanness and malice; while pru-dence understands better how to conceal this. And how often, on the other hand, the perversity of the heart prevents man from seeing truths to which his understanding would be quite equal.

However, let no one be too proud, since every one, even the greatest genius, is unquestionably limited in some sphere of knowledge, and thereby proclaims his relationship with the essentially perverted and absurd human race. Each one bears something morally bad within him, and even the best, the noblest character, will surprise us at times by individual traits of badness, in order, as it were, to indicate its kinship with that human race in which every degree of unworthiness and cruelty occurs. For precisely owing to this bad within him, this evil principle, he was compelled to become a man. And for this same reason the world is exactly that which my true mirror of it has shown it to be.

In spite of all, however, the differences between men remain incalculably great, and many a one would be shocked if he saw another as he himself is. O for an Asmodeus of morality who not alone made roofs and walls transparent to his favored one, but the veil of the Presentment spread out over all falseness, hypocrisy, double-facedness, lying and deception, and who would let him see how little true honesty is to be found in the world, and how often, even where one least expects it, behind all the virtuous outworks, secretly and in the innermost recess unrighteousness sits at the helm. Hence come the four-footed friendships of so many of the better kind of men, for on what indeed should one refresh oneself from the endless deceit, falseness, and cunning of men if it were not for the dogs into whose faithful countenance one may look without distrust? Our civilized world is then only a great masquerade. One meets there knights, parsons, soldiers, doctors, advocates, priests, philosophers, and what not! But they are not what they represent themselves; they are mere masks under which are hidden, as a rule, money-makers. One will assume the mask of justice which he has borrowed from his advocate, merely in order to crush another; a second, with the same object, chooses the mark of public weal and patriotism; a third that of religion, of purity, of faith; many a one has for a variety of purposes donned the mask of philosophy, of philanthropy, etc. Women have less choice; they mostly employ the mask of purity, of bashfulness, domesticity, and modesty. There are, moreover, universal masks with no special character, as it were the dominos that one meets with everywhere. To this character belong strict integrity, politeness, disinterested sympathy, and grinning friendship. Manufacturers, commercial men, and speculators, only are, for the most part, hidden behind all these masks. In this respect the merchants constitute the only honorable class, for they alone admit themselves to be what they are; they go about unmasked, and, therefore, stand low in rank. It is very important to be taught early in youth that one is living in a masquerade. For otherwise many things will be unable to be understood and come at; but one will stand before them puzzled, and the longest he who *cui ex meliori luto dedit præcordia Titan.* Such is the favor which baseness finds, the neglect which merit even the rarest and the greatest suffers from the men of its department, the detestation of the truth, and of great capacities, the ignorance of the learned in their own branch that genuine wares are almost always despised, and the merely apparent sought after. The youth should, therefore, be taught that in this masquerade the apples are of wax, the flowers of silk, the fish of paste, and all is trifling and jesting; and that of those yonder whom he sees so earnestly engaged with each other, the one gives nothing but false wares, and the other pays for them with counters.

But more serious considerations are to be brought forward and worse things told. Man is at bottom a wild, horrible creature. We know him merely as broken in and tamed by what we call civilization, and hence the occasional outbreaks of his nature shock us. But where and when the padlock and chain of legal order fall off and anarchy enters, then he shows himself what he is. He who in the meantime without this opportunity would like to inform himself thereupon, can acquire the conviction from hundreds of ancient and modern narratives, that man yields in cruelty and pitilessness to no tiger and no hyena. An important instance from modern times is furnished by the answer which the British Anti-Slavery

Society received to its questions as to the treatment of the slaves in the slave-holding states of the North American Union from the North American Anti-Slavery Society in the year 1840: "Slavery and the internal slave trade in the United States of North America, being replies to questions transmitted by the British Anti-Slavery Society to the American Anti-Slavery Society in London, 1841." This Book constitutes one of the heaviest indictments against human nature. No one will lay it aside without horror, few without tears. For what the reader has heard or imagined or may have dreamt, as to the unhappy state of the slaves or of human harshness and cruelty in general, will seem insignificant to him when he reads how those devils in human shape, those bigoted church-going, strict sabbath-observing scoundrels, especially the Anglican parsons among them, treat their innocent black brethren who by injustice and violence have come into their devil's claws. This book, which consists of dry but authentic and substantiated accounts, inflames all human feeling to such a degree that with it in the hand one could preach a crusade for the conquest and punishment of the slave-holding States of North America. For they are a disgrace for all humanity. Another example from the present time — for the past will not seem to many any longer valid — is contained in Tschudi's "Travels in Peru," 1846. In the description of the treatment of the Peruvian soldiers by their officers.* But we do not require to seek for examples in the new world, that reverse side of the planet. In the year 1848 it came to light that in England within a short space of time, there had been not one, but a hundred cases in which a husband poisoned a wife, or a wife a husband, or both together their children, or slowly tortured their children to death by hunger or bad treatment, merely to receive from the burial clubs the funeral expenses guaranteed to them in case of death, for which purpose they bought a child into several, sometimes as many as twenty of such

---

* A most recent instance may be found in Macleod's "Travels in Eastern Africa" (2 vols., London, 1860), where the unheard-of cold, calculating, and truly devilish cruelty with which the Portuguese in Mozambique treat their slaves is narrated.

clubs. See on this matter the "Times," 20th, 22d, 23d September, 1848, which journal merely on this account presses for the abolition of burial clubs. It repeats the same charge in the strongest manner on the 12th December, 1853.

Reports of this kind certainly belong to the blackest pages in the criminal annals of the human race, but the source of them, and of everything similar, is nevertheless the inner and inborn nature of man, this κατ' ἐξοχήν, this God of the Pantheists. There rests directly in every one a colossal egoism which overleaps the boundaries of justice with the greatest ease, as daily life teaches on a small scale, and history at every page on a large scale. Does there not lie, indeed, in the recognized necessity of the so anxiously-watched European equilibrum, the confession that man is a wild beast, which as soon as it has espied a weaker one near it, infallibly falls upon it? And do not we daily receive the confirmation of this in a small way? But to the limitless egoism of our nature there allies itself yet again the store of hatred, anger, envy, rancor, and malice present more or less in every human breast, and collected like the poison in the gland of the snake's tooth and only awaiting the opportunity to free itself, and then like an unchained demon to ramp and rage. If no great opportunity for it presents itself it will at last use the smallest, enlarging it by its imagination,

"Quantulacunque adeo est occasio, sufficit iræ."
"Juv. Sat." xiii. v. 183.

and will then carry things as far as it can and dare. We see this in daily life where such eruptions are known under the expression "to pour out one's gall on something." It has been observed, moreover, that when it has met with no resistance the subject of it finds himself much better after it. That anger is not without pleasure Aristotle has observed: τὸ ὀργίζεσθαι ἡδύ ("Rhet." I., 11, II., 2), where he also quotes the passage from Homer which declares anger to be sweeter than honey. But one does not devote oneself *con amore* merely to anger, but also to hatred, which is related to it as the chronic to the acute disease.

«Now hatred is by far the longest pleasure:
Men love in haste, but they detest at leisure.»
Byron, «Don Juan,» c. xiii. 6.

Gobineau ("Des Races Humaines") has called man
l'animal méchant par excellence, which people take offense
at because they feel it touches them. But he is right,
for man is the only animal which causes others pain
without any further object than that of doing so. The
other animals never do it otherwise than to satisfy their
hunger or in the heat of conflict. Although it is said of
the tiger that he kills more than he eats, yet he strangles
everything with the intention of eating it so that it is a
case merely to be expressed by the French phrase *ses
yeux sont plus grands que son estomac*. No animal ever
tortures for the sake of torturing but man, and this constitutes the DEVILISH character in him which is far worse
than the merely animal. We have already spoken of the
matter on a great scale, but on the small it is no less
clear, as everyone has daily opportunity of observing.
For instance, two young dogs are playing with one another — a peaceful and pretty sight — and a child of three
or four years comes upon the scene; the child will almost
inevitably strike in violently with its whip or stick and
thereby show it is already *l'animal méchant par excellence!*
Even constant purposeless teasing and mischief spring
from this source. For example, if one has expressed
one's dislike of something disturbing, or some other
small unpleasantness, people will not be wanting who will
bring it about for that very reason — *animal méchant par
excellence!* This is indeed so certain, that one has to be
careful of expressing one's annoyance at small discom-
forts; as also on the other hand, one's gratification at
any trifle. For in the latter case they are likely to do
as the jailer who as soon as he discovered that his pris-
oner had completed the difficult task of taming a spider
and found pleasure in it, at once crushed it: *l'animal
méchant par excellence!* Hence all animals instinctively
fear the look or indeed even the trace of man, the *animal méchant par excellence*. Instinct does not deceive
here; for only man hunts prey which is neither useful to
him nor injures him.

There really resides in the heart of each of us a
wild beast which only waits the opportunity to rage and
rave in order to injure others, and which if they prevent it, would like to destroy them.   Hence arises all the
pleasure in fighting the war; and it is this which gives
the understanding, its special keeper, always enough to
do to overcome and to hold it in some measure within
bounds.   One may indeed call it the radical evil, with
which those for whom a word takes the place of an explanation may be contented.   But I say it is the Will to
live which, embittered more and more by the constant
sorrows of existence, seeks to lighten its own suffering
by causing the same to others.   In this way it gradually
develops genuine malice and cruelty.   One may also observe in this connection that as, according to Kant, matter only obtains by the antagonism of expansive and
contractive force, so human society only exists through
that of hatred or anger or fear.   For the ferocity of our
nature would probably make every one a murderer at
once were it not mingled with the necessary dose of fear
to hold it within bounds, and this again would make it
the mock and plaything of every child if anger were not
ready to hand, and keeping watch.

But the worst trait in human nature is the malicious
pleasure in mischief which is nearly akin to cruelty, and
indeed distinguishes itself therefrom only as theory from
practice, and which appears generally where sympathy
ought to find a place, sympathy, as its opposite, being
the only true source of all genuine righteousness and human love.   In another sense ENVY is opposed to sympathy
in so far, namely, as it is called forth by the opposite occasion.   Hence its opposition to sympathy rests directly
on opportunity, and displays itself in feeling also as a
consequence of this.   Hence moreover envy, although to
be condemned, is at least capable of an excuse and eminently human, while the mere pleasure in mischief is
diabolical and its mockery the laughter of hell.   It presents itself, as already said, just where sympathy should
appear; envy, on the contrary, only there where no occasion for the latter exists, but rather for its opposite,
and as this opposite it arises in the human breast, and

is therefore in so far a human emotion; I fear, indeed, that no one will be found entirely free from it. For that Man in looking upon alien enjoyment and possession should feel his own want the more bitterly is natural and indeed inevitable; only it ought not to excite his hatred against the more fortunate, but precisely in this envy properly-speaking consists. But envy should least of all find a place where, not the gifts of fortune, or of chance, or the favor of others, but where that of nature is the cause of them, since everything inborn rests upon a metaphysical basis, that is, has a justification of a higher kind, and is, so to say, of God's grace. But unfortunately with envy it is exactly opposite. To personal advantages it is most irreconcilable; hence understanding, and even genius, have at first to beg for forgiveness of the world, wherever they are not in a position to venture proudly and boldly to despise the world. When, namely, envy has been excited merely by riches, rank, or power, it is often damped by egoism, inasmuch as the latter sees, that in certain cases help, enjoyment, assistance, protection, advantage, etc., is to be hoped for, or that at least by association with it one is illumined by the reflection of its importance and may even enjoy honor. There is, moreover, always the hope of at sometime or other attaining these good things oneself. On the other hand with natural gifts and personal excellences such as, with women beauty, with men intellect, the envy directed upon them derives no consolation of the one kind or hope of the other, so that nothing remains for it but to hate those so privileged, bitterly and irreconcilably. Hence its only wish is to take revenge on its object. But in this it finds itself in the unfortunate position that all its blows fall powerless as soon as it appears that they have proceeded from it. Hence it hides itself as carefully as secret sins of lust, and is an inexhaustible inventor of devices, tricks, and dodges in order to mask and conceal itself so that it may wound its object unseen. The excellences, for example, which consume its heart it will ignore with the most innocent mien, it will not see them nor know them, it will never have noticed or heard of them, and will show itself a past master in dissimulation.

With the greatest refinement it will entirely overlook the
brilliant qualities which gnaw at his heart, seemingly as
though they were insignificant, it will be quite unaware of
them and have opportunely quite forgotten them.   But
it will above all things be concerned carefully to remove
by secret machination all opportunity for these excellences
to show themselves and become known.   It will then eject
from the darkness blame, mockery, contempt, and calumny,
like the toad that spits forth its poison from its hole.
None the less will it enthusiastically praise insignificant
men, or the mediocre, or the bad, in the same class of
achievement.   In short it becomes a Proteus in stratagem
in order to wound without showing itself.   But what does
it avail ?   The practiced eye recognizes it notwithstanding.
Its fear and fight before its object already betrays it,
the object which stands by so much the more alone, the
more brilliant it is.   For this reason pretty girls have no
female friends.   Its hate without any occasion betrays it,
a hate which breaks out in the most violent explosion at
the least, often indeed, a merely imaginary, occasion.
For the rest, however widespread its family may be, one
recognizes it in the universal praise of modesty, that sly
virtue invented for the benefit of flat commonplaceness,
which nevertheless by the necessity that displays itself
of sparing mediocrity brings it rather into the light.
There can assuredly be nothing more flattering for our
conceit and our pride than the sight of envy lurking and
carrying on its machinations in its hiding place.   But
one should never forget that where envy is, hate accompanies it, and one should guard against allowing the en-
vier to become a false friend.   His discovery is therefore
of importance for our safety.   One should therefore study
him in order to be up to his tricks, for he is everywhere to be found, and always goes about *incognito*, or,
like the poisonous toad, lurks in dark holes.   He deserves
indeed neither consideration nor sympathy, but let the
motto be :—

> « No mortal envy can appease;
> 'Twere best to scorn her at your ease,
> Thy fame and fortune are her pain;
> Thus in her torment find your gain! »

If, as we have here done, we keep human badness before our mind's eye, and feel inclined to be horrified at it, one must cast a glance at the misery of human existence, and again at the former, if one is shocked at this. We shall then find that they keep each other in equilibrium, and shall become aware of eternal justice when we observe that the world itself is the world-tribunal, and we shall begin to understand why all that lives must pay the penalty of its existence, first in life, and then in death. The *malam pœne* appears therefore in agreement with the *malam culpæ*. From the same standpoint our indignation at the intellectual incapacity of the majority which so frequently disgusts us in life becomes dissipated. Hence *miseria humana*, *nequitia humana* and *stultitia humana* completely cover one another in this Sansara of the Buddhists, and are of equal amount. But if we once on special occasion keep one of these in mind and sample it specially, it then seems to exceed both the others in amount, but this is illusion and merely the consequence of their colossal range.

Everything proclaims this *Sansara*, but more than anything the human world in which, morally, badness and baseness, intellectually, incapacity and stupidity, dominate to a frightful degree. Nevertheless, there appear in it, sporadically perhaps, but yet surprising us ever, anew, phenomena of honesty, of goodness, of nobility, as also of great understanding of the thinking intellect, and even of genius. These never become quite extinct, they glitter at us like isolated shining spots from out of the great dark mass. We must take them as a pledge that a good and saving principle is hidden in this *Sansara*, which can manifest itself, and fill and free the whole.

The readers of my " Ethics " know that the foundation of morals rests with me finally on the truth which has its expression in the Veda and Vedanta in the established mystical formula *Tat twam asi* (this art thou), which is pronounced with reference to every living thing, be it man or animal, and is there termed the *Maha-vakya*.

One may, indeed, regard conduct in accordance therewith, as for instance benevolence, as the beginning of

mysticism. Every benevolent action practiced from a
pure motive proclaims that he who practices it stands in
direct contradiction to the phenomenal world in which
other individuals are entirely separate from himself, and
recognizes himself as identical with them. Every quite
disinterested service is accordingly a mysterious action, a
mysterium; and hence in order to give an explanation of it
men have had to take refuge in all sorts of fictions. After
Kant had removed from Theism all other supports he
merely left it this one, namely, that it afforded the best
explanation of the above and all mysterious actions similar to it. He admitted it accordingly as a theoretically
unprovable, but for practical purposes valid assumption.
But that he was altogether serious in this I am inclined
to doubt. For to support morals by means of Theism is
equivalent to reducing them to egoism: although the
English, like the lowest classes of society with us, do not
see the possibility of any other foundation.

The recognition above referred to, of one's own true
essence in a strange individuality manifesting itself
objectively appears especially clear and beautiful in those
cases where a human being already hopelessly sacrificed,
concerns himself with anxious care and active zeal for
the welfare and rescue of others. There is a well-known
story in this connection of a servant girl, who at night,
in the courtyard, being bitten by a mad dog, giving herself up for lost, seizes the dog, drags it into the stable,
and locks it up there that no one else might become its
victim. Similarly that incident in Naples which Tisch-
bein has perpetuated in one of his water color drawings.
Flying before the lava as it streams toward the sea, a
son carries his old father on his back; but as at last only
a narrow strip of land divides the two destructive elements, the father tells his son to lay him down in order
that he may save himself by running, since otherwise
both would be lost. The son obeys, and as he goes
throws a last parting look at the father. This is represented in the picture. Of this kind also is the historical
fact which Walter Scott depicts with masterly hand in
" The Heart of Midlothian," chapter ii., where of two
delinquents condemned to death the one who by his

clumsiness had been the cause of the capture of the other, successfully frees him in the church after the death sermon, by vigorously overpowering the watch without making any attempt for himself. We may reckon also in this connection, although it may offend the occidental reader, the often reprinted engraving of a soldier already kneeling to be shot zealously driving back his dog, who is running toward him, with a handkerchief. In all cases of this kind we see an individual who is approaching his immediate personal destruction with complete certainty, thinking no more of his own preservation and directing his whole care and endeavor to the preservation of another. How could the consciousness more clearly express itself that this destruction is only that of a phenomenon, and is therefore itself phenomenon, while the true essence of the perishing being remains untouched, continues in the other, in which even now, as its action shows, it so clearly recognizes itself! For how, if this were not so, but if we had a being before us in the throes of real annihilation, could such a one by the supreme exertion of its last powers show such an intense interest in the welfare and continuance of another ?

There are indeed two opposite ways in which to become conscious of one's own existence: firstly, in empirical intuition as displayed from the outside as an infinitely small being in a world limitless in time and space; as one among the thousand millions of human beings which run to and fro on this earth for a very short time, renewing themselves every thirty years; secondly, in so far as one sinks oneself within oneself and becomes conscious of being all in all and in very deed the only real being, which sees itself again in the other given it from without, as in a mirror. Now the first mode of knowledge embraces merely the phenomenon mediated through the *principium individuationis*, but the other is an immediate consciousness of itself as the thing-in-itself — is a doctrine in which I, as regards the first part, have Kant with me, but in both the Vedas. The simple objection to the latter mode of knowledge is that it presupposes that one and the same being can be in different places at the same time. But although, from the empirical standpoint, this is the most palpable impossibility and, indeed, absurdity, it remains, notwithstanding, perfectly true of the thing-in-itself; because this impossibility and absurdity merely rests on the forms of the phenomenon which constitute the *principium individuationis*. For the thing-in-itself, the Will-to-live, is in every being, even the least —is present, whole and undivided as completely as in all that ever were, are, and will be, taken together. On this is based the fact that every being, even the least, says to himself, *Dum ego salvus sim pereat mundus*. And in truth of all other beings perished, in this one that remained, the whole essence in itself of the world, uninjured and unlessened, would laugh at its destruction as at a play of jugglery. This is certainly a conclusion *per impossibile* to which one is equally justified in opposing the opposite that if any being, even the least, were wholly destroyed the whole world would perish with it. In this sense the mystic Angelus Silesius says:

> «I know that not one moment can God live from me apart
> If I to nothingness am brought, His spirit must depart.»

But in order that this truth, or at least the possibility, that our own self may exist in other beings, whose consciousness is separate and distinct from ours, may be seen to some extent even from the empirical standpoint, we only require to recall to mind the magnetized somnambules whose identical I after they are awakened knows nothing of all that which a moment before they have themselves said, done, and suffered. The individual consciousness therefore is so entirely phenomenal a point, that even in the same I, two such may arise, of which the one knows nothing of the other.

Considerations, however, like the foregoing, retain in our Judaized west a strange appearance; but not so in the fatherland of the human race, in that land where an entirely different faith dominates, a faith in accordance with which even to-day, after the burial, the priests before all the people and with the accompaniment of instruments chant the Veda Hymn which begins:

"The embodied spirit which has a thousand heads, a thousand eyes, a thousand feet, has its root in the human breast and nterpenetrates at once the whole earth. This being is the world and all that was and will be. It is that which grows by nourishment and which confers immortality. Such is its greatness, and hence it is the most noble embodied spirit. The elements of this world constitute one part of his being and three parts are immortality in heaven. These three parts have raised themselves from the world; but the one part has remained behind and is that which (by transmigration) enjoys and does not enjoy the fruits of good and evil deeds," etc. See Colebrooke on "Religious Ceremonies of the Hindoos," in vol. v. "Asiatic Researches," p. 345 of the Calcutta edition, also in his "Miscellaneous Essays," vol. i., p. 167.

If one compares such hymns with our hymn-books it will no longer be wondered at that the Anglican Missionaries on the Ganges do such bad business, and with their sermons on their "maker" made no impression upon the Brahmin. He, however, who would enjoy the pleasure of seeing how forty-one years ago an English officer boldly and emphatically opposed himself to the absurd and shameless pretensions of these gentlemen should read, "The Vindication of the Hindoos from the Aspersions of the Rev. Claudius Buchanan, with a refutation of his arguments in favor of an ecclesiastical establishment in British India; the whole tending to evince the excellence of the moral system of the Hindoos; by a Bengal Officer. Lond. 1808." The author there explains with rare independence the advantages of the doctrines of the Hindoo faith over those of the European. The little work, which in German would fill about five sheets, deserves still to be translated, for it expounds better and more honestly than any other known to me the benevolent practical influences of Brahminism, its effect on life and on the people — very differently to the reports emanating from clerical pens which for that very reason deserve little credence, but agreeing notwithstanding with what I have heard verbally from English officers who have spent half their life in India. In order to know how jealous and furious is the Anglican Church, trembling for its benefices, at Brahminism, one should have heard the loud bellowing which some

years ago the bishops raised in Parliament, continued
for months together, and as the East Indian authorities,
as usual on such occasions, showed themselves unyield-
ing, set up again and again, and all merely because the
English authorities, as was only fair in India, displayed
some external signs of honor toward the ancient venerable religion of the country — *e. g.*, that when the procession of the gods passed by, the watch with the officer at
its head came out and saluted with a roll of the drum;
also that a red cloth was furnished to cover the Car of
Juggernaut, etc. The latter has really been done away
with together with the pilgrim dues which were raised
in connection with it in order to please these gentlemen.
In the meantime the independent driveling of these self-
styling right-reverend holders of benefices and surplices
over such things, together with the quite mediæval manner, which nowadays sounds so rough and brutal, in
which they expressed themselves, also the bitter annoyance which it caused them that Lord Ellenborough, in
1845, brought back in a triumphal procession to Bengal
and gave up to the Brahmins the Gate of the Pagoda of
Sumenaut destroyed by Mahmud the Gahznewid; all this,
I say, let us suppose that it is not unknown to them
how much the majority of Europeans who live long in
India are predisposed in their hearts toward Brahminism
and how they only shrug their shoulders at the religion,
as at the social prejudices, of Europe. "That all falls
off like scales after one has lived two years in India,"
said such a one to me on one occasion. Even a Frenchman, that very obliging and cultivated gentleman who
about ten years accompanied the Dewardussi (*vulgo* Bay-
aderes) to Europe, as I was speaking with him respecting the religion of the country, exclaimed immediately
with fiery enthusiasm, "Monsieur, c'est la vrai religion!"
It is nevertheless extremely droll, by the way, to see the
comfortable smiling self-sufficiency with which certain
servile German philosophasters, as also some cut and
dried Orientalists, look down from the heights of their
rationalistic Judaism, upon Brahminism and Buddhism.
To such mediocrities I would seriously venture to pro-
pose an engagement with the apes' comedy at the Frank-

fort Fair, if indeed the successors of Hanuman would tolerate them among them.

I think that if the Emperor of China or the King of Siam and other Asiatic monarchs concede to the European power the permission to send missionaries into their lands they would be quite justified in doing so, only under the condition that they might send exactly as many Buddhist priests with equal rights into the European land in question, choosing for this purpose naturally those who were previously well instructed in the particular European language with which they had to do. We should then have before our eyes an interesting competition, and see which of them achieved the most.

Even the fantastic and sometimes quaint Hindoo mythology as it to-day, no less than thousands of years ago, makes up the religion of the people, is, if one goes to the root of the matter, only the allegorized (*i. e.*, clad in images, and so personified and mythisized as to be suited to the capacity of the people) doctrine of the *Upanishads*, which every Hindoo, according to the measure of his powers and education, either feels, or has a presentiment of, or seeing through it, clearly understands; while the coarse and narrow-minded English reverend mocks and blasphemes it as IDOLATRY, in the belief that he alone is in the right box. The purpose of the Buddha SAKYA MUNI, on the contrary, was to separate the kernel from the shell, to free the high doctrine itself from all admixture with images and gods, and to make its pure content accessible and comprehensible even to the people. In this he succeeded wonderfully, and hence his religion is most excellent, and represented by the greatest number of adherents upon earth. He can say with Sophocles:

> — θεοῖς μὲν κᾂν ὁ μηδὲν ὢν ὁμοῦ
> κράτος κατακτήσαιτ'· ἐγὼ δὲ καὶ δίχα
> κείνων πέποιθα τοῦτ' ἐπισπάσειν κλέος.
> **"Ajax,"** 767-69.

Christian fanaticism, which seeks to convert the whole world to its faith, is irresponsible. Sir James Brooke (Rajah of Borneo), who colonized and, for a time, ruled a portion of Borneo, delivered an address in September,

19

1858, at Liverpool, before a meeting of the Society for the Propagation of the Gospel—that is, the centre of Missions—in which he said: "You have made no progress with the Mahometans, and with the Hindoos you have made no progress at all, but are precisely at the point where you were on the first day on which you set foot in India" ("Times, 29th September, 1858). The emissaries of the Christian faith have nevertheless shown themselves very useful and praiseworthy in another direction, since some of them have furnished us with excellent and complete reports on Brahmanism and Buddhism and true and careful translations of the holy books such as could only have been possible to have been done *con amore*. I dedicate the following rhyme to these worthy persons:

> "As teachers ye went hither,
> As pupils ye came hither,
> From the unveiled sense
> Fell what ye took from hence."

We may, therefore, hope that there will be a time when all Europe will be purified from Jewish mythology. The century has perhaps come, in which the peoples of Asia springing from the Japhetic stem will again receive the holy religions of their home, for after long wandering from the path they are again ripe for them.

After my prize essay on "Moral Freedom" it can remain doubtful to no thinking man that this is to be sought for nowhere in nature, but only outside of nature. It is a metaphysical fact, but in the physical world an impossibility. Nevertheless our individual acts are in no sense free. But the individual character of each is to be regarded as his free act. He himself is such, because he once for all wills to be such. For the Will exists in itself even in so far as it appears in an individual: it constitutes, that is to say, the original and fundamental Will of the same, independent of all knowledge, because preceding it. From knowledge it receives merely the motives by which it successively develops its essence, and makes itself known, or becomes visible; but it is itself as lying outside time, unchangeable so long as it exists at all. Hence each one, since as such he exists only once, and under the circumstances of his time, but which on their side appear with strict necessity, can never do anything else but precisely what he does now. The entire empirical course of the life of a man is accordingly, in all its events, great and small, as necessarily predetermined as the works of a clock. At bottom this arises from the fact that the manner in which the aforesaid metaphysically free act comes into the cognizing consciousness is a preception which has time and space for its form, by means of which the unity and indivisibility of that act displays itself as torn asunder into a series of states and events which follow the clue of the principle of cause in its four forms — and this is termed NECESSITY. But the result is a moral one, viz, this; by that which we do we know what we are, in the same way that by that which we suffer we know what we deserve.

From this it follows further that the INDIVIDUALITY does not rest alone on the *principio individuationis*, and hence is not through and through mere phenomenon, but that it has its root in the thing-in-itself, in the will of the individual, for even his character is individual. How deeply its roots penetrate here belongs to those questions whose answer I do not undertake; but it deserves here to be borne in mind that even Plato in his way presents the individuality of each as his own free act, since he makes him to be born in consequence of his heart and character, such as he is, by means of Metempsychosis ("Phædr.," p. 325 *seq.* vol. x. ed. Bip.; "De Legib." x. p. 106, ed. Bip.). Even the Brahmins on their side express the unchangeable determination of the inborn character mythically, in that they say that Brahma has in the generation of every man impressed his action and his suffering in written characters upon his skull, in accordance with which his course of life must follow. They point to the notches of the sutures of the skull bones as this writing. The content of it is a consequence of his previous life and conduct (see "Lettres Édifiantes," 1819, vol. vi. p. 149, and vol. vii. p. 135). This insight appears to lie at the foundation of the Christian (even Pauline) dogma of salvation by grace.

Another consequence of the above, which entirely confirms it empirically, is that all genuine merits, moral as
well as intellectual, have not merely a physical, or otherwise empirical, but a metaphysical origin, are accordingly *a priori* and not *a posteriori*—that is, are innate,
and not acquired, and consequently have their root not in
the mere phenomenon, but in the thing-in-itself. Hence
each one only accomplishes that which at bottom already
in his nature—that is, in his innate nature—is irrevocably fixed. Intellectual capacities, indeed, require
cultivation as many natural products require direction in
order to be enjoyable or otherwise useful. But as here
no direction can replace the original material, there also
not. For this reason all merely acquired, learned, affected
qualities—in other words, qualities *a posteriori*, moral no
less than intellectual—are, properly speaking, ungenuine,
empty appearance without content. Following as this
does from a correct metaphysic, it is taught by a deeper
glance into experience. It is evidenced, indeed, by the
great weight which all lay on physiognomy and the external appearance—that is, the innateness of every man
in any way distinguished—and hence by their eagerness
to see him. The superficial, indeed, and for good reasons, the commonplace natures will be of the opposite
opinion, in order to be able to console themselves in
what they lack that it will come in good time. This
world is, therefore, not merely a battle ground for whose
victories and defeats prizes will be distributed in the future, but it is itself already the last judgment in which
each brings with him reward and shame according to
his merits; and Brahminism and Buddhism, in so far as
they teach Metempsychosis, do not know anything different.

The question has been mooted as to what two men
who had each grown up quite alone in the wilderness
and who met each other for the first time would do.
Hobbes, Pufendorf, and Rousseau have answered it in
opposite senses. Pufendorf believed they would meet
each other lovingly; Hobbes, on the contrary, inimically;
Rousseau that they would pass each other by in silence.
All three are right and wrong; for here precisely **the**

immeasurable diversity of the innate moral dispositions of individuals would show itself in so clear a light that we should here have, as it were, the rule and measure of them. For there are men with whom the look of man at once excites a hostile feeling, inasmuch as their innermost being expresses itself "not I!" And others there are with whom this look at once excites friendly interest; their innermost being says "I once more!" In between there lie numberless degrees. But that we are in this chief point so fundamentally different is a great problem, indeed a mystery. Respecting this A PRIORITY of the moral character, the book of the Dane, Bastholm, "Historical Contributions toward Knowledge of the Savage State," affords material for a variety of reflections. It surprises him that the intellectual culture and moral goodness of nations exhibit themselves as quite independent of each other in that the one is often to be found without the other. We shall explain this from the fact that moral goodness does not in any sense arise from reflection, the development of which is dependent upon intellectual culture; but directly from the Will itself, whose structure is innate and which is in itself incapable of any improvement through culture. Bastholm describes most nations as very vicious and bad. He has, on the other hand, from certain savage peoples the most generally excellent characteristics to report, as from the Orotchyses, the inhabitants of the island Sawu, the Tumguses, and the Pelew Islanders. He then attempts to solve the problem whence it comes that particular races are so exceptionally good while all their neighbors are bad. It seems to me it may be explained from the fact that since the moral qualities of the father are hereditary, that in the above cases such an isolated race has arisen from one family, and, therefore, sprung from the same ancestor, who happened to have been a good man, and has maintained itself unmixed. The English have often reminded the North Americans on the occasion of unpleasant incidents, such as repudiation of state debts, robber enterprises, etc., that they are descended from an English criminal colony, although this is only true of a small portion of them.

It is wonderful how the individuality of every man (*i. e.*, this determinate character with this determinate intellect) precisely determines like a penetrating die, all his actions and thoughts down to the most insignificant; in consequence of which the whole course of life, that is, the external and internal history of the one turns out so total.y different from that of the other. As a botanist knows the whole plant from one leaf; as Cuvier constructed the whole animal from one bone; so from one characteristic action of a man one can attain to a correct knowledge of his character and thus, to a certain extent, construct him from it. Even if this action concerns a trifle it is possible, indeed it then often succeeds best, for in more important things people take more care, but in trifles they follow their nature without much consideration. Hence the accuracy of Seneca's saying: "Argumenta morum ex minimis quoque licet capere" (Ep. 52). If anyone show in such things by an absolutely reckless egoistic conduct that just views of things are foreign to his heart, one ought not to trust him with a single groschen without adequate security. For who will believe that he who in all other matters which do not touch property shows himself daily unjust, that one whose boundless egoism everywhere peeps out from the small actions of ordinary life for which he is not called to account, like a dirty shirt out of the holes in a ragged jacket—that such a one will be honorable in matters of *meum* and *tuum* without any other impulse than that of Justice? He who is inconsiderate in small things will be without scruple also in great. He who leaves small traits of character unnoticed has himself to thank if he afterward learns to know the character in question to his own disadvantage from the great. On the same principle one should also at once break, even with so-called good friends, if they betray, be it only in trifles, a malicious or bad or low character, in order thereby to avoid their bad turns on a larger scale, which only await the opportunity to produce themselves. The same applies to servants. One should always think, "better alone than among traitors."

The foundation and *propædeutic* of all knowledge of

men is the conviction that the conduct of man as a whole and essentially is not guided by his reason and its dictates. Hence no one becomes this or that because he has the wish to be so, however strong it may be; but his action proceeds from his innate and unchangeable character, is more closely and in detail determined by motives, and is consequently the necessary product of these two factors. One may accordingly compare the conduct of men to the course of a planet which is the result of the tangential and centripetal force which accrues to it by the operation of its sun, the former force representing the character, the latter the influence of motives. This is almost more than a mere metaphor, inasmuch, namely, as the tangential force from which the motion properly proceeds while it is limited by gravitation is, taken metaphysically, the Will displaying itself in the body in question.

He who has understood this will also see that we, properly speaking, never have more than a supposition as to what we shall do in a future position of affairs, although we often regard this as an intention. If, for example, a man in consequence of a proposal has, with perfect honesty, and even quite willingly incurred the obligation upon the occurrence of certain events still in the future to do this or that, it is not by any means assured thereby that he will fulfill it unless he be of such a nature that his promise given, of itself and as such, would be always and everywhere a sufficient motive for him, in that it, by means of his regard for his honor, acted upon him as a foreign compulsion. But apart from this what he will do on the occurrence of those circumstances may, nevertheless, be forseen with perfect certainty solely from a correct and exact knowledge of his character and of the external circumstances under whose operation he has come. This is indeed very easy if one has ever seen him once in a similar position; for he will infallibly do the same a second time, presupposing that on the first occasion he had known the circumstances accurately and completely, for as I have often remarked: " *Causa finalis non movet secundum suum esse reale, sed secundum esse cognitum* " (Suarez, " disp. metaph. disp." xxiii., sect. 7.

et 8), what, namely, he has not known or understood the first time could not operate upon his will. Just as an electrical process stops, if some isolating body intercepts the action of a conductor. The unchangeability of character and the necessity of action proceeding from it impresses itself with uncommon clearness upon him who on some occasion has not conducted himself as he ought, inasmuch as he has perhaps failed in decision or firmness, or courage, or other qualities demanded by the moment. Now after it is over he knows and honestly regrets his wrong conduct and thinks, perhaps, "If only that occurred to me again I would act differently!" It does occur to him again, the same thing happens, and he acts again exactly as before,—to his great astonishment. (Compare "World as Will and Presentment," ii., p. 226, *et seq.;* 3d ed. ii., p. 251, *et seq.*) By a long way the best explanation of the truth here under discussion is furnished us by Shakespeare's dramas. For he was penetrated by it and his intuitive wisdom speaks it *in concreto* on every side. I will, notwithstanding, here exemplify it in a case in which it stands out with special clearness, although without intention and affectation, since he as a true artist never starts from conceptions except obviously in order to satisfy the Psychological truth as he apprehended it perceptually and immediately, unconcerned that it would be by few rightly regarded and understood, and without any presentiment that in Germany dull and stupid persons were destined to appear who would elaborately explain that he had written his pieces in order to illustrate moral common-places. What I here refer to, is the character of the Earl of Northumberland which we see carried through three tragedies, without his appearing as a leading personage, but only in a few scenes which are distributed over fifteen acts, so that he who does not read with all his attention the character displayed between such long intervals may easily lose sight of its moral identity, notwithstanding the firmness with which the poet has kept it in view. He makes this Earl everywhere enter with noble knightly mien, use a language suited thereto, and has even put into his mouth at times very beautiful and even sublime passages, since he is so

far removed from doing as Schiller does who is fond of
painting the devil black, and whose moral approval or
disapproval sounds through the very words of the characters portrayed by him.   But with Shakespeare and also
with Goethe each one, so long as he is present and speaks,
is perfectly right even if he be the devil himself.   Compare, in this respect, the Duke of Alva with Goethe and
with Schiller.   We make the acquaintance of the Earl of
Northumberland already in " Richard II." where he is the
first to stir up a conspiracy against the King in favor of
Bolingbroke, afterwards Henry IV., whom he also (act
ii., scene 3), personally flatters.   In the following act he
suffers a correction because, speaking of the King, he
simply said " Richard," but gives the assurance, however,
that it was only done for the sake of brevity.   Soon afterward his cunning speech moves the King to capitulation.
In the following act he treats him in the act of abdica-
tion with such hardness and contempt that the unhappy
broken monarch for once loses patience and exclaims,
" Devil! thou plaguest me already before I am in hell."
At the conclusion he reports to the new King that he
has sent the decapitated heads of the adherents of the
former to London.   In the following tragedy, " Henry
IV.," he sets a conspiracy on foot in the same way as
before, against the new King.   In the fourth act we see
the rebels united, preparing themselves for the great
battle of the following day and waiting impatiently for
him and his army division.   There comes finally a letter
from him; he is himself ill and could not trust his men
to any one else; they should, however, courageously continue and proceed bravely to the attack.   They do it, but
are considerably weakened by his absence, are completely
beaten most of their leaders are taken, and his only son,
the heroic Hotspur, falls by the hand of the Crown
Prince.   Again, in the following piece, the " Second Part
of Henry IV.," we see him plunged into the wildest
rage by the death of this son and madly breathing
out revenge.   Hence he stirs up the rebellion afresh;
the leaders of it assemble themselves once more.   As
these, in the fourth act, have to fight the decisive
battle, and only await his joining himself to them,

there comes a letter; he has not been able to collect sufficient forces, and will therefore, for the present, seek his safety in Scotland, but wishes their heroic undertaking from his heart the best success. Upon this they surrender themselves to the King under an agreement which is not kept and they perish.

So far, then, from the character being the work of rational choice and reflection, the intellect has nothing more to do with its conduct than to hold up motives before the will. But then it must, as mere onlooker and witness, observe how from its effect on the given character the course of life shapes itself, all the processes of which when correctly considered occur with the same necessity as the movements of a clock-work, on which point I refer my readers to my prize essay on "Freedom of the Will." The illusion of a complete freedom of the Will, which nevertheless obtains here, with every single action, I have there reduced to its true significance and its origin, and thereby indicated the active cause of it, to which I will only here add the final cause in the following teleological explanation of the above natural illusion. The freedom and originality which in truth alone accrue to the intelligible character of a man, the mere apprehension of which by the intellect is his course of life appear to attach to every particular action, and so the original work is for the empirical consciousness apparently repeated anew in every particular action. Our course of life receives thereby the greatest possible moral νουτέθησις, since all the bad sides of our character become in this way first really perceptible to us. Conscience, namely, accompanies every action with the commentary, "thou mightest act differently," although its real meaning is, "thou mightest be another man." Now since, on the one hand, by the unchangeability of character, on the other by the strict necessity whereby all the circumstances in which he is successively placed occur, the course of life of each is precisely defined from A to Z; but notwithstanding one life will in all its conditions, subjective as well as objective, turn out incomparably happier, nobler, and worthier than the other. This leads, if one does not wish to eliminate all justice, to the assumption axiomatic in Brahminism and Buddhism, that no less the subjective conditions with which, as the objective condition under which each one is born, are the moral consequences of a previous existence.

Macchiavelli, who does not seem by any means to have concerned himself with philosophical speculations, is by virtue of a penetrating acuteness of his so unique intellect led to the following truly deep-thinking utterance which presupposes an intuitive knowledge of the entire necessity by which, with given characters and motives, all actions take place. He begins the prologue "Clitia" with it: "Se nel mondo tornassino i medesimi uomini, come tornano i medesimi casi, non passarebbono mai cento anni, che noi non oi trovassimo un altra volta insieme, a fare le medesime cose, che hora." ("If the same men reappeared in the world as the same events reappear, a hundred years would never pass without our finding ourselves again together, doing the same things as we are doing now.") A reminiscence, however, of what Augustine says ("De Civitate Dei," libr. xii. c. 13) seems to have led him on to this.

The Fate (the εἱμαρμένη) of the ancients is nothing else than the assurance brought to consciousness, that all that happens is firmly bound by a causal chain, and therefore happens with strict necessity, and that accordingly the future is already perfectly fixed, is determined certainly and exactly, and that as little can be changed in it as in the past. It is only the foreknowledge of it that can be looked upon as fabulous in the fatalistic myths of the ancients, if we eliminate the possibility of clairvoyance and second sight. Instead of trying to set aside the fundamental verity of fatalism by stupid talk and empty evasions, one should rather try to recognize and to understand it clearly, for it is a demonstrable truth which furnishes us with an important datum for the understanding of our so enigmatical existence.

Predestination and fatalism are not in the main distinct, but only in that the given character and the determination of human action which comes from without, proceed, the former from a knowing, the latter from a knowingless being. In the result they are the same: that

happens which must happen. The conception of a MORAL
FREEDOM is, on the contrary, inseparable from that of
ORIGINATION. For that a being is the work of another,
but in its willing and acting is free notwithstanding, may
be said with words, but not comprehended in thought.
He, namely, who called it into being from nothing has
thereby also created and determined its nature, that is,
all its qualities. For one can never create without creating something — that is, a being precisely determined
throughout, and in all its qualities. But from these qualities which are thereby determined flow afterward with
necessity its entire manifestations and defects, inasmuch
as these are simply the same qualities brought into play,
which only required a stimulation from without in order
to manifest themselves. As man is so must he act, and
thus fault and merit cleave not to his individual acts, but
to his essence and being. Hence Theism and the moral
responsibility of man are incompatible, because responsibility always falls back upon the author of the being as
the place where it has its centre of gravity. It has been
in vain attempted to throw a bridge between these two
incompatibilities by means of the conception of the moral
freedom of man, for it always breaks down again. The
free being must also be the original being. If our will
is free our primary nature is so also, and conversely.
Even the pre-Kantian dogmatism which would have kept
these two predicaments asunder was compelled to assume
two freedoms that, namely, of a first-world cause for
Cosmology, and that of the human will for morals and
theology. In accordance with this Kant also treats the
third no less than the fourth antimony of freedom.

In my philosophy, on the other hand, the straightforward recognition of the strict necessitation of actions
involves the doctrine that, even in consciousless beings,
that which manifests itself is Will, otherwise the action
of this obvious necessitation would be placed in opposition to willing, if, namely, there were really such a freedom of individual action, and this were not rather as
strictly necessitated as any other effect. On the other
hand, the same doctrine of the necessitation of the act
of Will renders it necessary that the existence and

nature of man be itself the work of his freedom — that is, of his Will — and that the latter, therefore, has *aseity*. On the opposite assumption, all responsibility would, as already shown, be done away with; and the moral, like the physical, world would be a mere machine, which its outside artificer made to work for his amusement. Truths thus all hang together, require each other, complete each other, while error strikes itself against every corner.

Of what kind the influence is which MORAL TEACHING can have on conduct, and what are its limits, I have sufficiently investigated in my treatise on the foundation of Morality. Essentially analogous to this is the influence of EXAMPLE, which is nevertheless more powerful than that of teaching, and therefore deserves a short analysis.

Example acts directly, either hindering or promoting. The first, when it determines the man to leave undone what he would willingly do. He sees, namely, that others do not do it, from which he infers in general that it is not advisable, in other words, that it must bring danger to his person, or his property, or his honor; to this he holds, and gladly sees himself relieved from independent investigation. Or he sees that another who has done it has suffered evil consequences from it. This is the terrifying example. Example acts advantageously in two ways: either in moving men to do what they would gladly leave undone by showing them that its omission would bring them into some danger or injure them in the opinion of others; or it acts so as to encourage them to do what they would willingly do, but hitherto from fear of danger or disgrace have left undone; this is the seductive example. Lastly, example may bring to a man's notice something which would otherwise not have occurred to him. In this case it obviously acts directly only on the intellect; the effect on the Will is secondary, and is, when it occurs, brought about by an original act of judgment or by confidence in him who sets the example. The entire very powerful effect of example rests on the fact that the man as a rule has too little faculty of judgment, often, also, too little knowledge to explore his way himself, and hence he is glad to tread in the footsteps of

others   Every one will, therefore, be the more open to
the influence of example the more he lacks the above
two qualifications.   The guiding star of most men is, however, the example of others, and their whole conduct in
great things as in small, is reducible to mere imitation:
they don't do the least thing on their own judgment.*   The
cause of this is their horror of every kind of reflection, and
their well-grounded mistrust of their own judgment.   At
the same time this bears witness to the surprisingly strong
imitative tendency of man, as also to his relationship to the
ape.   But the mode in which the example acts is determined by the character of each; hence the same example
can act upon one seductively and on the other repellently.
Certain social mispractices which, not previously existent, gradually force their way, readily give us the opportunity of observing this.   On first noticing something of
the kind, one thinks, "Ah, how can he do it! How egoistic, how inconsiderate! I will certainly take care that
I will never do any such thing." But twenty others will
think, "Aha! he does that, I may do it also."

In a moral respect, example, like teaching, though it
indeed promotes a civil or legal improvement, does not,
nevertheless, further the inner, which is properly the
moral, improvement.   For it only acts as a personal motive, and consequently under the presupposition of receptivity for this class of motive.   But it is precisely whether
a character is more receptive for this or that class of
motive which is decisive for its proper and true, but
nevertheless always innate, morality.   Example acts in
general advantageously for the bringing into prominence
of good and bad characteristics, but it does not create
them, and hence Seneca's utterance, " *velle non discitur*,"
holds good here also.   That the innateness of all genuine
moral qualities, of the good as of the bad, suits the doctrine of Metempsychosis, of the Brahminists and Buddhists, according to which, " The good and the bad
actions of a man follow him from one existence to another like his shadow," better than Judaism, which rather
requires that man should come into the world as a moral

---

* Imitation and habit are the impelling motives of most of the actions
of men.

zero in order by virtue of an unthinkable *liberi arbitri indifferentiæ*, that is, as a consequence of rational reflection, to decide whether he wills to be an angel or a devil, or whatever else may lie between them,—this I know well enough, but do not trouble myself about it, for my standard is the truth. I am no professor of philosophy, and, therefore, do not recognize my calling to consist in, before all other things, making sure the fundamental ideas of Judaism even if these should block the way forever to all and every philosophical cognition. *Liberum arbitrium indifferentiæ*, under the name of "Moral Freedom," is a very favorite toy for the professors of philosophy which we must leave to them—the deep-thinking, the honest, and the upright!

ON THE DOCTRINE OF THE INDESTRUCTIBILITY OF OUR TRUE NATURE BY DEATH.

ALTHOUGH I have treated this subject thoroughly and in its connection in my chief work, I nevertheless believe that a small selection of separate reflections upon it, which always throw back some light on an exposition, will not be without value for many.

One must read Jean Paul's "Selina" in order to see how an eminently great mind becomes the victim of the absurdities of a false conception, which he will not give up because he has set his heart upon it, but is all the same perpetually disturbed by absurdities which he cannot digest. It is the conception of the individual continuance of our entire personal consciousness after death. Precisely the fighting and struggling of Jean Paul proves that such concepts compounded of the false and true are not, as is alleged, wholesome errors, but are rather decidedly noxious. For not only is the true knowledge — resting on the distinction between appearance and the thing in itself — of the indestructibility of our proper nature as untouched by time, causality, and change, made impossible by the false opposition of soul and body, as also by the raising of the whole personality to a thing in itself which must eternally exist; but this false conception cannot even be firmly held as the representative of the truth, since the reason ever anew rises indignant against the absurdity lying in it, and then has to give up therewith the truth which is amalgamated with it. For in the long run truth can only subsist in its purity; mixed up with errors it participates in their fallibility as the granite crumbles when its felspar is decayed, although quartz and mica are not subject to such decay. It goes badly therefore with surrogates of the truth.

When in daily intercouse it is asked by one of those many people who wish to know everything, but do not want to learn anything, as to continued existence after death, the most suitable and indeed, in the first instance, the most correct answer is: "After your death you will be what your were before your birth." For it implies the wrong-headedness of the demand that a species of existence which has a beginning shall be without end, besides containing the implication that there may be two kinds of being and two kinds of nothing according with it. Similarly one might answer, "Whatever you will be after your death, even if it be nothing, will be just as natural and suitable to you as your individual organic existence is now, thus you will have at most to fear the moment of transition. Yes, since a mature consideration of the matter affords the result, that complete non-existence would be preferable to an existence such as ours. Thus the thought of the cessation of our existence, or of a time when we shall no longer be, ought, as far as reason goes, to trouble us as little as the thought of the time when we were not. But since the existence is essentially a personal one the end of the personality is not to be regarded as a loss."

To him, on the contrary, who on the objective and empirical path had pursued the plausible clue of materialism, and now full of alarm at complete destruction by death which confronts him therein, turns to us, we should perhaps procure for him satisfaction in the shortest way and one most suited to his empirical mode of thought, if we demonstrated to him the distinction between matter and the metaphysical force which is always temporarily taking possession of it; as, for example, in birds, where the homogeneous formless fluidity as soon as it attains the requisite temperature, assumes the complicated and exactly determined shape of the genus and species of its bird. This is indeed, to a certain extent, a kind of *generatio æquivoca*, and it is exceedingly probable that the hierarchical series of animal forms arose from the fact that once in primitive times and in a happy hour it overleaped the type of animal to which the egg belonged, to a higher one. At all events something distinct from matter appears here most prominently, especially in that by the least unfavorable circumstance it comes to nothing. In this way it becomes explicable that after an operation that has been completed

20

or subsequently prevented it can deviate from it without injury, a fact which points to a totally different permanence than that of the persistence of matter in time.

If we conceive of a being which knew, understood, and saw everything, the question whether we endure after death would probably have no meaning for such a one, since beyond our present temporal individual existence enduring and ceasing would have no significance, and would be indistinguishable conceptions. And accordingly neither the concept of destruction nor that of continuance, would have any application, since these are borrowed from time, which is merely the form of the phenomenon. In the meantime we can only think of the INDESTRUCTIBILITY of this core of our phenomenon as a continuance of it, and indeed, properly speaking, only according to the *schema* of matter which under all changes of its form maintains itself in time. If we deny it this continuance we regard our temporal end as an annihilation according to the *schema* of form which vanishes when the matter in which it inheres is taken away from it. Both are nevertheless μετάβασις εἰς ἄλλο γένος, that is, a transference of the forms of the phenomenon to the thing in itself. But of an indestructibility which would be no continuance we can hardly form even an abstract idea, since all perception by which we might confirm it fails us.

In truth however the constant arising of new beings and the perishing of those already existent is to be regarded as an illusion produced by the apparatus of two polished lenses (brain-functions), by which alone we can see anything. They are called space and time, and in their reciprocal interpenetration — causality. For all that we perceive under these conditions is mere phenomenon; but we do not know the things as they may be in themselves, that is independently of our perception. This is properly the kernel of the Kantian philosophy which, together with its content, one cannot too often call to mind in a period when venal charlatanry has by its stupefying process driven philosophy from Germany with the willing assistance of people for whom truth and intelligence are the most indifferent things in the world, and wage and salary the most important.

How can we suppose on beholding the death of a human being that a thing-in-itself here comes to nothing? That a phenomenon in time, that form of all phenomena, finds its end without the thing-in-itself being thereby affected is an immediate intuitive cognition of every man; hence men have endeavored to give utterance to it at all times, in the most diverse forms and expressions, but these are all derived from the phenomenon in its special sense and only have reference thereto. Everyone feels that he is something different from a being who has once been created from nothing by another being. In this way the assurance arises within him that although death can make an end of his life it cannot make an end of his existence. Man is something else than an animated nothing; and the animal also. He who thinks his existence is limited to his present life regards himself as an animated nothing. For thirty years ago he was nothing and thirty years hence he will be again nothing.

The more clearly one is conscious of the transience, nothingness and dreamlike nature of all things, by so much the more clearly is one conscious also of the eternity of one's own inner nature. For only in opposition to this is the foregoing structure of things known, as the rapid motion of the ship one is on, is only perceived when one looks toward the fixed shore and not when one looks at the ship itself.

The present has two halves, an OBJECTIVE and a SUBJECTIVE. The objective alone has the perception of time for its form, and hence rolls ceaselessly forward. From this arises our vivid recollection of what is very long past, and the consciousness of our imperishability, in spite of our knowledge of the transience of our existence.

Everyone thinks that his innermost core is something that the PRESENT contains and carries about with it. Whenever we may happen to live we always stand with our consciousness in the centre of time, never at its terminations; and we might assume from this that everyone bore within himself the immovable centre of infinite time. This is, moreover, at bottom what gives him the confidence with which he lives on without continual fear of death.

But whoever by virtue of the strength of his memory and imagination can recall the most vividly the long past of his own life, will become more clearly conscious than others of the IDENTITY OF THE NOW IN ALL TIME. Perhaps, indeed, this proposition is more correct taken conversely. But at all events such a clearer consciousness of the identity of all now is an essential requirement of the philosophic mind. By means of it we apprehend that which is most fleeting — the now — as the only persistent. He who is in this intuitive way aware that the present moment, which is the only form of all reality in the narrowest sense, has its source in US, and springs, that is, from within and not from without, cannot doubt of the indestructibility of his own nature. He will rather understand that by his death the objective world, indeed, with the medium of its presentment, the intellect, perishes for him, but that this does not touch his existence, for there was as much reality within as without. He will say with complete understanding: ἐγώ εἰμι πᾶν τὸ γεγονὸς, καὶ ὂν, καὶ ἐσομενον ("Stob. Floril. Tit." 44, 42; vol. ii. p. 201).

He who does not admit this to be true must maintain the opposite, and say: " Time is something purely objective and real, which exists quite independently of me. I am only accidentally thrown into it, have only become participant in a small portion of it, whereby I have attained to a transient reality like thousands of others before me who are now no more, and I shall also very soon be nothing. Time, on the contrary, is the Real. It goes further without me."

In accordance with all this, life may certainly be regarded as a dream and death as an awakening. But then the personality, the individual, belongs to the dreaming and not to the waking consciousness, for which reason death presents itself to the former as annihilation. It is still, at all events from this standpoint, not to be regarded as the transition to a state entirely new and strange to us, but rather only as the return to our original one, of which life was only a short episode.

If in the meantime a philosopher should, perhaps, think that he would find in dying a consolation peculiar to him alone, or at least a diversion, and that then a problem would be resolved for him which had so frequently occupied him, we can only say that it will probably fare with him as with one, who as he is about to find what he is seeking, has his lantern blown out.

For in death the consciousness assuredly perishes, but not by any means that which till then had produced it. The consciousness, namely, rests immediately on the intellect, but the latter on the physiological process. For it is obviously the function of the brain, and hence conditioned by the co-operation of the nerve and cellular system, though more directly by the brain, which is nourished, animated, and continuously agitated by the heart. It is by the artistic and mysterious construction of the brain as described by anatomy, but which physiology does not understand, that the phenomenon of the objective world and the trend of our thoughts is brought about. An INDIVIDUAL CONSCIOUSNESS, that is, a consciousness as such, cannot be conceived in an INCORPOREAL BEING, since knowledge, the condition of every consciousness, is necessarily brain-function — for the simple reason that the intellect objectively manifests itself as brain. Now as intellect appears physiologically — that is, in empirical reality or in the phenomenon — as a secondary, as a result of the process of life, so it is also psychologically secondary in opposition to the Will which is alone the primary and ever the original. The organism itself is really only the Will displaying itself perceptually and objectively in the brain, and therefore in its forms of space and time, as I have often explained, especially in " Will in Nature," and in my chief work (vol. ii. chap xx.). Since, then, the consciousness is not immediately dependent upon the Will, but this is conditioned by the intellect, and this again by the organism, there remains no doubt that consciousness is extinguished by death, as also by sleep and swoons.* But let us be consoled! For what kind of a consciousness is this ? A cerebral, an animal consciousness — one a little more highly developed than that of the beasts, in so far as we have it as regards all essentials in common with

* It would certainly be very pleasant if the intellect did not perish with death: one would then bring the Greek which one had learned in this world all ready with one into the other.

the whole series of animals although it attains its summit
in us. It is the same, as I have sufficiently demonstrated,
with respect to its purpose and origin — a mere μηχανή of
nature, a means of knowing how to help the animal nature to its requirements. The state, on the contrary,
into which death throws us back is our original state —
that is, it is the state peculiar to our nature, whose original force displays itself in the production and maintenance of the life that is now ceasing. It is, in short, the
state of the thing-in-itself in opposition to the phenomenon. Now in this primal state such an assistance as the
cerebral, a cognition so extremely mediate, and for this
reason merely supplying phenomena, is without doubt entirely superfluous; hence we lose it. Its disappearance is
the same as the cessation of the phenomenal world for
us, of which it was the mere medium, and can serve for
nothing else. If in this our original state the retention
of the animal consciousness were even offered us, we
should reject it as the lame man who is cured does the
crutch. He therefore who bemoans the loss in question
of this cerebral consciousness, which is merely phenomenal and adapted to the phenomenal, is to be compared to
the converted Greenlanders who did not wish for heaven
when they heard that there were no seals there.

Moreover, all that is here said rests on the assumption
that we cannot even conceive of a now-conscious state except as a knowing one, which therefore bears the root-form
of all knowledge — the separation of subject and object,
of a knowing and a known. But we have to consider that
this entire form of knowing and being known is conditioned merely by our animal, and hence very secondary
and derived, nature, and is thus in no way the original
state of all being and all existence, which may therefore
be quite different, and yet not without consciousness. If
then our own present nature, so far as we are able to
trace it to its core, is mere WILL; and this in itself is a
knowingless thing; when through death we sacrifice the
intellect, we are only thereby transplanted into our original
consciousless state, which is therefore not simply consciousless, but rather above and beyond this form — a state in
which the antithesis of subject and object disappears, be-

cause here that which is to be known would be really and immediately one with the knowing, and thus the fundamental condition of all knowing (which is precisely this opposition) would be wanting. Herewith may be compared by way of elucidation "The World as Will and Presentment," vol. ii, p. 273 (3d ed. 310.) The utterance of Giordano Bruno (ed. Wagner, vol. i, p. 287): "*La divina mente, e la unità assoluta, senza specie alcuna è ella medesimo lo che intende, e lo ch' è inteso.*"

Perhaps every one is now and then aware in his innermost heart of a consciousness that would be suited to an entirely different kind of existence than this so unspeakably beggarly, timely, individual one, occupied as it is altogether with misery; on which occasions he thinks that death might lead him to such a one.

If we now in opposition to this mode of contemplation which is directed inward, again turn our attention outward and apprehend the world displaying itself objectively, death will then certainly appear to us a passage into nothing: But birth also none the less as a proceeding out of nothing. The one like the other, however, cannot be unconditionally true since it only has the reality of the phenomenon. That in some sense we should survive death is really no greater miracle than that of generation which we daily see before our eyes. What dies goes hence, where all life comes from, its own included. In this sense the Egyptians called *Orchus Amanthus*, which, according to Plutarch ("de. Is. and Osir," c. 29), signifies ὁ λαμβάνων καὶ διδούς, "the taker and giver," in order to express that it is the same source into which everything returns and from which everything proceeds. From this point of view our life might be regarded as a loan received from death; sleep would then be the daily interest on this loan. Death announces itself without any concealment as the end of the individual, but in this individual lies the germ of a new being. Hence nothing of all that dies, dies forever. But neither does anything that is born receive a fundamentally new existence. The dying perishes but a germ remains over from which proceeds a new being which now enters into existence without knowing whence it comes and why

it is exactly such as it is. This is the mystery of the Palingenesis for the explanation of which the 42d chapter of
the 2d volume of my chief work may be consulted. It
appears from this that all beings at this moment living con-
tain the true germ of all that will live in the future, which
are thus to a certain extent already there. Similarly every
animal existing in its full perfection seems to cry out to us:
" Why dost thou complain of the perishability of the living ?
How could I exist if all those of my species which were
before me had not died ? " However much, therefore, the
pieces and the masks on the stage of the world change, the
Actors remain the same in all. We sit together and talk
and excite each other and eyes gleam and voices become
louder; exactly so others have sat thousands of years ago;
it was the same, and they were the same. Just so will it
be thousands of years hence. The arrangement owing to
which we are not aware of this, is time.

One might very well distinguish Metempsychosis as the
passage of the entire so-called soul into another body — and
Palingenesis as the decomposition and reformation of this
individual, inasmuch as his Will persists, and assuming the
shape of a new being, receives a new intellect. Thus the
individual decomposes like a neutral salt, the basis of which
combines itself with another acid into a new salt. The
difference between Metempsychosis and Palingenesis which
Servius the commentator of Virgil assumes, and which is
shortly indicated in " Wernsdorffii dissertat de Metempsy-
chosi," p. 48, is obviously fallacious and nugatory.

From Spencer Hardy's " Manual of Buddhism " (pp.
394–96 with which may be compared pp. 429, 440, 445,
in the same book), also from Sangermano's " Burmese
Empire " as well as from the " Asiatic Researches," vol.
vi., p. 179, and vol. ix., p. 256, it appears that in Buddhism an exoteric and esoteric doctrine obtains regarding
continuance after death. The former is Metempsychosis
as in Brahminism but the latter is a Palingenesis much
more difficult of comprehension, which is very much in
agreement with my doctrine of the Metaphysical existence of the Will, of the merely physical structure of the
intellect, and the perishability which accords with it.
Παλιγγενεσια occurs in the Old Testament.

But if, in order to penetrate deeper into the mystery of Palingenesis we seek aid from the 43d chapter of the 2d vol. of my chief work, the matter, more closely considered, will appear to be that throughout all time the male sex has been the bearer of the Will, the female of the Intellect of the human race, whereby it receives perpetual subsistence.   Every one, therefore, has a paternal and a maternal element, and as these are united in generation they are also separated in death, which is thus the end of the individual.   This individual it is whose death we so much deplore with the feeling that it is really lost, since it was a mere combination which irrevocably ceases.   But we must not forget in all this, that the transmissability of the Intellect of the mother is not so decided and unconditioned as that of the Will of the father, on account of the secondary and merely physical nature of the intellect and its complete dependence on the organism, not only in respect of the brain but also otherwise, as has been shown by me in the chapter in question.   I may mention here, by the way, that I so far agree with Plato in that he also distinguishes in his so-called soul, a mortal and an immortal part.   But he comes into diametrical opposition with me and with the truth, in that he, after the manner of all philosophers who have preceded me, regards the intellect as the immortal, and the Will, that is, the seat of the appetites and passions, as the mortal part; as may be seen from the "Timæus" (pp. 386, 387, 395, ed. Bip.).   Aristotle has the same idea. *

But though the physical may strangely and wonderfully rule things by procreation and death, together with the visible combination of individuals out of Will and Intellect and their subsequent dissolution, yet the metaphysical principle lying at its basis is of so entirely heterogeneous a nature that it is not affected by it, so on this point we may be consoled.

One can accordingly conceive every man from two oppo-

---

* In the "De Anima" (I. 4. p. 408), his real opinion escapes accidentally at the beginning that the νοῦς is the true and immortal soul — which he confirms with fallacious assertions. Hatred and love belong not to the soul, but to their organ, the perishable part.

site points of view: from the one, he is an individual beginning and ending in time, fleeting and transitory, σκιᾶς
ὄναρ besides being heavily burdened with failings and
pains. From the other, he is the indestructible original
being which objectivises itself in everything existent, and
may, as such, say, like the statue of Isis at Sais: ἐγώ εἰμι
πᾶν τὸ γεγονὸς, καὶ ὄν, καὶ ἐσομενον. Such a being might indeed
do something better than manifest itself in a world like
this. For this is the finite world of sorrow and of death.
What is in it, and what comes out of it must end and die.
But what is not of it, and what never will be of it,
pierces through it, all-powerful like a flash of lightning,
which strikes upward, and knows neither time nor death.
To unite all these antitheses is properly the theme of my
philosophy.

Short Concluding Dialogue.

Thrasymachos—To be brief, what am I after my death?
be clear and precise.

Philalethes—Everything and nothing.

Thrasymachos — There we have it! as the solution of a
problem, a contradiction. The trick is played out.

Philalethes—To answer transcendent questions in the
language created for immanent knowledge may certainly
lead to contradictions.

Thrasymachos—What do you call transcendent and what
immanent knowledge? These expressions are indeed
known to me from my professor but only as predicates
of Almighty God, with which his philosophy, as was only
suitable, was exclusively concerned. If, namely, he remains
in the world he is immanent, but if he sits anywhere
outside it he is transcendent. Only look, that is clear,
that is comprehensible! One knows what one has to hold
by. But your old-fashioned Kantian artificial language
no human being any longer understands. The time-
consciousness of the modern world, from the metropolis
of German science—

Philalethes (*aside*) — German philosophical windbaggery.

Thrasymachos — Through a whole succession of great
men, especially through the great Schleiermacher and the
giant intellect Hegel has been brought back from all that,

or rather, has been brought so far forward that it has left it all behind and knows no more of it. So what do you mean by it?

Philalethes — Transcendent knowledge is that which proceeding beyond all possibility of experience, seeks to determine the nature of things as they are in themselves. Immanent knowledge on the other hand, is that which keeps itself within the bounds of the possibility of experience, and therefore can speak of phenomena. You as individual end at your death, yet the individual is not your true and ultimate nature, but rather merely a manifestation of it. It is not the Thing-in-itself, but only its phenomenon which displays itself in the form of time, and accordingly has a beginning and end. Your true nature in itself knows neither time, nor beginning, nor end, nor the limits of a given individuality, and hence it can be excluded from no individuality, but is there in each and all. In the first sense you become by your death nothing; in the second you are and remain all things. Hence I said that you, after your death, would be everything and nothing. Your question scarcely admits of a more correct answer in so short a compass than this one, which, however, certainly contains a contradiction; because while your life is in time, your immortality is in eternity. This may be termed therefore an indestructibility without continuance, which again results in a contradiction. But so it is when the transcendent has to be brought into immanent knowledge, for it sustains thereby a kind of violence, since it is misused for that to which it was not born.

Thrasymachos — Do you hear, without the continuance of my individuality, I would not give a single heller for all your immortality.

Philalethes — But perhaps we may still do business together. Granted I guaranteed you the continuance of your individuality but made it a condition that before its reawakening there was to be a perfectly consciousless death-sleep of three months?

Thrasymachos — That would do.

Philalethes — But since in a perfectly consciousless state we have no measurement of time it is quite the same to us whether while we lay in that death-sleep three months or ten thousand years had passed. For we must accept the one thing like the other on trust and faith, on awakening. It must therefore be indifferent to you whether your individuality is given back to you after three months or after ten thousand years.

Thrasymachos — In the last resort that cannot be denied.

Philalethes — But now if after the lapse of the ten thousand years you were forgotten to be awakened, I believe that when after so short an existence you had become accustomed to so long a non-existence the misfortune would not be great. But certain it is; that you could know nothing of it. And you would be quite consoled as regards the question if you knew that the secret machinery which maintains your present phenomenon in motion had not ceased one moment during those ten thousand years to produce and set in motion other phenomena of the same kind.

Thrasymachos — So ? And in this way you think to swindle me out of my individuality by smooth talk, without my noticing it ? I am not to be taken in in that way. I have stipulated for the continuance of my individuality, and no machinery and phenomena can console me for the loss of it. It lies closest to my heart, and I will not part from it.

Philalethes — You regard your individuality then as so pleasant, excellent, perfect and incomparable that there could be nothing preferable to it, and hence you would not like to exchange it for any other, with which it might be asserted that it was possible to live better and more comfortably.

Thrasymachos — But surely my individuality, whatever it is, is myself,

> «Nothing in the world is above me,
>   For God is God and I am I.»

I, I, I desire existence! This it is which concerns me and not an existence which has first of all to be proved to me that it is mine.

Philalethes — But consider the matter! What is it that cries, " I, I, I desire existence," that is, not you alone, but everything, simply everything, that has a trace of consciousness. Consequently this wish in you is precisely that which is NOT individual, but common to all without distinction. It does not spring from the individuality but from existence generally, is essential to everything that exists, is indeed that WHEREBY it exists, and will accordingly be satisfied by existence IN GENERAL to which alone it refers, and not exclusively by any determinate individual existence. For it is not at all directed to the latter, although it always has the appearance of being so because it cannot attain to consciousness otherwise than in an individual being, and therefore always seems to have reference to such. But this is a mere illusion, to which indeed the crudity of the individual cleaves, but which reflection can destroy and free us from. That, namely, which so madly desires existence is merely MEDIATELY the individual! Immediately, and properly speaking, it is the Will to live in general, which is one and the same in all. Now since existence itself is its free work, is indeed its mere reflection — it follows that existence cannot escape it, but it is provisionally satisfied by existence in general, so far that is to say, as it, the eternally unsatisfied, can be satisfied. Individualities are the same to it, it does not really concern itself with them, although to the individual who immediately only perceives it in himself, it seems to do so. In this way it is brought about that the individual watches over his own existence with a care which would not otherwise be, and thereby secures the maintenance of the species. Hence it follows that the individuality is no perfection but a limitation, and that to be quit of it is no loss but rather a gain. Do not cherish therefore an anxiety which would truly appear childish and altogether ridiculous if you knew your own nature thoroughly and to its foundation, to wit, as the universal Will to live, which you are!

Thrasymachos — You yourself and all philosophers are childish and quite ridiculous, and it is only for fun and pastime that a staid man like myself occupies himself for a quarter of an hour with this sort of fools. I have now more important things to do, so good-bye!

ON SUICIDE

As FAR as I see it is only the monotheistic, that is, the Jewish religions, whose votaries regard suicide as a crime. This is the more surprising as neither in the Old, nor in the New Testament is there to be found any prohibition, or even any decided disapproval of it. Teachers of religion, therefore, have to base their condemnation of suicide on philosophical grounds of their own, with which, however, it goes so badly, that they seek to supply what in their arguments lacks strength, by the vigor of their expressions of disgust, that is, by abuse. We have to hear, accordingly, that suicide is the greatest cowardice, that it is only possible in madness, and similar twaddle, or even the entirely senseless phrase that suicide is " wrong," whereas obviously no one has a greater right over anything in the world than over his own person and life. Suicide, as already remarked, is even accounted a crime, and with it is allied, especially in brutal, bigoted England, a shameful burial, and the invalidation of the testament, for which reason the jury almost always brings in a verdict of insanity. Let us before anything else allow moral feeling to decide in the matter and compare the impression which the report that an acquaintance had committed a crime, such as a murder, a cruelty, a fraud, a theft, makes upon us, with that of the report of his voluntary death. While the first calls forth energetic indignation, the greatest disgust, a demand for punishment or for vengeance, the latter will excite only sorrow and sympathy, mingled more often with an admiration of his courage than with the moral disapproval which accompanies a bad action. Who has not had acquaintances, friends, or relations, who have willingly departed from the world ? And are we to think with horror of each of these as of a criminal ? *Nego ac pernego.* I am rather of the opinion that the clergy should, once for all, be challenged to give an account, with what right they, without being able to show any biblical authority, or any valid philosophical arguments, stigmatize in the pulpit and in their writings an action committed by many men honored and beloved by us, as a CRIME, and refuse those who voluntarily leave the world an honorable burial—it should, however, be clearly understood that reasons are required, and that no mere empty phrases or abusive epithets will be accepted in place of them. The fact that criminal jurisprudence condemns suicide is no ecclesiastically valid reason, besides being extremely ridiculous. For what punishment can frighten him who seeks death? If we punish the attempt at suicide, it is the clumsiness whereby it failed that we punish.

The ancients, moreover, were a long way from regarding the matter in this light. Pliny (" Histor. Nat.," lib. 28, c. 1; vol. iv., p. 351 Ed. Bip.), says: " *Vitam quidem non adeo expetendam censemus, ut quoque modo trahenda sit. Quisquis es talis, aeque morier, etiam cum obscoenus vixeris, aut nefandus. Quapropter hoc primum quisque in remediis animi sui habeat: ex omnibus bonis, quae homini tribuit natura, nullum melius esse tempestiva morte: idque in ea optimum, quod illam sibi quisque praestare poterit.*" He also says (lib. 2, c. 7; vol. i., p. 125): " *Ne Deum quidem posse omnia. Namque nec sibi potest mortem consciscere; si velit, quod homini dedit optimum in tantis vitae poenis,*" etc. In Massilia, and in the island of Chios, indeed, the hemlock was publicly handed to him who could give sufficient reasons for leaving life (" Val. Max.," 1. ii. c. 6, §§ 7 and 8).* And how many heroes and wise men of antiquity have not ended their lives by a voluntary death! Aristotle indeed says (" Eth. Nicom.," v. 15) that suicide is a wrong against the state, although not against one's own person. Stobæus, however, in his exposition of the Ethics of the Peripatetics, quotes the proposition (Ecl. eth. II., c. 7, p. 286): Φευκτὸν δὲ τὸν βίον γίγνεσθαι τοῖς μὲν ἀγαθοῖς ἐν ταῖς ἄγαν ἀτυχίαις· τοῖς δὲ κακοῖς καὶ ἐν ταῖς ἄγαν εὐτυχίαις. (*Vitam autem relinquendem esse bonis in nimiis quidem miseriis, pravis vero in nimium quoque secundis.*) And in a similar way, p. 312: Διὸ καὶ γαμήσειν,

* On the Island of Chios it was also the custom that the aged should voluntarily put themselves to death.

καὶ παιδοποιήσεσθαι, καὶ πολιτεύσεσθαι, etc., καὶ καθόλου τὴν ἀρετὴν ἀσκοῦντα καὶ μένειν ἐν τῷ βίῳ, καὶ πάλιν, εἰ δέοι πότε δι' ἀνάγκας ἀπαλλαγήσεσθαι, ταφῆς προνοήσαντα, etc. (*Ideoque et uxorem ducturum, et liberos procreaturum, et ad civitatem accessurum,* etc. *Atque omnino virtutem colendo tum vitam servaturum, tum iterum, cogente necessitate, relictarum,* etc.)

We find suicide celebrated by the Stoics as a noble and heroic deed, as might be confirmed by hundreds of extracts, the strongest being from Seneca. Again, with the Hindoo, as is well known, suicide often occurs as a religious action, especially as widow burning, also as immolation beneath the wheels of the Car of Juggernaut, as self-sacrifice to the crocodiles of the Ganges, or of the holy pond of the temple, and otherwise. In the same way, at the theatre, that mirror of life, where we see for example in the celebrated Chinese piece "L'Orphelin de la Chine" (trad. p. St. Julien, 1834), almost all the noble characters end by suicide without its being anywhere indicated, or its occurring to the onlooker, that they have committed a crime. On our own stage, indeed, it is not otherwise, *e. g.*, Palmira in Mahomet, Mortimer in Maria Stuart, Othello, the Countess Terzky. Is Hamlet's monologue the meditation of a crime? It says certainly that if we were sure to be absolutely destroyed by death it would, considering the structure of the world, be unconditionally to choose. "But there lies [*sic* tr.] the rub." The reasons, however, against suicide which have been put forward by the clergy of the monotheistic, that is, Jewish religion, and the philosophers who accommodate themselves to them, are feeble sophisms easy of refutation. (See my "Treatise on the Foundation of Morals," § 5.) Hume has furnished the most thoroughgoing refutation of them in his "Essay on Suicide," which first appeared after his death, and was immediately suppressed by the shameful bigotry and scandalous priestly tyranny of England, for which reason only a very few copies were sold, secretly and at a high price, so that for the preservation of this and of another treatise of the great man, we have to thank the Basel reprint: "Essays on Suicide and the Immortality of the Soul, by the late David Hume. Basel, 1799. Sold by James Decker, p. 124, 8vo." But that a purely philosophical treatise coming from one of the first thinkers and writers of England, refuting the current reasons against suicide, had in its native land to be smuggled through like a forbidden thing, until it found refuge abroad, redounds to the greatest shame of the English nation. It shows at the same time the kind of good conscience the Church has on this question. I have pointed out the only valid moral reason against suicide in my chief work, vol. i., § 69. It lies in that suicide is opposed to the attainment of the highest moral goal, since it substitutes for the real emancipation from this world of sorrow, a merely apparent one. But from this mistake to a crime, such as the Christian clergy seek to stamp it, is a very long way.

Christianity bears in its innermost essence the truth that suffering (the Cross) is the true purpose of life; hence it rejects, as opposed to this, suicide, which antiquity, from a lower standpoint, approved and even honored. The foregoing reason against suicide is, however, an ascetic one, and as such applies only to a much higher ethical standpoint than that which European moral philosophers have ever occupied. But if we descend from this very high standpoint there is no longer any valid moral reason for condemning suicide. The extraordinarily energetic zeal of the clergy of the monotheistic religions against it, which is supported neither by the Bible nor by valid reasons, must rest, it would seem, therefore, on a concealed basis. Might it not be that the voluntary surrender of life is a poor compliment for him who said πάντα καλὰ λίαν? Once more, then, it would be the obligatory optimism of these religions which arraigns suicide in order not to be arraigned by it.

We shall find on the whole that as soon as the terrors of life counterbalance the terrors of death, man makes an end of his life. The resistance to these terrors is nevertheless considerable; they stand as it were as warders before the gate of exit. There is no one living perhaps who would not have made an end of his life if this end were something purely negative, a sudden cessation of existence. But there is something positive in it — the

21

destruction of the body. This frightens men back simply because the body is the phenomenon of the Will-to-Live.

Meanwhile the struggle with these warders is not so hard as a rule as it may seem to us from afar, and indeed in consequence of the antagonism between intellectual and corporeal sufferings. When, for instance, we suffer corporeal pain severely and continuously, we are indifferent to all other trouble; our recovery alone seriously concerns us. Just in the same way severe mental sorrows make us unsusceptible to corporeal — we despise them. Even if they acquire the preponderance, this is a welcome diversion to us, a pause in our mental suffering. It is this which makes suicide easier, inasmuch as the corporeal pain associated with it loses all importance in the eyes of one tortured by excessive mental suffering. The above is especially noticeable with those who are driven to suicide through a purely morbid but none the less intense melancholy. It does not cost such persons any self-conquest, they do not require to form any resolution, but as soon as the keepers provided for them leave them for two minutes they quickly make an end of their life. When in disturbed, horrible dreams, anxiety has reached its highest pitch, it brings us of itself to awakening, and therewith all these horrors of a night vanish. The same thing happens in the dream of life, where also the highest degree of anxiety compels us to break it off.

Suicide may also be regarded as an experiment, a question which we put to nature, and to which we wish to compel the answer, to wit, what change the existence and the knowledge of man experiences through death. But it is a clumsy one, for it abolishes the identity of the consciousness which should receive the answer.

CONTRIBUTIONS TO THE DOCTRINE OF THE AFFIRMATION AND NEGATION OF THE WILL-TO-LIVE.

It is to a certain extent to be understood *a priori*, that is to say, it is obvious of itself, that that which now produces the phenomenon of the world must also be capable of not doing so, and therefore of remaining at rest — or, in other words, that to the present διαστολὴ there must also be a συστολὴ. If the first be the phenomenon of the Will-to-Live the other will be phenomenon of the non-Will-to-Live. This will be moreover, essentially the same with the magnum Sakhepat of the Veda doctrine (in the "Oupnekhat," vol. i., p. 163), with the *Nirvana* of the Buddhists, also with the ἐπέχεινα of the Neo-Platonists. As against certain silly objections I may observe that the negation of the Will-to-Live in no way involves the destruction of a substance, but the mere act of not-Willing — that which hitherto has willed wills no more, since we know this Being, the Will, as thing-in-itself merely in and through the act of willing, it is impossible for us to say or to comprehend what it is or does after having given up this act. Hence the Negation is for us who are the phenomenon of the Will a passage into nothing.

Between the ethics of the Greeks and the Hindoos there is a sharp opposition. The former (with the exception of Plato) has for its object to facilitate the leading of a happy life, *vitam beatam*. The latter, on the contrary, the liberation and emancipation from life altogether — as is directly enunciated in the very first proposition of the Sankhya Karika.

A similar, and, owing to its operating by means of the senses, a stronger contrast will be perceived on contemplating the beautiful antique sarcophagus of the gallery of Florence, whose reliefs represent the whole series of the ceremonies of a wedding from the first offer until the

time when Hymen's torch lights the way to the Thorus,
if one at the same time calls to mind the Christian coffin
with its black hangings in token of grief, and with the
crucifix on the top. The opposition is in the highest
degree significant. Both wish to console in death, each
in an opposite way, and each with justice. The one
signifies the affirmation of the Will-to-Live which life
throughout all time undoubtedly remains, however rapidly
its forms may change. The other indicates by the symbols
of sorrow and death the negation of the Will-to-Live, and
the emancipation from the world where sorrow and death
reign. Between the spirit of Græco-Roman heathenism
and that of Christianity is the special opposition between
the affirmation and negation of the Will-to-Live — as
regards which Christianity in the last resort is right.

My philosophy stands in the same relation to all the
ethics of European philosophy as that of the New Testament to the Old, according to the ecclesiastical conception
of this relation. The Old Testament, namely, places man
under the domination of the Law which nevertheless does
not lead to emancipation. The New Testament, on the
other hand, declares the law insufficient, indeed breaks
away from it — Romans vii., Galatians, ii. 3. It preaches,
on the contrary, the dominion of Grace which is to be
attained through faith, love of one's neighbor, and complete denial of oneself. This is the way to emancipation
from evil and from the world, for assuredly, in spite of
all rationalistic-protestant misrepresentations, asceticism is
peculiarly the soul of the New Testament; but this is
precisely the negation of the Will-to-Live, and the above
transition from the Old Testament to the New, from the
dominion of the law to the dominion of faith, from justification through works to salvation through the mediator,
from the dominion of sin and death to eternal life in
Christ, signifies *sensu proprio*, the transition from the
merely moral virtues to the negation of the Will-to-Live.
All the philosophical Ethics which have preceded me have
retained the spirit of the Old Testament with its absolute
(*i. e.*, foundationless and goalless) moral law, and all
its moral commandments and prohibitions to which tacitly
the ruling Jehovah is added in thought, however diverse

may be the forms and statements of the matter. My ethic, on the other hand, has basis, purpose, and goal. It first of all demonstrates theoretically the metaphysical basis of Justice and human love, and then points out the goal to which these, when fully accomplished, must finally lead. At the same time it admits straightforwardly the undesirability of the world, and indicates the negation of the Will as the way toward emancipation from the former. It is therefore really conceived in the spirit of the New Testament, while the rest hold in their entirety by that of the Old, and accordingly issue theoretically in mere Judaism — "naked despotic theism." In this sense my doctrines might be called the true Christian Philosophy, however paradoxical this may seem to those who do not go to the root of the matter, but remain standing on the surface.

He who is capable of deeper thinking will soon see that human desires cannot first begin to be sinful at that point where they, fortuitously crossing one another in their individual directions, occasion evil from the one and malice from the other side; but that, if this be so, they must be originally and in their very essence sinful and accursed, and that consequently the entire Will-to-Live must itself be accursed. The horrors and misery with which the world is full are then the necessary result of the sum of the characters in which the Will-to-Live objectifies itself, to which the circumstances occurring in the unbroken chain of necessity supply motives — in other words, are the mere commentary on the affirmation of the Will-to-Live (compare "German Theology,"* p. 93). That our existence itself implies a fault is proved by death.

A noble character will not readily complain of his fate, but rather what Hamlet boasts of Horatio will be true of him:

> " For thou hast been
> As one, in suffering all, that suffers nothing."

And this is explicable from the fact that such a one, recognizing his own being also in others, and therefore as sharing in their fate, beholds almost invariably round about him harder fate than his own, for which reason he

* Deutsche Theologia, Edited by Franz Pfeiffer, Stuttgart, 1851.

cannot bring himself to complain of the latter. An ignoble egoist, on the other hand, who limits all reality to himself, and regards others as mere wraiths and phantasms, will take no interest in their fate, but will devote his whole attention to his own, great sensitiveness and frequent complaints being the result. It is precisely this recognition of oneself in an alien phenomenon from which, as I have so often proved justice and human love directly proceed, which leads finally to the surrender of the Will; for the phenomenon in which this Will presents itself is so distinctly in a position of suffering, that he who extends himself to all such can no longer will its continuance — just as one who takes all the tickets in a lottery must necessarily suffer great loss. The affirmation of the Will presupposes the limitation of self-consciousness to one's own person, and reckons on the possibility of a favorable career in life from the hand of fortune.

If in our conception of the world we proceed from the thing-in-itself — from the Will-to-Live — we shall find as its kernel, as its greatest concentration, the act of generation which presents itself as the first thing, the point of departure; it is the *punctum saliens* of the world-egg, its mainspring. What a contrast, on the other hand, if one proceeds from the empirical world, the world of presentment, which is given us as phenomenon! For here the aforesaid act presents itself as an altogether individual and special one of subordinate importance — indeed, as a covert and secret bye-concern which only creeps in; a paradoxical anomaly, affording frequent material for laughter. It might even strike us that the devil only wanted to hide his game thereby, for coition is his currency, and the world his kingdom. For who has not remarked how *illico post coitum cachinnus auditur Diaboli?* which, to speak seriously, rests on the fact that the sexual desire, especially when by fixation of a particular woman it is concentrated into the passion of love, is the quintessence of the whole rascality of this noble world, for it promises so unspeakably, infinitely, and extravagantly much, and performs so contemptibly little.

The share of the woman in generation is, in a certain sense, more innocent than that of the man; in so far, namely, as the latter gives the Will to the being about to be procreated, the Will which is the primal sin, and hence the source of all wickedness and evil, while the woman gives the knowing faculty which opens the way to emancipation. The act of generation is the World-focus, inasmuch as it says: "The Will-to-Live has affirmed itself anew." In this sense a well-known Brahmanic saying laments: "Woe, woe! The Lingam is in the Yoni." Conception and pregnancy tell us, on the other hand, "To the Will is given once more the light of the Intellect," by means of which, it can again find its way out, and thus the possibility of emancipation appears once more.

From this is to be explained the significant phenomenon, that while any woman surprised in the act of generation would like to sink into the ground for shame, yet notwithstanding she will wear her pregnancy without a trace of shame, and even with a kind of pride. Since in every other case an infallibly certain sign is regarded as equivalent to the thing signified, so here every other sign of the completed coitus shames the woman in the highest degree; pregnancy alone does not do so. This is to be explained in that, as above said, pregnancy in a certain sense brings with it, or at least affords the prospect of, a purgation from the guilt which has been contracted in the coitus. Hence the coitus bears all the shame and disgrace in the matter, while the pregnancy which is so nearly related to it, remains pure and innocent, and indeed to a certain extent honorable.

The coitus is chiefly the affair of the man, pregnancy wholly that of the woman. From the father the child receives its Will, its character; from the mother its Intellect. The latter is the emancipating principle, the former is the binding principle. The symbol of the continuous existence of the Will-to-Live, in time, in spite of all increase of light through the Intellect, is the coitus; the symbol of the light of the understanding, and indeed in the highest degree of its clearness, which is ever anew allied to this Will, keeping up the possibility of emancipation, is the renewed birth of the Will-to-Live as Man. The sign of this is pregnancy, which goes about therefore in frankness and freedom, and indeed in pride, while the coitus slinks away like a criminal.

Some of the church fathers have taught that even marital cohabitation should only be allowed when it occurs merely for the sake of the procreation of children, ἐπὶ μόνη παιδοπιία as Clemens Alex. (Strom. 1, iii. c. 11.) says. (The passages referring to the subject will be found collected in P. E. Lind. de coelibatu Christianorum c. 1). Clemens (Strom. iii. c. 3) attributes this view to the Pythagoreans. This is, however, strictly speaking, incorrect. For if the coitus be no longer desired for its own sake, the negation of the Will-to-Live has already appeared, and the propagation of the human race is then superfluous and senseless, inasmuch as its purpose is already attained. Besides, without any subjective passion, without lust and physical pressure, with sheer deliberation, and the cold-blooded purpose to place a human being in the world merely in order that he should be there — this would be such a very questionable moral action that few would take it upon themselves; one might even say of it indeed that it stood in the same relation to generation from the mere sexual impulse as a cold-blooded deliberate murder does to a death-stroke given in anger.

The condemnation of all unnatural sexual pleasures is based on the opposite ground; since though by these the impulse is satisfied, that is, the Will-to-live is affirmed, propagation is eliminated through which alone the possibility of the negation of the Will is maintained. From this is to be explained that it was not before the appearance of Christianity, whose tendency is asoetic, that pederasty was recognized as a deadly sin.

A cloister is an assemblage of human beings who have embraced poverty, chastity, obedience (*i. e.*, the surrender of the individual Will), and who seek through living together to lighten partly the existence itself, but still more this state of severe renunciation, since the sight of those holding like views and surrendering themselves in a similar manner strengthens their resolution and consoles them, inasmuch as the companionship of common living, within certain limits, is suited to human nature and affords innocent recreation amid many severe sacrifices. This is the normal conception of the cloister. And who can call such a society a union of fools and idiots, as one must do according to any philosophy but mine?

The inner spirit and meaning of the genuine cloister life, as of asceticism generally, is this: That one has recognized oneself as worthy and capable of a better existence than ours is, and desires to maintain and strengthen this conviction by despising what this world offers, by casting away from us all its pleasures as worthless, by awaiting the end of this our life deprived of its empty bait in rest and confidence, in order that when at last the hour of death comes we may welcome it as that of emancipation. Saniassism has entirely the same tendency and significance, as also the monasticism of the Buddhists. Certainly in no case does practice so seldom conform to theory as in that of Monasticism, simply because its fundamental conception is so exalted, and *abusus optimi pessimus*. A true monk is a being in the highest degree honorable. But in by far the majority of cases the cowl is a mere mask, behind which there is as little of the real monk as there is in one at a masquerade.

The notion of devoting and surrendering the individual Will entirely and without reserve to that of another is a physical means of facilitating the negation of one's own Will, and therefore a suitable allegorical vehicle of the truth.

The number of regular Trappists is indeed small, yet notwithstanding this the half of mankind consists of UNWILLING TRAPPISTS. Poverty, obedience, lack of all enjoyments, or even of the most necessary comforts, often combined with compulsory chastity, or one brought about through defect, is their lot. The distinction is merely that the Trappists conduct the thing of their own free choice, methodically and without hope of betterment, while the other class are to be reckoned to that which I in my æsthetic chapters have designated by the expression δεύτερος πλοῦς; to effect which nature has already sufficiently taken her measures through the fundamental principles of her order, particularly if one reckons to the evils directly springing from the latter those others which the dissension and malice of man produce in war and in peace. But precisely this necessity of involuntary suffering for eternal salvation is expressed in that saying of the Savior (Matth. xix. 24): "εὐκοπώτερόν ἐστι κάμηλον διὰ τρυπήματος ῥαφίδος διελθεῖν, ἢ πλούσιον εἰς τὴν βασιλείαν τοῦ θεοῦ εἰσελθεῖν." ("Facilius est, funem ancorarium per foramen acus transire, quam divitem regnum divinum ingredi.") Those there are who have taken their eternal salvation with great seriousness, have voluntarily chosen poverty when fate had denied it to them, and when they had been born in wealth. Thus Buddha, Sakya Muni who, born a prince, willingly took to the beggar's staff; and Francis of Assisi, the founder of the mendicant orders, who as a young gallant at the ball where the daughters of the notables were sitting together, when asked: "Now Mr. Francis, will you not soon find a choice among these beauties?" replied, "I have selected for myself one much more beautiful!" "Who?" "La poverta!" Upon which he soon afterward left everything, and wandered through the land begging.

He who through such considerations has realized how necessary to our salvation, sorrow and suffering mostly are; he will recognize that we should envy others not so much on account of their happiness as of their unhappiness.

For the same reason the stoicism of the view which defies fate is indeed a good armor against the sorrows of life, and serviceable for making the present better to be borne; but it stands opposed to the true salvation. For it hardens the heart. How shall this latter be bettered by suffering, if, covered by a strong coating, it does not feel it? For the rest, a certain degree of stoicism is not very rare. It may be affected and turn out to be bonne mine au mauvais jeu. Where, however, it is genuine, it arises mostly from mere feelinglessness, from a lack of energy, brightness, sensibility, and imagination, which are requisite to a heartfelt sorrow. The phlegma and heaviness of the Germans are especially favorable to this kind of stoicism.

Unjust or malicious acts are, in respect of those who perform them, signs of the strength of the affirmation of their Will-to-Live, and accordingly of the distance which separates them from the true salvation which consists in its negation, and therewith in emancipation from the world; and hence of the long school of understanding and of suffering which they have to pass through before they reach it. But in respect of him who has to suffer through the above actions, they are, although physically an evil, metaphysically a good, and at bottom a benefit, since they help to lead him to his true salvation.

World-Spirit — Here then is the measure of thy labor and thy suffering; for this must thou exist as all other things exist.

Man — But what have I from existence ? If I am occupied I have trouble; if I am unoccupied tedium; How canst thou offer me for so much labor and so much suffering such a miserable reward ?

World-Spirit — And yet it is an equivalent for all thy troubles and all thy sorrows; and it is this precisely by reason of its emptiness.

Man—Indeed? That really exceeds my powers of comprehension.

World-Spirit—I know it. (*Aside.*) Ought I to tell him that the value of life consists exactly in that it teaches him not to wish for it? For this highest dedication life itself must prepare him.

If now, we can, through considerations such as the above, that is to say, from a very high standpoint, see a justification for the sorrows of mankind, this does not extend to the animals, whose sorrows, caused indeed in great measure by human beings, but also without their co-operation, are considerable. (Compare "World as Will and Present-ment," 3rd ed., vol. ii., p. 404, *seq.*) The question there-fore arises: wherefore this tormented anxious Will in such thousandfold shapes without the freedom of emanci-pation which is conditioned by reflection? The suffering of the animal world is to be justified merely from the fact that the Will-to-live, because out of itself in the phe-nomenal world, finds nothing to hand; and since it is a

hungry Will must devour its own flesh.   Hence the scale
of its phenomena, each step of which lives at the cost of
another.   For the rest I refer the reader to my " Contributions to the Doctrine of the Suffering of the World," in
which will be found demonstrated that the capacity for
suffering in the animal is much less than in the man.
What might be added further than this might appear hypo-
thetical or even mythical, and may thus be left to the
private speculation of the reader himself.